POLITICS AND PEACE IN NORTHERN IRELAND

Manchester University Press

POLITICS AND PEACE IN NORTHERN IRELAND

Political parties and the implementation of the 1998 Agreement

DAVID MITCHELL

Manchester University Press

Copyright © David Mitchell 2015

The right of David Mitchell to be identified as the author of this work
has been asserted by him in accordance with the Copyright,
Designs and Patents Act 1988.

Published by Manchester University Press
Altrincham Street, Manchester M1 7JA
www.manchesteruniversitypress.co.uk

British Library Cataloguing-in-Publication Data
A catalogue record for this book is available from the British Library

Library of Congress Cataloging-in-Publication Data applied for

ISBN 978 0 7190 8526 0 hardback
ISBN 978 1 5261 2282 7 paperback

First published 2015

The publisher has no responsibility for the persistence or accuracy of
URLs for any external or third-party internet websites referred to in this book,
and does not guarantee that any content on such websites is, or will remain,
accurate or appropriate.

Typeset Perpetua Std
by Out of House Publishing
Printed in Great Britain
by CPI Group (UK), Ltd, Croydon CR0 4YY

In memory of my mother, Doreen Mitchell, 1951–2014

Contents

Acknowledgements		ix
Abbreviations		x
Figure		xi
	Introduction	1
1	A theory of post-Agreement Northern Ireland	10
2	Ulster Unionist Party	51
3	Social Democratic and Labour Party	85
4	Sinn Féin	108
5	Democratic Unionist Party	137
6	Alliance Party of Northern Ireland	167
	Conclusion	193
References		202
Index		222

Acknowledgements

The origins of this book lie in doctoral research carried out at Ulster University, Magee, between 2004 and 2008. That project, funded by the Northern Ireland Department for Employment and Learning, analysed the experience of the four main parties between 1998 and 2003. Thanks are therefore due to my supervisors, Professor Paul Arthur and Dr Emmet O'Connor, and to Professor Tom Fraser and Dr David Roberts who supervised me in the early part of the PhD.

This book, however, bears little resemblance to that thesis. Over half of the material presented here is entirely new and the rest has been revised and restructured. That work was done alongside and between other (more lucrative) research projects, and thus the greatest debt is to my wife, Louise, and little Maria for inspiration and support throughout.

I have also benefited from the belief and encouragement of academic colleagues and friends, including Matt Hill, Sandra Buchanan, Gerry Leavey, John Brewer, Owen Hargie and Ian Somerville, and my wider circle of family and friends. Mining the Northern Ireland Political Collection at the Linenhall Library, Belfast, was the central activity of this project, and so gratitude is owed to the staff there who manage and maintain this valuable resource.

Understanding of this material was enriched through interviews with a number of political actors including Gregory Campbell, Jeffrey Donaldson, Mark Durkan, Chris Lyttle, Mitchel McLaughlin, Duncan Morrow, Dermot Nesbitt and Trevor Ringland. All were generous with their time and insights. Shane Kirby, Allan Leonard and Derek Bell provided me with important unpublished material. Finally, I am grateful for the comments of the anonymous reader and to the staff at Manchester University Press for supporting this project and bringing it to publication.

Abbreviations

DUP	Democratic Unionist Party
ECHR	European Convention on Human Rights
EU	European Union
FPCU	Free Presbyterian Church of Ulster
GAA	Gaelic Athletic Association
IICD	Independent International Commission on Decommissioning
IMC	Independent Monitoring Commission
IRA	Irish Republican Army
MEP	Member of the European Parliament
MLA	Member of the Legislative Assembly
MP	Member of Parliament
NDP	National Democratic Party
NSMC	North–South Ministerial Council
OFMDFM	Office of the First Minister and Deputy First Minister
PSNI	Police Service of Northern Ireland
PUP	Progressive Unionist Party
RUC	Royal Ulster Constabulary
SDLP	Social Democratic and Labour Party
TUV	Traditional Unionist Voice
UCUNF	Ulster Conservatives and Unionists – New Force
UDA	Ulster Defence Association
UDP	Ulster Democratic Party
UDR	Ulster Defence Regiment
UKUP	United Kingdom Unionist Party
UUC	Ulster Unionist Council
UUP	Ulster Unionist Party
UVF	Ulster Volunteer Force

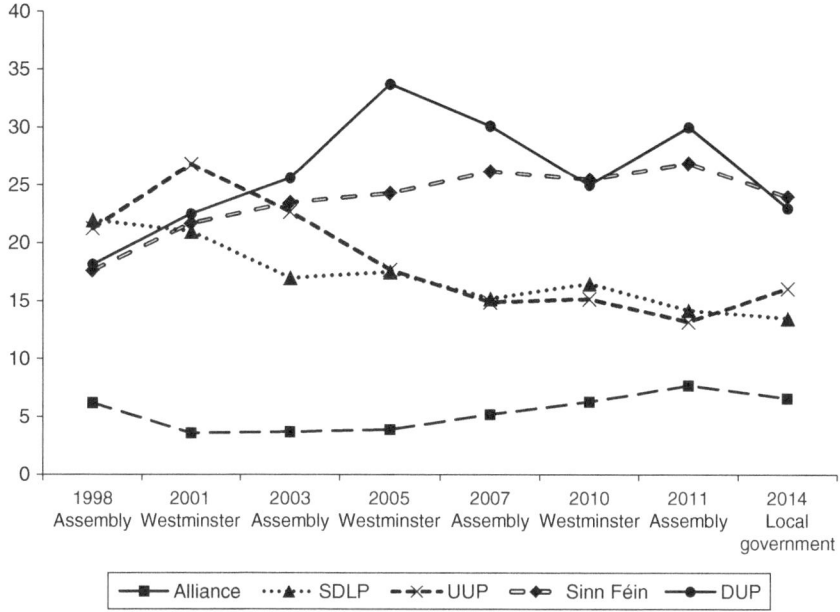

Percentage vote share of main parties since 1998
(*sources*: www.ark.ac.uk/elections; *Belfast Telegraph*).

Introduction

On Saturday, 11 April 1998, the *Irish Times* announced the multi-party agreement reached in Belfast the day before with the headline 'Easter 1998'. It was, of course, a factual statement; the negotiators had missed the Holy Thursday midnight deadline and the document had been finalised on Good Friday. However, to those well versed in Irish history, the headline had a greater depth of meaning.

The rebellion led by Patrick Pearse against the British in April 1916 is often referred to as 'Easter 1916'. The *Irish Times*' implication was that the 1998 Agreement could be as significant a turning point in the centuries-long conflict as Pearse's Rising that shaped twentieth-century Ireland. Yet, at the same time, by conjuring a comparison between Easter 1916 and Easter 1998, the *Irish Times* drew attention to the dramatic contrast between the natures and meanings of those two events. Pearse, a fervent Catholic, imagined himself as a Christ figure, shedding his (and others') blood for the redemption of the Irish people during the very season in which Christians celebrate the death and resurrection of Christ. Eastertide 1998 had a different theological resonance. This time, the sacrifice was not of blood but of enmity and hatred, or at least of maximal political demands. It appeared to be a historic compromise that heralded new relationships and a society resurrected from the violent past, set free for the future. In sum, the headline captured the twin hopes that many people placed in the Agreement in its immediate aftermath: that it would be historic in significance and reconciliatory in effect.

The historic nature of the Agreement, at least, is beyond doubt. Although the accord is best understood as an important stage in what was a prolonged process, with political battles continuing long after the Agreement and political convergence evident long before it, the pivotal nature of the Good Friday 'moment' is certain. Never before had power-sharing arrangements and constitutional change enjoyed such broad support, encompassing most Northern Ireland parties, the paramilitary groups that had fought for the thirty years of the 'Troubles', and the British and Irish states. Earlier 'historic' junctures anticipated it and later ones flowed from it. Perhaps an even more significant date in 1998 than 10 April was 22 May, the day the people of the North and South of Ireland endorsed in simultaneous referenda what the politicians had negotiated behind closed doors.

Of course, there have been good reasons, and many occasions, to doubt the Agreement. Again and again, the new Assembly was suspended by London when the Northern Ireland parties were unable to agree on how the deal should be implemented. Most notably, the electoral victory of the ostensibly anti-Agreement Democratic Unionist Party (DUP) in November 2003 made the realisation of stable, inclusive government difficult to imagine. Yet the strong electoral mandates won by the DUP and Sinn Féin actually led to the resumption of power-sharing in 2007 and the strange and cold alliance of the erstwhile 'wrecker' factions. The post-Agreement era continues.

But while a new chapter in political history may have opened, the 'Easter 1998' headline's second intimation – that the Agreement had reconciliatory potential – is still to be fully borne out. Over fifteen years on, the accord has not yet brought the kind of inter-communal reconciliation that many assumed was its ultimate purpose. Sporadic street violence, paramilitary attacks and residential and educational segregation have all continued, despite the operation of the Good Friday institutions, while those institutions themselves have frequently been paralysed by Orange versus Green disputes (see Nolan, 2014). Indeed, some argue that patterns of conflict have survived *because* of the new arrangements, which are said to cement the two-community dichotomy, leave identities and constitutional aspirations as they were pre-1998 and fail to engender a spirit of collective endeavour among political leaders (see, for example, Alliance, 2004; Taylor, 2009a; Wilson, 2010). In its baldest forms, that argument is unconvincing (critiques include McGarry and O'Leary, 2009; Clancy, 2010; see also Chapter 6 of this book), but the reality of the unfulfilled, or yet-to-be-fulfilled, promise of the Agreement is inescapable.

So some things have changed and some things have stayed the same – yet that is to say nothing about *how* we got from there to here. That story is extremely complex – in two respects. One is the sheer expansiveness of the process. The players include political parties, governments, militant groups, international facilitators and commissions; the episodes include rounds of talks, press conferences, weapons destruction, parliamentary proceedings, police raids and elections; the locations include Belfast, Dublin, London, Washington and a number of other talks venues. At a very basic level, some order can be brought to post-Agreement events by dividing the period into three phases. The first was from 1998 until the November 2003 Assembly election. This period saw stop–start devolution, limited acts of decommissioning by the Irish Republican Army (IRA) and deepening unionist disaffection with the Agreement, all culminating in the victory of the DUP in late 2003. The second phase was from 2003 until 2007, in which the DUP and Sinn Féin edged towards the point where power-sharing could be re-established, and the IRA, most notably, took the steps necessary to facilitate this. The third phase covers the current period of relatively stable devolution from May 2007 to the present.

But a more profound complexity resides in the contradictory meanings that were apparent in all those events. The moderate parties sealed the Agreement but lost support. Paramilitaries were on ceasefire yet highly active. Talk of peace co-existed with words of war. The extreme parties triumphed but they also moderated. Northern Ireland was peaceful yet divided. This twilight character of post-Agreement Northern Ireland is expressed in the titles chosen by writers on the period: it was a 'reluctant peace' (Cochrane, 2013); there was 'peace without consensus' (Clancy, 2010); there was 'no war, no peace' (Mac Ginty, 2006a); it was a 'long peace' (Cox *et al.*, 2000); it was an 'armed peace' (Rowan, 2003); reconciliation was an 'elusive quest' (Porter, 2003). One of the most common descriptions of Northern Ireland's condition was that of 'cold peace'. Indeed, the abundance of contradictory indicators was the theme of the Peace Monitoring Reports produced by the Community Relations Council and the Joseph Rowntree Foundation (Nolan, 2012, 2013, 2014) that sought to assess the progress that had been made since the end of the 'Troubles'. Political violence had declined, the Assembly was reasonably stable, town centres were increasingly relaxed and cosmopolitan, but segregation persisted, there was a conspicuous lack of trust and shared vision between political leaders and localised territorial clashes continued. At any point during the Agreement's implementation, the direction of the process was debatable and signs of change were ambiguous. Hence, when Ian Paisley and Martin McGuinness took power on 8 May 2007, there was both a sense of inevitability about the occasion and surreal surprise.

There is, then, plenty to write about. John Whyte (1991: viii) famously called Northern Ireland 'the most researched area on earth'; how much more relevant this dubious accolade is today. In terms of daily commentary, the post-Agreement period saw the traditional media joined by round-the-clock blogging and tweeting. At another level, academic theorising proliferated. The precise form of power-sharing instituted by the Agreement fed vigorous debates concerning the best form of democracy for a divided society such as Northern Ireland (McGarry, 2001; McGarry and O'Leary, 2004; Taylor, 2009b), while there was considerable discussion about whether there were lessons to be drawn from the Northern Ireland experience that may help other protracted conflicts (Bew *et al.*, 2009; Mitchell, 2010; LSE IDEAS, 2011). Tonge (2005) and Aughey (2005) provided comprehensive and incisive explorations of the nature of the 'new' politics post-1998, while Clancy (2010) illuminated how the decisions and perceptions of actors outside Northern Ireland – in London, Dublin and Washington – influenced the course taken by the Agreement's implementation. A number of edited collections (Ruane and Todd, 1999a; Wilford, 2001a; Cox *et al.*, 2006; Carmichael *et al.*, 2007; Coulter and Murray, 2008; Edwards and Bloomer, 2008; Farrington, 2008; McGrattan and Meehan, 2012) have offered detailed accounts of various facets of contemporary Northern Irish politics and society, collections that exemplify the multi-dimensional nature of social and political change in the region. And writing at a more popular level has included numerous journalistic accounts of aspects of the post-Agreement story, as well as memoirs from individuals involved in the events.

The present work builds on this body of knowledge, but is distinguished first by its theoretical approach (explained below) and, second, by its focus on the political parties. For the latter there are three reasons. First, political parties are important. This is the case in any jurisdiction; parties both reflect and shape public opinion, they provide the personalities that hold the levers of power, they rise and fall according to social, political and economic change. To study parties is to study competing philosophies of human nature, economics and security, and differing experiences of the past and visions of the future. In Northern Ireland, this is doubly the case, given the ethnic divide. This cleavage means that there is in truth not one party system but an 'ethnic dual party system' (Mitchell, 1995) in which parties are vehicles of ethno-national and religious identity and in which elections are first and foremost contests over which party will be on top *within* the respective ethnic blocs because few voters stray from the political community of their birth. As we explore in Chapter 1, the 1998 Agreement was purposefully ambiguous in certain key areas, which meant that the parties held opposing interpretations of its meaning, how it should be implemented and its likely long-term outcome. These clashing visions characterised post-Agreement politics and, indeed, are likely to do so for many years to come. The structure of this book is designed to foreground the divergence in understandings, hopes and fears reflected in, and amplified by, the Agreement. Each perspective is considered seriously, described and appraised in detail.

The second reason for focusing on the main Northern Ireland political parties is the pivotal role they played in the peace process. Indeed, it has been observed that this role was a distinctive feature of peace-making in Ireland:

> In other peace processes, such as Sri Lanka and Colombia, political parties played a subsidiary role to other actors – governments, armies and insurgents. In the case of Northern Ireland, political parties were the chief medium through which communities were represented. It was the parties who attended negotiations, had prime

> ministerial access and were invited to make submissions to the peace process-related commissions.
>
> (Darby and Mac Ginty, 2002: 65)

Why were parties so important? The goal of the peace process was to secure agreement on devolved political arrangements within Northern Ireland, i.e. between the local political organisations for which people cast their votes. This was the agreed desire of the British and Irish Governments which were driving and managing the process. Other options that might have bypassed the North's parties, such as an all-Ireland state, joint British–Irish authority or ongoing rule by London, were not on the table; they were judged unlikely to secure cross-community support or, crucially, stop political violence. The consociational thrust of the peace process and Agreement that envisaged a grand, all-inclusive coalition further enhanced the importance of parties and the agreements and disagreements between them. While one may wish to argue that the process was too focused on political elites to the exclusion of the public and civil society, the reality in any case was that parties were centre-stage.

A third reason for a party-by-party examination of post-Agreement politics is the remarkable degree of change wrought by the Agreement context in the political landscape, a landscape that had been fairly static for three decades. The period of peace implementation witnessed the end of the domination of unionism and nationalism by the Ulster Unionist Party (UUP) and the Social Democratic and Labour Party (SDLP), respectively, and the spectacular success of their long-standing junior rivals, the DUP and Sinn Féin. Given these reversals, the post-Agreement phase must be viewed as a critical time of accelerated political change akin to the other pivotal periods such as the decade 1912–22 or the late 1960s and early 1970s. The realignments within unionism and nationalism that were catalysed by the peace process demand the comprehensive examination that this book seeks to provide.

As for the choice of parties, those to which full chapters are dedicated here are those which are part of the power-sharing Executive. Unlike other political groups that have come and gone, or come recently, the five are also the parties that have been active since the early years of the 'Troubles' and have played the greatest role in shaping political change. Admittedly, this approach excludes a large number of post-Agreement groupings: fringe unionist parties (Progressive Unionist Party, Ulster Democratic Party, United Kingdom Unionist Party and Traditional Unionist Voice), minor centre parties (Women's Coalition, the Green Party, NI Conservatives, NI21) and dissident republicans (Éirígí), though many of these are discussed at appropriate junctures in the book. But the dominance of the five main parties is clear. In the 2011 Assembly election their combined vote share was 92 per cent.

The book begins with theory; a long opening chapter sets out and applies, in overview, the conceptual framework of security dilemma theory. This may seem an odd choice for a study of political parties. The security dilemma is usually employed to explain the insecurity of the international system or the outbreak of ethnic violence. However, Chapter 1 argues that the concept's key contribution is the spotlight it trains on the nature and impact of the relational dynamic between groups in conflict, and that, accordingly, it reveals much about the unstable, delicate process of implementing the Good Friday Agreement. Indeed, as the first chapter will show, to explore the security dilemma and the wealth of material that has been written about it is to tour the elemental components of ethnic strife: the role of state weakness in igniting conflict; the social-psychological aspects of inter-group relations; the nature and consequences of groups' drives for both military and identity security; and the insurmountable uncertainty that all political entities and individuals face. Most of all, as will be shown, a security dilemma-guided analysis focuses attention on the essential irony of ethnic (all?) conflict: the manner in which rival actors' identities and postures are mutually reinforcing, and how actors' pursuits of exclusively defined notions of security are cyclical and self-defeating.

Thus, drawing on some recent developments in the concept, especially Bilgic's (2013) use of Booth and Wheeler's (2008) three 'logics of insecurity' or ways of thinking about the uncertainty of international affairs – fatalist, mitigator and transcender – the chapter offers a new definition of the security dilemma that understands it is a spiral of hostility driven by interdependent, fatalist conceptions of group security – ethno-centric, fearful and belligerent. With this conceptual architecture in place, the chapter moves on to the Northern Ireland case. The conflict of nationalisms in Ireland is portrayed as a 'societal security dilemma' (Roe, 2005) in which the rival identity groups were locked into a bitter quest for security at each other's expense. The peace process sought to disrupt this pattern by providing mutual and interdependent assurances to each side and incentivising new understandings of group security, yet lingering ethno-centric ambitions led to certain issues being left unresolved in the 1998 Agreement.

As a result, the post-Agreement years saw the return of the security dilemma, albeit in a form of reduced intensity, as the groups continued to protect and project their identities, frequently in relation to the raft of political and moral quandaries left behind by the 'Troubles'. Although stable power-sharing was finally established, and much of the violence's volatile legacy was defused, antagonistic identity politics continued. The security dilemma has been stabilised and contained; resolution, characterised by inclusive identities and mutual trust, is yet to come, but remains probable. A concluding section of Chapter 1 draws out broader implications of the analysis. Based on the Northern Ireland experience, six features of the security dilemma after a peace settlement that distinguish it from its pre-settlement counterpart are identified, features that, it is proposed, make it appropriate to refer to a 'post-settlement security dilemma'.

The remainder of the book is more empirical, consisting of a blend of re-creative history, documentary analysis and critical commentary, all with the aim of understanding the motivations, behaviour and fates of the principal political parties in the wake of the Agreement. Each chapter stands on its own terms but also builds on the themes introduced in Chapter 1: a distinct context of uncertainty, clashing conceptions of group security, interdependent postures. The chapters are similarly structured: first, the party's historical and ideological background is presented; second, its position on the Agreement is explored; third, key aspects of the party's post-Agreement experience are examined. The order of the chapters reflects the chronological importance of the parties, with the parties most prominent in the early part of the period under study, the UUP and SDLP, coming first, Sinn Féin and the DUP next and the Alliance Party, most significant after 2007, last.

It is fitting to begin with the UUP given that it was the largest party at the time of the Agreement and its acceptance of the Agreement, and subsequent internal turmoil caused by that acceptance, proved so influential on the wider course of events. Chapter 2 begins by briefly tracing the UUP's trajectory from political dominance throughout the pre-1972 Stormont years to marginalisation and insecurity during Direct Rule and the peace process. It then examines the reasons for the party's decision to conclude a power-sharing agreement with nationalism. The chapter explores the UUP's expectations and concerns regarding the deal's implementation and the party's mode of pursuing its two central post-Agreement concerns: IRA disarmament and the preservation of the British character of Northern Ireland. Lastly, the formidable challenges facing the party following electoral defeat by the DUP and the latter's acceptance of the basic framework of the Agreement are assessed.

The SDLP, the subject of Chapter 3, was the party caused the least discomfort by the Agreement; it had long been advocating such an accommodation that might allow the transcendence of the security dilemma. The chapter's opening examination of the SDLP's political thinking is structured according to John Hume's threefold formulation of the party's aims: reform, reconciliation and reunification – a departure from traditional Irish nationalism. The chapter notes the great extent to which this vision was realised in the Agreement and how this very fact threatened the post-Agreement vitality of the party. The SDLP's controversial decision not to exclude Sinn Féin from the Executive despite the lack of progress on IRA decommissioning is considered, as is how its interpretation of the Agreement manifested itself in its approach to the policing and symbols issues.

Finally, the chapter analyses the political, organisational and financial dimensions of the SDLP's electoral contest with its nationalist rival, Sinn Féin, and the party's future prospects. The latter party is the subject of Chapter 4. Beginning with a discussion of Sinn Féin's ideological and militaristic roots, the chapter examines how and why the party moved from its historic fatalism towards a willingness to co-operate with enemies and support the Agreement. It assesses the party's central claim that the Agreement could be transitional to a united Ireland, and describes and explains Sinn Féin's fixation on promoting equality. The complex and disruptive role of the party's military arm, the IRA, after the Agreement, is also analysed. Lastly, the chapter discusses the most important part of Sinn Féin's post-Agreement strategy: electoral progress.

The DUP was the outlet of most of those in the Protestant community who rejected the ambiguities and compromises of the Good Friday deal. Yet, as Chapter 5 explores in detail, the party progressed from vowing to destroy the 1998 Agreement to assenting, in 2007, to arrangements that were extremely similar in content. The chapter begins by examining the background of the party within hard-line unionism and conservative Protestantism. What were the sources of its popularity and intense aversion to compromise? It then discusses the DUP's view of the Agreement as fatal for the Union and corrosive of democracy, and how the DUP's approach to post-Agreement politics indicated a more nuanced strategy than its rhetoric implied. The chapter examines the twin phenomena of the DUP's gathering electoral strength and its growing openness to co-operation with Sinn Féin, processes that culminated in the St Andrews Agreement of 2006. The nature of that agreement and how it compared with its 1998 predecessor are examined, before a final section that identifies the consequences, for the party and the political process, of the DUP's historic decision to enter government in 2007.

Chapter 6, on the cross-community Alliance Party, begins by exploring the party's founding purposes, and its diagnosis of the Northern Ireland problem as residing in the existence and persistence of two opposing identity groups. Alliance's position on the Agreement is then set out with a focus on how the party regarded the document as falling short of its own proposals for creating an integrated society. The chapter assesses the merits of this critique, especially the party's contention that the Agreement gave succour to the very ideologies that had driven the conflict – unionism and nationalism. Other significant themes, including the party's commitment to promoting a shared society, joining the Executive in 2010 and its experience of the flag protests of 2012–13, are analysed. A final chapter reviews the overall approaches of the parties in light of the conceptual framework, and offers some concluding thoughts built around a phrase that has become prevalent in Northern Ireland political discourse and which, in a way, captures the essence of what post-Agreement politics has been, and this book is, about: dealing with the past.

A final word on terminology. The rival identity groups in Northern Ireland are usually referred to as 'unionist' (pro-British and mainly Protestant) and 'nationalist' (pro-Irish and mainly Roman Catholic). Those terms are used here and, as is conventional, sometimes used interchangeably with 'Protestant' and 'Catholic'. While there is some scholarly debate on the nature of unionism as an ideology and identity, it is treated here, as is also conventional, as a form of nationalism. 'Loyalist' usually refers to working-class unionists, especially the paramilitary groups and their associated political parties that have been based in working-class Protestant areas. This is how the word is used here. However, it is worth noting that some who would be regarded as loyalist question the term, viewing it as a way for middle-class unionists to distance themselves from the working class of their own community. In any case, loyalists are unionists.

'Republican' generally refers to nationalists who espouse violence in pursuit of their objectives. In terms of this book, that usually means Sinn Féin and the Provisional IRA, though 'republican' is also the appropriate term for various Irish separatist factions in the past, as well as 'dissident' republicans in the present. The latter are those who have disagreed with Sinn Féin's abandonment of the armed struggle, some of whom have sought to continue that struggle. However, just to complicate matters, having renounced violence, Sinn Féin can be and is now often described as a nationalist party, though the republican label still holds. In what follows, then, 'nationalism' refers to all those who support Irish unity, with 'republicanism' used when specifying nationalism's more extreme manifestation.

The agreed document produced on 10 April 1998 by the multi-party talks participants goes by a range of titles – 'Good Friday Agreement', 'Belfast Agreement', '1998 Agreement', or just 'the Agreement'. Here it is usually referred to as 'the Agreement', except where some stylistic variation is deemed necessary. It is well known that nationalists tended to call the accord 'Good Friday' while unionists preferred the more prosaic 'Belfast'; 'Good Friday' is most common in academia and journalism. Due to the absence of an explicit author or publisher, and for ease of identification, the Agreement is cited as (Agreement, 1998), the St Andrews Agreement of 2006 as (St Andrews, 2006) and the Governments' joint declaration of December 1993, known as the 'Downing Street Declaration', as (Joint Declaration on Peace, 1993).

1

A theory of post-Agreement Northern Ireland

Introduction

In ethnic conflict, the identity and behaviour of one group shape the identity and behaviour of the other. This fact may be plain to outside observers but is missed by those caught in conflict, faced with threat, filled with fear and blinded by history. The security dilemma, a conceptual tool that brings to light the interdependence of warring groups' postures, identities and fears, has become a popular means of analysing intra-state conflict. It has not, however, been widely used in relation to Northern Ireland, presumably because, as we will see, it is associated with situations of 'anarchy' and state disintegration and those conditions – so destructive in other parts of the world – have never prevailed in Northern Ireland. Nevertheless, this chapter shows how security dilemma theory provides a penetrating framework with which to analyse not just the historic conflict in Ireland, but the nature of post-Agreement politics. Accordingly, the chapter eschews narrative in favour of a fresh theoretical analysis of the conflict, the Agreement and its implementation that foregrounds the self-fulfilling dynamics of inter-communal competition and the key motifs of mutuality, intersubjectivity and reciprocal fear, threat and conciliation. First, however, we investigate the meaning of the security dilemma itself.

The security dilemma

The possibility that self-protective moves will provoke rather than deter is of course an unavoidable hazard of human interaction, but it was in the 1950s that scholars began to examine this dynamic in relations between states (Butterfield, 1951; Herz, 1951). In subsequent decades, the security dilemma came to occupy a central place within International Relations, largely due to its apparent explanatory power in relation to the most pressing political question of the day – the Cold War – and the (related) dominance of Realist thinking, which emphasised the self-interestedness of states in an insecure world (Roe, 2005: 4). With the end of the Cold War and the subsequent spread of conflicts within, rather than between, states in the 1990s, the focus of security dilemma theorists shifted accordingly (for example, Posen, 1993; Lake and Rothchild, 1998; Walter and Snyder, 1999). Despite the concept's apparent simplicity, an expansive literature has emerged around how the security dilemma works and the conditions in which it arises, with new conflicts providing new laboratories for scholars to explore, refine or challenge the concept (for a critical overview, see Tang, 2009).

But what is it? A security dilemma is defined as a situation in which an actor's efforts to increase its security actually cause it greater insecurity because its actions, perceived as threatening, provoke counter-measures (Jervis, 1978: 169; Posen, 1993: 28). This dynamic is a consequence of 'the existential condition of *unresolvable uncertainty*' (Booth and Wheeler, 2008: 5; emphasis in original); we cannot read other people's minds, yet despite not knowing whether they mean us good or harm, we must devise ways to co-exist – peacefully or otherwise. This uncertainty is manifest in the 'anarchic' structure of the international system. While inter-personal insecurity may be reduced to some extent through law and the state, there exists no authority over states to enforce co-operation or provide security guarantees, making it difficult for state decision-makers to trust their counterparts. Even if an actor is sure of another's innocent intentions, this does not remove uncertainty because it cannot be sure of the other's intentions in the future. Uncertainty between political units is heightened by the ambiguity of weapons. They can be used for defence or attack, or indeed both, if offence is judged as the best defence.

Rationalist explanations of ethnic conflict emphasise that the demise of a strong state can create an anarchic, sovereign-less situation analogous to the anarchy of the state system, giving rise to the same patterns of confusion and confrontation witnessed in the international system. In a situation of state collapse, groups face 'information failures' and 'problems of credible commitment' that prevent co-operation, fuel mutual fears and may lead to misconceived and provocative security actions, i.e. the security dilemma (Lake and Rothchild, 1998). In this view, ethnic violence results from groups' quite reasonable fears for safety and their rational calculations that they must 'self-help' to protect their own security. Nowhere more than the crumbling Yugoslavia appeared to demonstrate the link between insecurity, fear and violence, and the Balkan conflicts are analysed again and again in the security dilemma literature (including Posen,

1993; Kaufman, 1996; Melander, 1999; Woodward, 1999; Rose, 2000; Roe, 2005; Smith, 2006; Bilgic, 2013). Indeed, given the concept's relevance to identity conflicts, not simply inter-state military confrontations, some scholars have spoken of a 'societal security dilemma' (notably Roe, 2005), something to which we return presently.

Yet, is the claim at the heart of the security dilemma – that conflict may be caused solely by actors' security-seeking behaviour – really plausible? Such is the strict definition of a security dilemma: a situation in which actors come into conflict inadvertently due to their desire to protect themselves – neither side actually wishes confrontation. If actors do not have 'benign', security-seeking intentions then, in some accounts, it is not a security dilemma (see especially Roe, 1999; Tang, 2009). But writers on the concept highlight two difficulties with operationalising the security dilemma if defined in this way. One is that identifying a security dilemma becomes rather tricky. How can one be sure that an actor has innocent intentions? Analysts can read minds no better than decision-makers, and hindsight and archival research may be insufficient to illuminate the considerations of actors in the past. The 'goodness' or 'evilness' of actor intentions is in the eye of the beholder anyway, dependent on what sources are consulted and the personal prejudices of the observer (Bilgic, 2013: 192–3).

An even greater difficulty is that the very idea of benign and malign intentions is, on closer inspection, illusory. Snyder and Jervis (1999: 16) point out that in the real world of ethnic conflict, actors are not motivated purely by security but that their security motives tend to be 'intertwined with their predatory goals'. Actors may pursue aggression now believing that this is the only way to protect their security in the future – the pre-emptive strike. Or they may pursue aggression now in response to the threat provoked by their security-seeking behaviour in the past. Furthermore, most writers on the security dilemma note the role of social-psychological factors, in addition to rational self-protection, on a group's response to its insecurity. This undermines the security–greed distinction in that a group's interpretations of threats are distorted by its collective memory, which may be laced with grievance, resentment and a prejudiced image of the other group. Security fears may also be 'artificially' inflamed by the manipulation of that collective mythology by ethnic elites who stand to profit politically from an intensified awareness of threats from outsiders (see especially Kaufman, 2001, 2006). For all these reasons, Kaufman (2006: 54) argues that in civil conflict, 'security' and 'greed' motives are indistinguishable: 'Chauvinist leaders always claim to be driven by security motives, but what makes them chauvinists is that they define their group's security as requiring dominance over rival groups which is, naturally, threatening to the others.'

In light of these difficulties with separating actors into benign (security-seeking) or malign (expansionist) categories, Bilgic (2013: 195) offers a fruitful alternative way to deploy the security dilemma that does not depend on claiming to know *whether* an actor is pursuing security but that asks *how* the actor is pursuing security:

> When actors experience insecurity in relation to another, how do they think about themselves? How do they position themselves in relation to another? What do they think about the political structures? What kind of solutions [do] they envisage to the insecurity problem they face?

And to classify how actors answer these questions, Bilgic uses Booth and Wheeler's (2008: 10) three 'logics of insecurity', or ways of thinking about the uncertainty of international politics. These are fatalist ('the idea that insecurity can never be escaped in international politics'), mitigator ('the idea that insecurity can be ameliorated for a time, but not eliminated') and transcender ('the idea that human society on a global scale can become what it wants to be and is not determined'). The logics and how they may be incorporated into the security dilemma merit some expansion as they inform the analysis of the rest of the book.

Logics of insecurity

Fatalist logic assumes that 'the nature of relations between states and other entities is essentially competitive, sometimes violent and always insecure' (Booth and Wheeler, 2008: 12). The absence of authority over states and political entities forces all to seek power and advantage in order to survive. In such a Hobbesian 'state of nature', to be rational is to fear, and so fatalism is biased towards pessimism and negative constructions of others' intentions. Actors must assume the worst and act accordingly, for the alternative is to risk death. As well as these structural assumptions, a fatalist outlook may be informed by a philosophical belief in the unrelenting selfishness of human nature; collaborative impulses will always be eclipsed by greed and power-lust. While fatalism believes that competition between political units is fated and inevitable, security is possible, but only through the accumulation of power, especially military power, an assumption that gives fatalist logic its propensity towards violence. In sum, fatalism is characterised by the expectation of conflict and the preference for mistrust and self-reliance in response.

By contrast, mitigator logic contends that while uncertainty cannot be eliminated, it can be managed through the development of processes, norms and institutions. Mitigator thinking may share the fatalist assumptions about the insecure world and selfish human nature, but it believes that diplomacy, state responsibility and international regimes can bring a degree of predictability to the international order and stave off the worst excesses of insecurity such as arms racing and war. Examples of mitigator logic in action offered by Booth and Wheeler include the European Concert in the first half of the nineteenth century, superpower detente in the 1970s and the nuclear non-proliferation regime since the 1960s (2008: 107–36). The most instructive example, suggest the authors, is the end of the Cold War in which a combination of factors, including empathic relationships between leaders, successful signalling of de-escalating intent and mutual fear of future disaster, permitted the mitigation of the seemingly immutable superpower competition (pp. 165–70). The authors stress that the distinction between fatalist and mitigator logics is porous; most fatalists are in practice mitigators, eager to try to ameliorate insecurity by whatever means possible, even if it is assumed that competition and conflict will eventually re-emerge (p. 15).

Transcender logic departs radically from the other two, strongly rejecting the idea that competition between political entities is ordained by fate. Rather, it sees global insecurity as a result of the deformed evolution of human thinking and relations: 'humans constructed through patriarchy, capitalism, the Westphalian system, nationalism and other powerful ideas and structures, a world politics of division and suspicion. Better alternatives were always possible' (2008: 17). Thus, Booth and Wheeler include under transcender logic the feminist, anarchist and Marxist critiques, though they find these approaches unsatisfactory for they rely on single-cause explanations of international strife and accordingly provide 'reductive' solutions (p. 225). A more compelling example of transcender logic for the authors is the security community approach exemplified by the European Union (EU). This, they argue, provides a powerful riposte to fatalist prophecies of eternal power competition. The co-operative institutions through which European countries bound themselves to each other after the Second World War not only provided collective security and economic advantages, but transformed the identities of member states by demonstrating the principle that the best outcome for all was achieved by acting together. The identities of many European states were based on self-reliance, domination and hostility to others, but participation in the EU sculpted new, multi-layered identities – regional, national, European – and redefined states' notions of what was in their best interests. While tensions and disputes between states continue, war as an instrument of resolving them is now unthinkable.

The possibility of new identities defines transcender logic – fatalism, with its assumption that the future will follow the pattern of the past, has a more static conception of identity. And creating a new identity is at the heart of what Booth and Wheeler call 'the ultimate transcender strategy': trust (2008: 171). Trust is:

when a relationship shifts from being solely based on rational egoism, which produces common interests which may or may not last, to becoming a relationship embedded in a sense of a shared identity: this is what we earlier described as two parallel *I's* becoming a *we*.

(p. 172)

Trust, they argue, is neglected in the study of International Relations, often dismissed as naive or impossible. Yet the EU and other instances of conflict resolution (the authors cautiously include, incidentally, Northern Ireland) show otherwise. Trust is the key distinction between mitigator and transcender logics. Mitigator logic entails 'contingent co-operation' – co-operation between political leaders, contingent because it may last only while those particular leaders are in power. Transcender logic entails 'embedded trust' – when trust between leaders is reflected in trust between societies, a state of affairs that characterises the EU (p. 197). Trust overcomes the ambiguous meaning of weapons, since actors are assured that they will not be used against them. Weapons come to be no more threatening than 'somebody holding a bread knife in a kitchen' (p. 256).

In delineating these logics of insecurity, Booth and Wheeler obviously capture aspects of a range of more familiar epithets used to distinguish between actors: Realists and Idealists; hawks and doves; hardliners and moderates; ethnic nationalists and civic nationalists. However, they are careful to stress that the logics are ideal types: they are classifying ideas rather than people. This is because, in reality, few individuals, whether scholars or political actors, show consistent commitment to only one of the logics, but give voice to more than one at different times or even the same time. In employing these three logics, Booth and Wheeler's overarching purpose is to show that actors are not propelled towards mutual competition by the inexorable forces of anarchy (as in the Realist/fatalist argument), but actually possess agency. Determined to do the same, Bilgic (2013) adopts the three logics as a framework for analysing actor behaviour in civil conflict, thus reframing our understanding of the intra-state security dilemma.

While traditional security dilemma theorising entailed, as Bilgic puts it, 'inconsequential endeavours to determine whether actors had malign or benign intentions', focusing instead on which of the three conceptions of security they hold has the advantage of allowing observers to 'pass judgements on actor responsibility in current societal confrontations by analysing actors' discourses and practices'; hindsight and historical research aimed at discovering 'real' intentions are not needed (2013: 200). The implications of the logics pursued by actors are as follows:

> If actors choose to act in accordance with the fatalist logic, the security dilemma can result in mutual tension accompanied by arms racing at best, and conflict at worst.

> Actors choosing to act within the confines of the mitigator logic can break the vicious cycle of conflict and war. They can mitigate but not transcend the security dilemma. In order to transcend the security dilemma, actors have another choice: to construct a common we-feeling through trust-building at societal level. Actors adopting the transcender logic choose to act in a way that existing identities and interests are redefined in order to pursue common security.
>
> (p. 197)

It is the fatalist approach to an uncertain political environment that will recreate and perpetuate that very environment, manifesting itself in ethno-centric security policies that disregard and demonise the other group, heightening the threat and insecurity faced by all. As Booth and Wheeler (2008: 170) comment of so-called 'offensive realism', the fatalist strategy par excellence, it 'is a self-fulfilling prophecy, a self-replicating prescription and a self-confirming theory'. Expecting conflict and meeting the challenge offensively embitters and provokes others, an outcome that is then taken as proof that the belligerent approach was the correct one. For instance, in Yugoslavia, ethnic war arose from the insecurity caused by state collapse; yet, at the same time, it was rivalry between identity groups that caused the state to collapse in the first place (for a discussion of this point, see Roe, 2005: 38–9). Snyder and Jervis (1999: 24) point out such circularity: 'the security dilemma is a cause of behaviour, yet it is also an outcome to be explained'; it is 'a social situation with social and perceptual causes, not simply a fact of nature'. Chauvinist ethnic leaders deepen the insecurity of their environment by following the fatalist logic of insecurity. However, 'there are always different choices' (Bilgic, 2013: 198); actors may pursue alternative policies that mitigate or transcend the cycle of threat.

On the basis of these considerations, a new formulation of the security dilemma may be stated. Given the difficulties with defining a security dilemma as a situation in which actors solely and benignly pursue security, and incorporating the logics of insecurity approach that emphasises the fact and nature of actor agency, the security dilemma may be defined as:

> *a situation in which an actor's pursuit of security according to a fatalistic logic of insecurity sustains another actor's pursuit of security according to a fatalist logic of insecurity, thus preventing both actors from regarding themselves as secure.*

This shifts the focus of the concept away from the problematic idea that actors may clash despite being devoid of malign intent, towards the relational dynamic inherent in all conflict: the mutually reinforcing nature of rival actors' identities and postures, and the cyclical and self-defeating quality of actors' quests for exclusively defined notions of security. Accordingly, the new formulation raises a suite of incisive questions to bring to an arena of ethnic strife. What is the nature of the insecure environment facing actors and how have they contributed to its creation? Why do they respond to insecurity in the ways that they do – according to fatalist, mitigator and transcender logics? In what ways are actors' responses to their insecurity a reaction to the behaviour of others? And why does a particular logic come to dominate within a political entity and alternatives come to be marginalised? Before we pose these questions of the centuries and cycles of identity conflict in Ireland, we take a closer look at how the security dilemma operates at the intra-state level and the nature of the security sought by ethnic groups in conflict.

Identity and the societal security dilemma

In the 1990s, the traditional security dilemma scenario – arms racing between states – appeared increasingly dated as identity concerns and intra-state conflict came to be the dominant features of international politics. In the host of violent inter-group conflicts that broke out in the aftermath of the Cold War, the protagonists were not states but 'societies' – ethno-national or religious groups – that were apparently motivated by fears for their identity or their very survival. Accordingly, scholars of international security began to talk about 'societal security', defined as:

> the ability of a society to persist under changing conditions and possible and actual threats. More specifically, it is about the sustainability, within acceptable conditions for evolution, of traditional patterns of language, culture, association and religious and national identity and custom.
>
> (Waever, 1993: 23)

Societal security is the capacity of a society to reproduce itself, as itself, through the generations. Thus, according to Roe (2005: 73), a societal security dilemma is 'when the actions that groups take to secure their identity cause reactions in others which in the end leave all parties less secure'.

Roe, who provides the fullest account of the societal security dilemma, still seeks to determine actors' 'real' intentions as malign or benign, proposing three types of societal security dilemma depending on how those intentions are judged. Bilgic (2013) is critical of this; we have seen the pitfalls of trying to label actors' intentions as security-seeking or predatory, and the preferability of examining instead how actors define their own security and hope to achieve it – whether they follow the fatalist, mitigator or transcender logics. But the societal security dilemma concept nonetheless captures the potentially decisive role of non-military threats/reactions in triggering inter-group tension at the substate level. In a multi-ethnic state, a dominant group may repress the cultural or political rights of other groups, restricting religious or linguistic freedom, ethnic symbols and so on, while globalisation, economic stagnation and/or demographic decline may also contribute to a society's diminishing confidence and perception of threat. Responses to these threats may take the form of cultural or ethnic nationalism that may then stimulate a similar intensification of identity in the other group.

The societal security dilemma, then, mimics the inter-state, military security dilemma in certain key respects. First, it is uncertainty that gives rise to the societal security dilemma, but that uncertainty is not due to the anarchy of the states system but state collapse or just the weakness of the state. A weak state is one in which 'the substance of citizenship – legal, political and social rights – has not been provided'. In this context, 'when the state does not deliver, people turn elsewhere for the satisfaction of material and non-material needs, predominantly towards ethnic communities' (Brock et al., 2012: 17). Second, the ambiguity of offence and defence is evident in the societal security dilemma, not only in relation to military preparations but assertions of group identity: it cannot be known whether such an assertion is benign, motivated by identity security, or malign, intended to sideline another group's identity. In fact, security and predatory motives may be one and the same since, in its fatalist logic, a group may believe that a strong identity *requires* the weak identity of another group. Third, the action–reaction process is present, not necessarily in the form of an arms race (though this may feature) but in terms of a reciprocal intensification of identities: 'For the societal security dilemma, the action-reaction process can therefore be conceived in terms of *escalating nationalisms*' (Roe: 2005: 69; emphasis added). If the only way for 'us' to be ourselves is to make it harder for 'them' to be themselves, an ideological 'arms race' may result as rivals scramble to protect and project their identities.

And so at the heart of the societal security dilemma is the interdependent nature of competing ethnic identities. The role of an out-group in defining identity is well known, particularly for populations that inhabit and seek control over the same territory. Wendt (1992: 406–7) describes how mutually hostile identities arise from:

> cycles of interaction in which each party acts in ways that the other feels are threatening to the self, creating expectations that the other is not to be trusted. Competitive or egoistic identities are caused by such insecurity; if the other is threatening, the self is forced to 'mirror' such behaviour in its conception of the self's relationship to that other.

This is a point worth emphasising: insecurity can transform identity, a process described by a number of writers on the security dilemma in Yugoslavia. After the incendiary combination of rival ethnic identities, elite manipulation and state collapse led to the outbreak of violence, that violence led to the hardening of identities and forced many who held a cosmopolitan or Yugoslav identity to revert to more particularistic, ethnic identities (Kaufmann, 1996: 143; Lake and Rothchild, 1998: 6; Kuran, 1999; Booth and Wheeler, 2008: 78). This demonstrates how:

> group identities may become increasingly important not only intrinsically but because the security of individuals becomes implicated with the fates of the contending groups. *Group identity can then be a consequence of conflict* as much as a cause of it and can be fuelled by security concerns.
>
> (Snyder and Jervis: 1999: 22; emphasis added)

Security fears lead ethnic groups to 'close ranks', restrict travelling to areas perceived as safe, suspect outsiders. Ethnic and/or religious narratives of grievance and glory that have perhaps lain dormant for generations are revived to interpret current threats (Kinnvall, 2004). The perception of threat triggers feelings of victimhood and undeserved suffering, moulding group cultures of intransigence, self-righteousness, violence, fear and paranoia – a deep, in-group solidarity and a corresponding out-group hostility. In other words, threat feeds the fatalistic logic of insecurity, which is itself acutely sensitive to perceiving threat. People turn towards strengthening identity as a means to strengthen security.

Yet this hardening of identity simply conforms to and encourages the pessimistic and hostile attitudes held by the rival group:

> in responding to perceived threats, the Other embarks on a course of action that corresponds with those negative images propounded by the first group. In other words, insecurity among Others can stimulate similar processes, which, in turn subject them to increased Othering.
>
> (Roe, 2005: 69)

Like a Chinese finger trap, identities become locked in a security dilemma of mutually reinforcing enmity, with each group competing to imitate the other. The antagonistic relationship becomes institutionalised and extremely resistant to change. In fact, actors can become deeply attached to that competitive relationship because of the clarity of purpose and identity it gives them. States and ethnic groups can prefer the familiarity of war or a hostile relationship with an Other to the crisis of identity that would result from forming a new relationship (Mitzen, 2006). Ethnic conflicts come to be intractable and the fear of peace is fear of a new identity: if we are not to be victims/challengers of the Other, who are we to be?

Fatalism: the conflict of nationalisms in Ireland

A brief historical overview will suffice to illustrate the outworking of the societal security dilemma in Ireland and its dimensions just described: mutually competitive identities, state weakness, fatalist logic and reciprocal fear and threat. The zero-sum competition between the two traditional group identities in Ireland – British and Irish – is traceable to their emergence from Protestant and Catholic religious identities, respectively, identities that were inherently conflictual (Elliott, 2009; English, 2011). Protestantism's *raison d'être* was to resist the theology, practices and structure of the Catholic Church. In Ireland, these theological divisions were given political grounding in the clash between Protestant settlers from Britain and the Catholic Irish in the sixteenth and seventeenth centuries. This instituted the combustible condition of overlapping ethnic and economic cleavages that has been so central to ethnic conflict around the world (Scarcelli, 2014). The victory of British Protestantism at the end of the seventeenth century 'locked-in and partially fused a complex set of cultural oppositions (religious, ethnic, cultural, colonial) and created a situation where rational self-interest (for security or economic livelihood or influence) led individuals to band together as Protestants or as Catholics' (Ruane and Todd, 2007: 11). This poisonous 'system of relationships', in which Protestants held power and Catholics remained culturally and politically subordinate, was self-sustaining: 'The exclusion of Catholics was justified by their disaffection and exclusion reinforced disaffection' (p. 11). Identification with one's ethnic/political/religious bloc came to be regarded as necessary for people's security and sense of belonging, and the deepening of identity in one side encouraged the same in the other. The system was constituted by cultural differences, power disparity and communal solidarity, 'with each of these reinforcing the others and being reinforced by it in return' (p. 12).

Locked into this pattern of relations, Catholic and Protestant identities came to be defined by suspicion, grievance and mutual, negative stereotyping. This is laid bare in Elliott's (2009: 4) exploration of 'how Irish Protestants' and Irish Catholics' sense of self was conditioned by their views of each other'. Recalling the self-fulfilling dynamics of the security dilemma, Elliott notes how stereotypes have a habit of making themselves come true: 'stereotypical perceptions of situations actually change them to become as we perceive them. Even those stereotyped believe them and conform to them' (p. 13). Centuries-old images

(Catholics are subversive, disloyal, dishonest; Protestants are domineering, bigoted, oppressive) evolved in tandem, each supporting the other, while fear and insecurity exacerbated difference:

> insecurities have often been the backdrop of aggressive and exclusive displays of heritage and culture. The idea that group identity lies in difference then produces a disproportionate emphasis on those differences and a fear of dilution or loss of status ..., any threat of loss creating the potential for violence, but also for cohesiveness within that community.
>
> (p. 8)

Insecurity led to cultural chauvinism – in Ireland, usually called sectarianism – which itself undermined the security of others.

The societal security dilemma in Ireland gave rise to repeated cycles of escalation, violence and intense identity conflict. For example, the pivotal decade 1912–21 witnessed mainly Protestant unionists and mainly Catholic nationalists mobilising in the context of uncertainty regarding the resolve of the British state to defend the status quo, and on the basis of doomsday predictions of what would occur should the other side get its way. These predictions were based on historic images of the Other and were to some extent self-fulfilling. Protestants' fear that the 'Home Rule' arrangements for all-Ireland autonomy proposed in the late nineteenth and early twentieth centuries would destroy their cultural identity, civil rights and economic advantages motivated them to organise and arm themselves. This inspired nationalists to do likewise, forming the Irish Volunteers, a force that was used to rebel against the British in 1916. That uprising was crushed and its leaders executed, yet public sympathy for the rebels led to the victory of Sinn Féin, a separatist party, in the 1918 election, that party's formation of the Provisional Government and, ultimately, the division of Ireland, with six northern counties (to become Northern Ireland) remaining in the United Kingdom and the South becoming autonomous.

Partition brought a measure of security to both unionists and nationalists – a 'Catholic parliament for a Catholic people' in the South and a 'Protestant parliament for a Protestant people' in the North, as their leaders famously described the new situation. However, the antagonisms were not resolved but frozen in a Cold War of suspicion between the two new political entities. Uncertainty about whether the partition arrangement was permanent enabled unionists and nationalists to 'indulge in self-delusion, self-pity and self-protection' (Arthur, 2000: 3) and the two parts of Ireland settled into dichotomous, ethno-religious identities (Walker, 2012). At the same time, a substantial population of Catholics found themselves under the 'wrong' parliament in the North, experiencing their own insecurity while adding to the fear and paranoia of the two-thirds Protestant majority. In his Nobel lecture in 1998, unionist leader David Trimble highlighted that the mutual fears of a security dilemma were at work in this period when he said: 'Ulster Unionists, fearful of being isolated on the island, build a solid house, but it was a cold house for Catholics. And northern nationalists, although they had a roof over their heads, seemed to us as if they meant to burn the house down' (Trimble, 2001a: 62). Northern Ireland was effectively a one-party state, with the electoral system ensuring a permanent unionist majority, and the Nationalist Party, perpetually in opposition, offering ineffective representation to Catholics. Then, as now, the ethnic fissure overran the possibility of cross-community class politics, with group unity in the face of threats promoted as essential for group security.

The spiral of tension that unleashed the 'Troubles' in the late 1960s/early 1970s again displayed many of the characteristics identified by the security dilemma theorists. The state did not collapse but it was weak and lacking legitimacy, a condition heightened by the rising demographic, educational and economic strength of the Catholic minority. Both sides, in different ways, were driven towards 'self-help' in search of security. Catholics (and some Protestants) organised street protests to secure equal political and economic participation. These were interpreted by many Protestants as attempts to destroy Northern Ireland and were met by a repressive response – by security forces and Protestant gangs – which only served to prove to many in the Catholic community that the Northern state was un-reformable. Thus, the unionist (over)reaction 'gave ironical substance to unionist fears about the future of their society, as a revitalised and increasingly radicalised nationalism began to demand much more than fair housing, employment and voting practices' (Porter, 2003: 187). A reinvigorated IRA exploited the heady climate and commenced an armed insurgency that sought nothing less than the reunification of Ireland. In his history of the outbreak of the 'Troubles', Hennessey (2005: 390) emphasises the snowballing, self-fulfilling impact of worst-case-scenario fatalism in the early months of street violence: 'There was no state-authorised or co-ordinated attacks on Catholics. And there was no IRA conspiracy to overthrow the state. Yet in the heat of battle, realities were replaced by such perceptions, which then entered the respective communal mythologies.'

As the civil unrest progressed, fear continued to create its own justification. Republican violence provoked security force repression and loyalist attacks, and stiffened unionist intransigence, thus 'proving' republican claims of Protestant sectarianism and the failure of the Northern Ireland state; the republican insurgency was, for Protestants, incontrovertible evidence of the real threat to their security and way of life. As Elliott (2009: 4) puts it, the 'Troubles' 'happened because both sides acted the way the stereotypes said they would'. Republicans acted out the Protestant image of Catholics as murderous and disloyal; unionists acted out the Catholic image of Protestants as sectarian and supremacist; and the ethnic narratives were restocked with new grievances, new myths and new prejudices that would form the basis of future calculations of threat and accusations of provocation. All the while, the paramilitaries justified themselves in the name of communal defence, yet the bloodshed only heightened the intractability and bitterness of the conflict, and pushed the communities further apart. The most blatant acts of aggression were excused as defensive since terrorising the other side was intended to sap its resolve to fight (Brewer *et al.*, 2013: 61). Violence – ostensibly defensive but experienced by the other side as offensive – decreased the likelihood of those on the receiving end understanding or acknowledging the validity of the other side's mistrust. Republicans would not acknowledge unionist fear for their British identity since that would be to concede some justification for the British 'occupation' of the six counties. Unionists would not acknowledge the political alienation of Catholics for that would be to concede a justification for IRA violence.

And because this conflict was ultimately a battle over identity – societal – security, culture played a defensive role no less important than bombs and bullets. As Ruane and Todd (1996: 202) write:

> The struggle in Northern Ireland is in part psychological, a battle of wills in which identity and morale are crucial resources. Each community believes that if it 'goes under' culturally, political collapse will soon follow; each hopes that its cultural strength will convince the other that the contest is hopeless and that it is best to yield – that nationalism is on an inexorable rise, or that 'the dogs on the streets' know that Northern Ireland is going to stay British.

Cultural and symbolic displays heightened – and advertised to the 'enemy' – communal morale, political conviction and territorial reach. The arts and media became a bloodless but fiercely fought battlefield where ideas and reasons and histories vied for national and international credibility. And information (or just perception) of the communities' relative demographic strength, now and in the future, hugely impacted their sense of confidence and resolve. The cumulative effect of the conflict was, as Ruane (2004: 122) puts it simply, 'to intensify the fear, hostility, bitterness and grievance which had produced it in the first place'. Between 1969 and 1998, 3,627 people were killed (McKittrick *et al.*, 1999: 1474).

Above, we noted that it is the fatalist logic of insecurity that is the engine of the security dilemma, and so it was in Ireland. Indeed, writers on unionism and nationalism have identified a fatalistic worldview as being among their defining traits. Aughey (2005: 49), for instance, describes a 'cult of inevitability' within nationalism, an inability to accept frustration of its forward march towards Irish unity and a corresponding willingness to use violence to force a way through, clashing with a unionist 'cult of resilience', a fearfulness that even minor compromise poses an existential threat. In a similar vein, Shanahan (2009: 58–9) observes that both extreme nationalism and extreme unionism were characterised and energised, as nationalist movements tend to be, by mutually exclusive notions of destiny. Republicans, holding a semi-mystical trust in the inevitability of their own victory, regarded conflict towards that goal as immutable, an automatic and unavoidable consequence of the British presence in Ireland. Unionists who understood the conflict as a spiritual battle between good (God's chosen people in Ulster) and evil (Roman Catholicism, republicans and their colluders) similarly thought conflict to be relentless and fated, and compromise to be unconscionable. Both movements at times invoked divine sanction, both movements' pursuit of security was defined by 'ourselves alone' (the meaning of 'Sinn Féin') and in both cases, the conviction of a national mission and victorious future shaped expectations of, and resolve for waging, ongoing conflict in the present.

But mutually exclusive notions of destiny are a recipe for mutual failure, and unionist and nationalist fatalisms have been both interdependent and self-defeating. For example, one of Ian Paisley's biographers calls him a 'self-fulfilling prophet' and 'midwife' of his great enemy, the IRA, on the basis that his virulent opposition to efforts to address nationalists' legitimate political grievances in the 1960s contributed to internecine violence and a radicalisation within the Catholic community that produced the Provisional IRA (Moloney, 2008: 514–15). Journalist and campaigner Eamonn McCann describes Paisley as 'co-creator of the IRA' (BBC Radio Ulster, 2014). Likewise, the armed campaign of the IRA, rather than meeting its intended goal of hastening Irish unity, most likely did the very opposite, for reasons including the facts that it sowed intense distrust and bitterness among the Protestant population and stymied the development of cordial economic and cultural relations between the two parts of Ireland. Noel Doran, editor of the nationalist *Irish News*, commented at the Progressive Unionist Party conference in October 2013 that it could be argued that reducing the driving time between Dublin and Belfast to ninety minutes was 'nationalism's greatest achievement in living memory' (Doran, 2013). That achievement was only possible due to the removal of security checkpoints and considerable infrastructural investment, i.e. peace. By contrast, the IRA regularly targeted transport links between Dublin and Belfast, thus expanding, not reducing, the actual and psychological distance between the two capitals. Hence, it is possible to surmise, as does Ruairí Quinn, a prominent Labour Party politician in the Republic, that if IRA violence achieved anything, it was 'probably the permanent partition of this country' (TV3, 2013).

At the same time, the logics of insecurity framework draws attention to individuals, groups and ideas that, at each stage of conflict, seek to advance alternative approaches to security against the clamour of fatalist mobilisation. As noted, the key contention of Bilgic's (2013) and Booth and Wheeler's (2008) analyses of the security dilemma is that actors enjoy agency – 'there are always different choices'. Indeed, the denial of agency (and thus responsibility) is a theme in the testimonies of members of violent groups in Northern Ireland (see, for example, Brewer *et al.*, 2013). During the 'Troubles', a range of political actors including the Social Democratic and Labour Party (SDLP), Alliance Party, liberal unionists and others, plus churches, trade unions and scores of other civil society groups, resisted and strove to de-escalate the spiral of enmity perpetuated by the minority of extremists on both sides. They wished to escape the zero-sum tyranny of the conflict and deadlocked political visions of the extremes, but they had to navigate an environment in which violent fatalism worked to overpower and sideline alternative perspectives. As put by the Alliance Party, 'violence in support of the "two communities" idea has forced generations of people into choices about security which have embedded hatred and condemned others to silence and marginalisation' (Alliance, 2013a: 13). However, the analysis of the moderates, which refused to reduce the conflict to a single cause, British colonialism or Irish irredentism, and recognised the mutual alienation and mistrust of the two identity groups, eventually became the guiding light of official British and Irish efforts to resolve the conflict in the 1980s and 1990s.

Explaining the peace process

For most of the 'Troubles', the pattern of the security dilemma appeared unbreakable. Its dynamics gained expression in conflict clichés that captured the dismal predictability of the violence and the attitudes that bred it: 'tit-for-tat killing', 'retaliation', the 'cycle of violence' and 'whataboutery' (the deflection of responsibility by blaming the actions of the other side). Change, however, did come, and it did so as a consequence of two processes. One was intensified co-operation between the British and Irish states on reaching a political solution in Northern Ireland. The other was the gradual realisation of the Northern Ireland parties that indefinitely pursuing exclusivist conceptions of their security was impossible. Each process had its own set of causes.

The partnership of the British and Irish Governments gathered pace in the 1980s due to a common interest in resolving the Northern Ireland 'problem', a problem that at times spilled over into both territories and was damaging to their international reputations. After several still-born political initiatives during the 'Troubles' and years of fighting the IRA, the British Government realised that a political solution that could command the support of both traditions in the North, jointly nurtured with Dublin, was essential and, indeed, was preferable to military victory. But common interests between London and Dublin crystallised in a context of deepening and widening ties over several decades, ties resulting in a relationship of 'complex interdependency' between the two states entailing multi-levelled and reciprocal economic, cultural and political relations (Gillespie, 2014).

In this process, an important factor was the EU. Membership of the EU facilitated contact between politicians and civil servants and enhanced the standing of the Irish vis-à-vis the British, undermining the asymmetry of the historic colonial relationship. With regard to Northern Ireland, the EU provided a model for the institutionalisation of cross-border relations and a fresh discourse on sovereignty, identity and borders that helped reframe how the states understood themselves and their territorial conflict (Meehan, 2006; Hayward, 2009; Gillespie, 2014). The EU's role is striking since, as we saw, the EU is looked to by Booth and Wheeler and several other security dilemma theorists as a paradigmatic example of transcending the security dilemma (Wendt, 1992: 417; Snyder and Jervis, 1999: 31; Mitzen, 2006: 363; Booth and Wheeler, 2008: 190–200). The proponents of power-sharing approaches to managing ethnic conflicts recognise the potential for shared institutions to embed norms of trust and co-operation, to shape new, 'we' identities, in much the same way as the EU has gone so far in achieving across Europe, including between Britain and Ireland (see, for example, McGarry and O'Leary, 2009).

The European context, combined with the British and Irish Governments' joint role as gatekeepers and guarantors of the peace process (on this, see Darby and Mac Ginty, 2002), meant that Northern Ireland had two advantages that have been identified as important to the slackening of security dilemmas: a benign regional environment and strong third-party commitment (Lake and Rothchild, 1998; Walter, 1999). Britain and Ireland were stable democracies between which there was no chance of a military confrontation that might exacerbate the conflict. Peace efforts and peace implementation also had the considerable resources of the British and Irish states at their disposal, plus huge European and American financial and diplomatic support. (Needless to say, these are conditions enjoyed by few other arenas of protracted ethnic conflict, the key fact that must be borne in mind when seeking 'lessons' from the Northern Irish case.) Moreover, the combined approach of the British and Irish Governments to resolving the conflict was informed by a tacit recognition of the dynamics of societal security dilemma, and the need for a balanced prescription for the mutual security and identity fears of both sides.

This was evident, for example, in what is regarded as the founding document of the 1990s peace process, the 1993 'Downing Street Declaration'. The Governments declared their goal to be 'a new era of trust, in which suspicion of the motives and actions of others is removed on the part of either community'; they recognised the 'need to engage in dialogue that would address with honesty and integrity the fears of all traditions'; and they held out the potential to 'break decisively the cycle of violence'. The Governments would initiate this process by pledging to address features of the Self that they knew to be sustaining of the hostile outlook of the Other: principally, the British Government reiterated that it had no selfish interest in retaining Northern Ireland and would not impede Irish unity if both parts of the island wished it; the Irish Government pledged to consider revising Articles II and III of its constitution that unionists found so threatening, and to examine any aspect of the Irish state that may be perceived by unionists as inimical to their way of life (Joint Declaration on Peace, 1993). In this way, the Governments sought to undermine the fatalistic logic driving parts of the communities in Northern Ireland, logics that arose from negative images of the other side.

However, the peace process would not have gained traction without a convergence of interest between the British and Irish states, and the parties of the North. The subsequent chapters examine in detail the motivations of the parties in accepting or rejecting the Agreement, but suffice to note at this stage the critical push and pull factors. The overriding significance of the Governments' joint commitment to a consensual, power-sharing solution lay in the fact that they (particularly the British) had, and exercised, considerable power to induce the parties towards that goal. The increasing success of the security forces in containing the IRA showed republicans that continuing armed action indefinitely would yield a future of pointless hardship for their community and few political rewards. Accordingly, republicans were disposed to taking the political avenues on offer – Government-sponsored all-party negotiations and, particularly, the opportunity to form a pan-nationalist alliance with the SDLP, Dublin and the United States to press for whatever political gains they could.

For their part, unionists were inclined to negotiate and eventually come to agreement for two reasons. First, they disliked Direct Rule from London and despised the Anglo-Irish Agreement of 1985 that gave Dublin a consultative role in Northern Irish affairs. The return of devolved government to Northern Ireland would solve both problems, but the British would only allow this to happen if unionists agreed to share power with nationalists. Second, unionists feared that if they stonewalled indefinitely, London might pursue policies that would be even less agreeable to unionists, such as joint British–Irish authority over Northern Ireland. Hence, despite the short-term vulnerabilities that would result, unionists judged that it was wisest to take the institutional arrangements on offer in which they at least would have a strong influence. The threat of Joint Authority, particularly in 2006, may have been a British ruse to pressurise unionists (see Chapter 5), but in any case, the British Government's capacity to determine the parameters within which parties had no choice but to work was key to progress.

It is worth noting how these motivating constraints placed on the parties by Government-moulded circumstances illustrate an observation by Booth and Wheeler on how de-escalation in intractable conflict can occur. Above, we noted how the security dilemma is compounded by future uncertainty – even if opponents appear trustworthy, they may defect in the future, arguably making it foolish to trust them even now. However, Booth and Wheeler (2008: 157) use the case of the end of the Cold War to argue that future uncertainty can also work to incentivise compromise. Actors may judge that the conditions of the conflict, the available terms of agreement and/or the leadership on the opposing side will be *less* advantageous in the future and so it is best to seek accommodation now. This observation is comparable to Zartman's (1985) theory of ripeness – that the perception of a 'mutually hurting stalemate' in which the costs of continuing conflict are worse than the costs of compromise facilitates accommodation.

That said, self-interested strategic calculations were not the only factors in unionist and republican thinking. On all sides, there was a degree of 'learning' regarding the unrealistic nature of their positions at the outset of the conflict (Ruane, 2004: 122–4) as well as a desire to spare future generations from what the 'Troubles' generation had lived through. Developments in the republican outlook included a less dismissive assessment of the unionist position, while unionism increasingly recognised the need to make the governance of Northern Ireland more palatable to nationalists. The experience of incarceration stimulated new ideas among both loyalist and republican prisoners regarding alternatives to violence that fed into their political movements on the outside (McKeown, 2001; Sinnerton, 2002), while track-two diplomacy (Arthur, 1999) and back-channel dialogue (Powell, 2008; Ó Dochartaigh, 2011) allowed key players to explore what solutions might be possible. These processes interacted with parties' perceptions of a future of potentially worsening societal security and helped to weaken the parties' fatalist logic in favour of an impulse towards co-operation. That impulse eventually came to fruition in the Good Friday Agreement.

Mitigation: the promise and limits of the Agreement

The 1998 Agreement was an ambitious apparatus through which to contain and stabilise the rival nationalisms, restraining the capacity of one side to pursue a conception of its own security that required the insecurity of the other. Parties that could not trust each other could trust in the apparatus and in the guarantees given them. The Agreement, then, embodied the mitigator logic of insecurity, designed to regulate and render predictable the relations between the parties while recognising that ethno-political competition would continue in the short to medium term. At the same time, it was widely believed that the Agreement had the potential to achieve more than this. Political stability and co-operation could allow unionists and nationalists to, eventually, transcend their societal security dilemma through an organic process of trust building and the flowering of a common identity and allegiance. As the Agreement itself stated, talks participants recognised that the deal offered 'a truly historic opportunity for a new beginning … in which we firmly dedicate ourselves to the achievement of reconciliation, tolerance and mutual trust' (Agreement, 1998: 1).

The centrepiece of the accord was a power-sharing Assembly within Northern Ireland replete with various 'safeguards to ensure that all sections of the community can participate and work together successfully' (Agreement, 1998: 5). It would be elected via the Proportional Representation (Single Transferable Vote) system, thus ensuring, unlike the Westminster system, that parties' representation reflected their vote and the strengths of the ethnic communities, while also allowing people to transfer votes across the communal divide. Committee chairs, ministers and committee members would be selected in proportion to party strengths via the d'Hondt method. Assembly members would be required to designate themselves as 'unionist', 'nationalist' or 'other' to allow cross-community decision-making and mutual vetoes. Key Assembly decisions would require 'parallel consent' (a majority of members, including a majority of unionist and nationalist designations) or a weighted majority (60 per cent of members, including at least 40 per cent of the unionist and the nationalist blocs). At least thirty members could force a decision to be taken on a cross-community basis using a mechanism called a 'petition of concern'. An Executive Committee of Ministers comprising all parties eligible under d'Hondt would be presided over by a First Minister and Deputy First Minister who would be jointly elected by the Assembly using parallel consent. Ministers would be required to comply with a Pledge of Office and Code of Conduct in which they would be committed to, inter alia, using exclusively peaceful means, serving all the people of Northern Ireland equally and promoting good relations and equality of treatment.

Relations between Northern Ireland and the Republic of Ireland would be addressed primarily through a North–South Ministerial Council (NSMC), a forum comprising ministers from the Assembly and from the Irish Government tasked to agree policies in a range of areas of mutual, mainly economic and cultural, interest. Crucially, the NSMC would be accountable to the legislatures in the North and South, and it and the Northern Ireland Assembly would be 'interlocking and interdependent' (Agreement, 1998: 1). The NSMC would be 'balanced' by an east–west institution, the British–Irish Council, comprising ministers from the Irish Government and the various UK jurisdictions. A British–Irish Intergovernmental Conference would be established to replace the Intergovernmental Conference set up under the Anglo-Irish Agreement, but with a similar purpose of joint consultation on matters within the powers of both Governments.

In a section dealing with 'rights, safeguards and equality', the Agreement spelled out a series of rights with the preface 'against the background of communal conflict, the parties affirm'. Those rights included the 'right to free political thought', the 'right to freedom of expression of religion', the 'right to pursue democratically national and political aspirations' and the 'right to equal opportunity in all social and economic activity' (Agreement, 1998: 16). The British Government would incorporate into Northern Ireland law the European Convention on Human Rights and would create a statutory obligation on public authorities to conduct themselves 'with due regard to the need to promote equality of opportunity in relation to religion and political opinion; gender; race; disability; age; marital status; dependants; and sexual orientation' (p. 16). A Northern Ireland Human Rights Commission and an Equality Commission would be established – replacing and expanding the remit of similar existing bodies – to protect and promote human rights and equality, particularly in relation to the new Assembly and public bodies. The Irish Government pledged to ensure that its human rights regime was on a par with that of Northern Ireland.

Policing and justice – issues too contentious for the parties to agree on – would be delegated to independent commissions of experts that would advise on necessary reforms. The Agreement did, however, contain terms of reference for these commissions. The policing commission's proposals 'should be designed to ensure that policing arrangements, including composition recruitment, training, culture, ethos and symbols, are such that in a new approach Northern Ireland has a police service that can enjoy widespread support from, and is seen as an integral part of, the community as a whole' (Agreement, 1998: 23). The British Government would conduct a review of the criminal justice system 'through a mechanism with an independent element' with the aim of ensuring, among other things, that system's independence (p. 23). Dealing with the weapons held by paramilitary groups had already been tasked to an independent international commission and the Agreement reaffirmed the parties' support for this body. The British Government promised to normalise security arrangements in Northern Ireland as soon as possible, dependent on the level of threat from paramilitaries. Support was affirmed for victims of the 'Troubles', while paramilitary prisoners would be given early release on condition that their organisations were on cease-fire at the time of the Agreement.

The entire Agreement would be submitted to the public for endorsement in two simultaneous referenda, one in the North, one in the South. This would reflect the constitutional position set out in the Agreement, that the constitutional status of Northern Ireland was dependent on the consent of the people of the two parts of the island, 'freely and concurrently given' (Agreement, 1998: 2). The Irish Government agreed to remove the Irish constitution's definition of the national territory as the whole of the island, so loathed by unionists, in favour of looser wording that expressed an aspiration to unite the people of Ireland. Northern Ireland would be remaining in the United Kingdom for the time being as a majority there wished it to, but if the desire of a majority in the North changed, the Governments promised to facilitate new constitutional arrangements and that, in any case, whichever Government held jurisdiction would exercise its power 'with rigorous impartiality on behalf of all the people in the diversity of their identities and traditions' (p. 2). Perhaps the most radical provision of the Agreement was that concerning identity. While the Agreement emphatically recognised the identity, ethos and aspirations of unionists and nationalists as equally legitimate, in a profound twist the Agreement also enshrined a third option:

> [the talks participants] recognise the birthright of all the people of Northern Ireland to identify themselves and be accepted as *Irish or British, or both*, as they may choose, and accordingly confirm that their right to hold both British and Irish citizenship is accepted by both Governments.
>
> (p. 2; emphasis added)

In this way, the Agreement attempted to decouple identity from territory and sovereignty, transforming the zero-sum conception of identity that drove the societal security dilemma. As Arthur (2000: 247) describes this provision, it was 'the genius of the 1998 Agreement … a movement away from exclusion and towards polycentric identities and a blurring of boundaries'.

Overall, the provisions of the Agreement represented an elaborate programme of balanced safeguards and protections designed to create a context conducive to the continuing weakening of the parties' tightly interlocked antagonism. Mutual fears were addressed at five levels. First, the political. Unionists secured their place in the United Kingdom and the removal of the Southern state's constitutional claim on the North. Nationalists' aspiration to a united Ireland was recognised and their identity given institutional expression in the form of the NSMC. Inclusive power-sharing meant that neither group would be excluded from government, and far-reaching human rights and equality protections meant that neither group would be discriminated against by government. Second, both sides' security fears were addressed. Signatories to the Agreement rejected the principle of seeking political change through violence, while parties could be assured that the thorny, emotive issues of policing and decommissioning would not be in the hands of their rivals but delegated to bodies of independent technocrats with international standing.

Third, both sides' cultural fears were addressed. Talks participants agreed to respect the legitimacy of both cultures, cultures that were to be treated with 'parity of esteem' but be expressed with awareness of the sensitivities of the other side, and the Irish and Ulster Scots languages were recognised (more so the former). Fourth, fears of economic and material malaise were addressed by the British Government's pledge of an energetic economic development strategy targeted at urban, rural and border areas. Fifth, the demographic concerns of both sides were addressed to the extent that both Governments assured the parties that regardless of which state held power in Northern Ireland in the future, neither side need fear that its rights or identity would be infringed. In sum, the Agreement recognised the underlying dynamics of the societal security dilemma that prevailed in Northern Ireland and wielded a range of innovative measures designed to counteract those dynamics. As Morrow (2001: 16–17) writes, it was 'an ingenious, almost miraculous, political package. Both Unionist and Nationalist ceded ground on previously non-negotiable territory and did so in such a way that both were able to glimpse a new security in the future'.

However, despite the Agreement's general clarity and comprehensiveness, there were chinks in its programme. As was evident at the time, and as the parties made their positions and interpretations clear in the weeks and months following the Agreement, the document was ambiguous and/or silent in two critical areas. The first concerned constitutional matters. While the principle of consent settled the constitutional question for the time being, by making the status of Northern Ireland dependent on the will of a majority there, the principle also entailed a fundamental ambiguity. Depending on one's expectation of future political and demographic developments, consent could be seen as a glass half full or half empty. The Agreement provided for future referenda, not less than seven years apart, on Northern Ireland's place in the United Kingdom in the event that the British Secretary of State for Northern Ireland deemed a majority for a united Ireland likely (Agreement, 1998: 3). Consent, therefore, was a device to manage the ethnic blocs' competing national aspirations, not a means of reconciling them. Unavoidably, the Agreement left the core issue of rival territorial claims unaltered, allowing 'the national question to exist as a ghost in the machinery of its operation' (Gilligan, 2003: 29).

Not only was the future insecure, but there was fuzziness about how the constitutional position of Northern Ireland should be manifested in the present. This emanated from the central trade-off in the Agreement, which may be explained as follows. The Agreement sought to lay a new foundation of legitimacy for Northern Ireland, and that legitimacy depended on certain standards being met with regard to both constitutional and institutional matters. The constitutional standard of legitimacy was majority consent. Securing the explicit acceptance of this by nationalists and the Republic was the major gain of unionism. The institutional standard of legitimacy, however, did not rest on majoritarianism, but on cross-community consent. This was nationalists' principal interest and victory – that the governance of Northern Ireland would be just and impartial and would be amenable to nationalists' political identity (on this, see Porter, 2003: 218–19). The Agreement was a package deal encapsulating both standards of legitimacy but it was unclear which should prevail should each community hold to its own standard as trumping the other's. This ambiguity was to reveal itself in the relentless post-Agreement dispute over the appropriate display of state flags and emblems, an issue that was itself fudged in the Agreement; the document made a vague call for sensitivity in their use and further monitoring and discussion (Agreement, 1998: 20). Thus, 'if the Agreement resolved the issue of sovereignty at the formal-legal level, it did not do so at the political-substantive level, nor has it removed it from the terrain of active political struggle' (Ruane and Todd, 2001: 936).

The second strand of ambiguity in the Agreement concerned several security related issues: paramilitary weapons decommissioning, policing and the normalisation of the state security regime. While the handling of decommissioning and policing was delegated to neutral bodies, how those bodies would deal with the issues was unknown and they had no power to enforce recommendations or compel compliance anyway. Decommissioning had long bedevilled the peace process. After an impasse following the IRA ceasefire in 1994, political progress was eased through a controversial twin-track approach that referred decommissioning to an international commission, allowing parties linked to paramilitary groups to participate in the talks without any arms being disposed of. But the Agreement brought no certainty to the issue; on decommissioning, 'constructive ambiguity took the strain' (Powell, 2008: 315). All the Agreement contained was a weak requirement for parties to 'use any influence they may have, to achieve the decommissioning of all paramilitary arms within two years following endorsement in referendums North and South of the agreement and in the context of the implementation of the overall settlement' (Agreement, 1998: 20). As for changes to policing and demilitarisation, the likely scope and pace of change in these areas was unknown and thus a source of anxiety on all sides. Ultimately, decisions on disarmament, policing, demilitarisation, and indeed the pace of paramilitary prisoner releases lay in the hands of the British Government. None of the parties in Northern Ireland could be confident that the British would enforce implementation as it desired.

As we explore presently, these 'constructive ambiguities' had profound causes and far-reaching implications, but the fact of imprecision in the Agreement text was not in itself surprising. Peace agreements often rely on deliberate textual ambiguity to prevent difficult issues from scuppering an overall agreement. Circumventing obstacles in this way may be unavoidable during difficult negotiations but entails considerable risk, given the likelihood that as soon as one side's interpretation of the accord is proven mistaken, the accord will unravel (see Mitchell, 2009). The ambiguity of the 1998 deal was such that Aughey (2005: 104–5) likens it to the perceptual puzzle used by Wittgenstein – an image of a duck that can also be seen as rabbit – to illustrate the depth of confusion. Like this puzzle, the Agreement displayed contradictory qualities, and looking at it, 'People may see only part of the picture and not the whole; they may see only what they choose to see; or they may wish the whole to be something other than what it is'. The contradictions came to be inscribed in the new political landscape and the opposing interpretations of the Agreement adopted by the political parties. But before turning to the politics of implementation, we must first set out why, when the Agreement was clear on so many other issues, these constitutional/symbolic matters and the security/legacy of violence matters were left vague and unresolved.

Party politics and the security dilemma after 1998

The argument here is that the instability of post-Agreement politics must be understood in terms of the continuing security dilemma. To restate our definition of a security dilemma, it is: *a situation in which an actor's pursuit of security according to a fatalistic logic of insecurity sustains another actor's pursuit of security according to a fatalist logic of insecurity, thus preventing both actors from regarding themselves as secure.* The security dilemma after the Agreement was recreated by the fatalist logic that had traditionally shaped the thinking of the parties. That logic prevented agreement on key issues and consequently rendered parts of the Agreement ambiguous and incomplete. At the core of fatalist orientation is a negative image of an Other, and it is from this image that emanate other fatalist themes – fear, mistrust, self-reliance, violence, exclusive identity and the pessimistic expectation of conflict. Without rehearsing the detailed exposition contained in subsequent chapters, we can briefly summarise the unionist and republican fatalist mindsets at the time of the Agreement, before exploring their impact on the Agreement and its aftermath.

For unionists, the foremost negative image of republicans, and sometimes all Catholics, was one of *subversion*. Republicans were dishonest and disloyal and their core impulse was violent destruction of Northern Ireland, the bulwark of unionists' British identity. Believing subversion to be the very essence of republicanism, and holding a static and fated view of identity, unionist fatalism dismissed the possibility that Sinn Féin's participation in the peace process meant that republicans had undergone or were undergoing any significant identity change. The strategy was the same as it had been for decades, only now, guaranteed a place in a power-sharing government, republicans would be able to pursue their sabotage agenda from within the corridors of power. Should they find their ambition to destroy Northern Ireland blocked, they had the leverage of weapons to find a way through. Unionist fatalism did not trust republicans and, more importantly, was uninterested in exploring whether trust could be built.

These fears were accompanied by a deep-seated sense of victimhood and self-righteousness. Despite having monopolised power for much of the twentieth century partly due to their fear of republican subversion, unionists regarded themselves as an embattled minority in Ireland, rather than, as nationalists saw them, a privileged majority within the six counties. Nationalists, therefore, deserved little or nothing in the way of redressing inequality. Since any disparity that existed was not to be explained by past or present discrimination, unionist fatalism saw nationalist achievements in the Agreement as a reward for republican terrorism; the same went for reform of the Royal Ulster Constabulary (RUC) and any diminution of the British character of Northern Ireland. British symbols and culture should be privileged in Northern Ireland, regardless of how they were experienced by nationalists. Unionist fatalism was coloured by an intense and raw awareness of suffering at the hands of the IRA, of justice unachieved and, indeed, now denied by the Agreement's provision to release paramilitary prisoners. Unionist fatalism found confirmation of its own veracity in the fact that its array of opponents – Dublin, Washington, Sinn Féin, the SDLP and moderate unionists – were firmly behind the Agreement.

In republican fatalism, the central negative image of unionists and their British sponsors was one of *domination*. Unionists were supremacist and bigoted and their chief impulse was to suppress the Catholic population within Northern Ireland. This was unionism's colonial *raison d'être*: to secure Northern Ireland for the Crown while enjoying the political, economic and cultural privileges that came with that role. Accordingly, republican fatalism did not regard unionist identity as a genuine expression of British national feeling or values, but a chimera hiding a rotten core of superiority and sectarianism. Unionists had no right to impede all-Ireland self-determination since they should never have been in Ireland in the first place. In the face of unionists' denial of Catholic rights, the IRA campaign was a righteous struggle for justice and equality, and republicans would end that struggle and lay down their weapons at a time of their own choosing. The appearance of defeat was unacceptable, yet in any case, the struggle for a united Ireland would run until its inevitable and successful conclusion. In the meantime, to redress the injustice of the British presence in Ireland and to raise nationalist consciousness, all vestiges of Britishness should be resisted and removed where possible within the six counties. The RUC deserved disbandment for its repressive role in enforcing Protestant ascendancy while the British army, an occupying force, should take its military machine and leave the island for good. While some unionists claimed to support the Agreement, the overwhelming inclinations of unionism were to inflict defeat on the IRA and maintain the second-class status of Catholics.

Now, what is paradoxical, and significant, about these fatalist logics is that they straddled the pro- and anti-Agreement boundary. The unionist fatalist logic was obviously endemic within the anti-Agreement Democratic Unionist Party (DUP) and was shared by the anti-Agreement section of the Ulster Unionist Party (UUP). Yet even unionists like Trimble, whose reasoning led them to support the Agreement, shared many of the fatalist assumptions or were politically pulled around by them. As Porter (2003: 208) wrote at the height of post-1998 intra-unionist division, despite their bitter and public differences, 'pro-Agreement unionism does not possess an interpretive framework that differs markedly from anti-Agreement unionism'. The same could be said of pro- and anti-Agreement republicanism. While they pursued very different political strategies, the foundational worldviews of Sinn Féin and republican dissidents were mostly the same. And the reason that fatalist logic could be found even in pro-Agreement parties was that the Agreement, through its ambiguous quality, permitted its supporters to regard themselves as securing not a compromise, but a victory. Parties could assent to the Agreement without disturbing their core goals or revising their desire to land blows on opponents. All this recalls Booth and Wheeler's (2008: 15) comment on the fine line between fatalist and mitigator logics. Even those who seek to mitigate insecurity likely share the fatalist belief that a common identity is impossible and that conflict management, not resolution, is the best that can be hoped for.

The fact that fatalist logic influenced even pro-Agreement parties is the key to understanding the limitations of the Agreement that they negotiated. While the parties, cajoled by the Governments, could agree to impressionistic principles of mutual respect and to institutions that would yield pragmatic benefits and enhance democracy, the constitutional/symbolic matters and security/legacy of violence matters were irresolvable because they pertained to the core meaning of the conflict. Pro-Agreement unionists and republicans could not agree those issues in the talks but they supported the deal because they trusted that those issues could be worked out in their favour after the Agreement through determined political action. Hence the tremendous ideological and moral significance with which the fudged and still-to-be-resolved symbolic and security issues were invested after the Agreement. It was through these that the quest for ascendancy in the struggle for societal security would continue.

So, on the uncertain matter of the constitutional future of Northern Ireland, Trimble declared that the principle of consent meant that 'We have sought and secured a permanent settlement, not a transitional arrangement' (Trimble, 2001a: 11). But Martin McGuinness concluded the very opposite, describing the consent principle as 'a clause limiting the life of the Union' (McGuinness, 1998: 14). Both sides knew that demographic change, cultural vitality and communal solidarity (translated into political strength) still mattered because these would ultimately tip the constitutional balance in one or other of the communities' favour. This fact charged all other disputes with intense import. On the question of how British sovereignty should be manifested, unionists contended that British constitutional status demanded the privileging of British symbols; without such privileging, they claimed that their identity was insecure and the Agreement's endorsement of British sovereignty was meaningless. Nationalists countered that the Agreement's standard of cross-community legitimacy required symbols that were either neutral or co-equal, and, moreover, stressed that the Agreement accorded equal legitimacy to the identities, cultures and political aspirations of both communities.

And in the absence of clarity on decommissioning, Sinn Féin contended that there existed no precondition for paramilitary groups to disarm before their allied parties entered the Executive. In any case, the party exploited the ambiguity of its relationship with the IRA by claiming that the IRA was an entirely separate organisation that had not signed any agreement. Unionists, who regarded Sinn Féin and the IRA as one and the same, argued that there was a precondition, pointing in the main to the Pledge of Office that required ministers to renounce violence. Republicans trumpeted the swift release of their prisoners; if prisoners must be released, said unionists, it should at least be conditional on the IRA surrendering its weapons of war. As for police reform, unionists regarded the RUC as a courageous and honest force that had suffered greatly during 'the Troubles' at the hands of republicans. They desired minimal policing reform. Regarding the RUC as illegitimate and oppressive, republicans sought total disbandment. Unionists were also wary about diminishing state military capability; republicans sought the rapid dismantling of the British security presence.

Contests over these issues, on the basis of these opposed positions, dominated post-Agreement politics and hamstrung the Agreement's implementation. Two points are critical. First, the contests were not separate and unrelated; constitutional and security issues were two fronts in the same post-Agreement battle for societal security, and each compounded the other. By digging in on the security issues – for instance, unionists seeking speedy decommissioning and minimal police reform, republicans seeking the opposite – the parties contested for the prize of vindication for its identity and its traditional narrative of the conflict. At the same time, the vexed nature of the symbols issue was due to the parties' feeling that to give ground in this area would be to confer legitimacy on the past violence inflicted by the other side. It would be a de facto concession that the other side's violence had not been in vain. The link between identity and security issues was evident in the fact that the unionists who were most anxious to see decommissioning were also those who held a strong ethnic identity, distrusted republicans and were concerned about the Agreement's impact on the Union. The republicans who were most hard-line on seeing maximum security reform were also those who held a strong ethnic identity, distrusted unionists and the British, and were eager to see maximum damage done to the Britishness of Northern Ireland.

A second crucial point is that the parties' fatalistically inflected positions were mutually reinforcing or, to borrow a phrase from the Agreement, 'interlocking and interdependent'. On the symbols controversy, unionist fatalism was determined to maintain the ascendancy of British symbols (sustaining republicans' perception of unionists' supremacist identity), but this determination contributed to republicans' determination to challenge British symbols (sustaining unionists' perception of republicans' subversive identity). Or, the other way around: republicans were insistent on undermining British symbols (sustaining unionists' perception of republicans' subversive identity) due to the fatalist anxiety that unionists sought to ride roughshod over Catholic-nationalist rights and expression, but this insistence sustained the fatalist unionist attachment to British symbols. The decommissioning impasse can be construed similarly. Unionist fatalism was wary of sharing power with republicans, at least while they kept their arsenal (sustaining republicans' perception of unionists' supremacist identity), but this wariness contributed to republicans' fatalist disinclination to give up that arsenal (sustaining unionists' perception of republicans' subversive identity). Or, the other way around: republicans were reluctant to decommission arms (sustaining unionists' perception of republicans' subversive identity) due to the fatalist anxiety that unionists sought only to humiliate them and exclude Catholics from power, but this reluctance sustained the fatalist unionist case against power-sharing.

These mutually sustaining fatalistic logics arose from conditions of uncertainty, and simultaneously recreated those conditions by producing deadlock on certain issues in the talks, causing the relevant parts of the Agreement to be ambiguous, permitting clashing interpretations, and then repeatedly destabilising politics and deepening post-Agreement uncertainty. In the light of this analysis, it is interesting to consider precisely how the post-Agreement environment exhibited the conditions of uncertainty noted in our initial discussion of the societal security dilemma: state weakness and the ambiguity of offence and defence. As we saw, a weak state (i.e. a state that lacks the confidence and allegiance of all its citizens) may result from intense identity conflict and at the same time exacerbate it, propelling the security dilemma. Despite the endorsement of the Agreement in the referenda, the Agreement's strong recognition and protection of the rival communities' identities, and the ongoing rule of law, post-Agreement Northern Ireland actually resembled a weak state.

To begin with, neither side, even the groupings that supported the Agreement, could be absolutely sure that the Agreement would protect its societal security. While 71 per cent of people in Northern Ireland supported the Agreement, almost half of all unionists rejected it, including many of the leading figures in the largest unionist (and officially pro-Agreement) party, the UUP. Although it was in favour of the Agreement, Sinn Féin was yet evasive about whether it in fact now recognised Northern Ireland's right to exist and was unequivocal that it still sought its ultimate demise. The various 'private armies' – the anti-state IRA and others and the pro-state Ulster Volunteer Force (UVF), Ulster Defence Association (UDA) and others – were officially on ceasefire but still intact and operational. The state police lacked legitimacy within the nationalist community and was in line for unspecified reforms that endangered its legitimacy within the unionist community. The Agreement promised stability and protection to both sides, but there were ambiguities in its provisions and its institutions had yet to prove themselves. Neither side could predict how or whether the Governments would enforce implementation. All this meant that many unionists and nationalists – as is the case within weak states – continued to feel their identities to be vulnerable after the Agreement, *because* of the Agreement, perhaps even more vulnerable than during the violent conflict that at least had the predictability of political impasse. Both sides still had reason to fear betrayal.

The ambiguity of offence and defence was, after the Agreement, perpetuated by the ongoing, mutually exclusive political aspirations and identities of the parties and intra-party division. The mutually exclusive aspirations meant that political and/or cultural assertion continued to be viewed in zero-sum terms – political/cultural defence was offence and vice versa. The Agreement had the ambition to transform identities and, as we saw, contained the radical clause allowing people in Northern Ireland to choose Irish or British citizenship, or both, as way of challenging the zero-sum logic of the conflict. But that would be a long-term process. The bitter emotions and competing historical narratives were all left intact after the Agreement, deepening the uncertainty of the environment and the propensity for people to detect threat from the other side. Moreover, intra-group division compounded the uncertainty facing the parties, intensifying the parties' dilemmas. How could the parties interpret the intentions of opponents if those opponents were themselves divided, ambiguous and contradictory? Pro-Agreement unionists and republicans knew that their counterparts were under pressure from in-group dissenters, dissenters who may be influencing the leadership and who at some point in the future could be in the ascendancy. And how could actors pursue a clear strategy and convey clear intentions to their opponents if the political movements they led were themselves split?

It was in this context of uncertainty that the parties operated. However, recalling the circular relationship between uncertainty and the fatalistic logic of insecurity, this was also a context *created by* the fatalistic positions of the parties. The parties were not exogenous to their uncertain environment but constituted it. It was the parties' inability to agree that put the ambiguities in the Agreement. It was the parties that held clashing, partisan interpretations of the Agreement. It was the parties that were repositories of exclusive identities and skewed communal memories. Hence, the complex reality was that each party had to interpret and respond to the intentions of others and, at the same time, each party's interpretation and response influenced the intentions of others.

In terms of party-political competition, the post-Agreement societal security dilemma manifested itself as 'ethnic outbidding', with support draining from the centre parties, the UUP and SDLP, to their rivals, the DUP and Sinn Féin. Outbidding occurs because, in an ethnic party-system like Northern Ireland's:

> there is one principal issue axis – the ethnic conflict axis – which pre-empts the others … The possibility of intragroup party competition creates strong incentives for parties to be diligent in asserting ethnic demands, the more-so when they consider the life-or-death implications of that competition for the party's fortunes. Outbidding for ethnic support is a constant possibility.
>
> (Horowitz, 2000: 346)

Thus, the ongoing security and symbolic contests could be fatalistically portrayed as matters of (at least political and cultural) life and death, and voters presented with a stark choice of which party was best equipped to ensure group survival. On the unionist side, the DUP trumpeted the fact that the UUP was apparently unable to implement a strongly pro-unionist version of the Agreement that yielded immediate IRA decommissioning and secured primacy for British culture. The UUP was lambasted for being unable to iron out the ambiguities of the Agreement in unionism's favour, and, indeed, for being responsible for those ambiguities in the first place through negotiating ineptitude. The implementation process proved, said the DUP, that the UUP was incapable of protecting unionism's vital interests and showed that a change of leadership was required. That DUP victory came in November 2003. Opinion was less volatile within nationalism, but Sinn Féin similarly cast itself as the most dogged advocate of nationalist interests at the expense of the SDLP, eclipsing the latter at the 2001 Westminster election.

Thus, while fatalist logic may have been 'genuine' on both sides, it was also knowingly promoted by ethnic elites as a means of garnering votes: 'The delicate psychological environment of a civil war or peace process may prompt rival bidders to construct narratives that deliberately play on fears and worst-case scenarios' (Gormley-Heenan and Mac Ginty, 2008: 46). It is well known that elections in Northern Ireland and elsewhere can resemble the 'prisoner's dilemma' scenario, in which people are reluctant to vote for any party other than a strong ethnic party due to their expectation that people on the other side will not vote for any party other than *their* strongest ethnic party. The DUP, and to a lesser extent Sinn Féin, capitalised on that fear to their mutual advantage. Polarisation occurred despite repeated attempts to de-escalate the security dilemma through 'choreography', 'sequencing' and reciprocal gestures, most notably in relation to weapons decommissioning and devolution. This was intended to publicly demonstrate mutuality and to protect each side from accusations of sell-out, yet the moves each side was willing to make did not go far enough, in part due to fear of in-group extremists.

It is worth highlighting one particular mechanism through which the Governments sought to assuage (mainly unionist) security fears during implementation: the Independent Monitoring Commission, a neutral international body established in 2004 that would publish periodic, impartial reports on paramilitary activity as well as British security 'normalisation'. This body proved to be a valuable and authoritative source of information that fed into the political process, though it came too late to shore up moderate political unionism; the Assembly had been suspended in 2002 in response to unionists' anger at allegations of republican spying at Stormont. Indeed, it can be argued that, in general terms, the British Government was deficient in taking account of declining unionist support for the Agreement and actually contributed to it. Most notably, the release of paramilitary prisoners before paramilitary groups had decommissioned was particularly demoralising for unionists, and violated pledges made by Tony Blair prior to the Agreement referendum (Dixon, 2013). This apparent prioritisation of republican sensibilities undermined

Trimble's ability to promote the Agreement to his constituency and answer the DUP's fatalist claims of UUP betrayal and failure, and the impending threat to unionism.

Transcendence? May 2007 and beyond

The 'triumph of the extremes' sowed widespread pessimism regarding whether the Agreement and its institutions could be resuscitated. In theory, the logic of outbidding promised indefinite political stalemate, with the rise of the hard-line parties proving, each party to the other, the folly of co-operation. This, however, is not what happened. The 'outbidders' eventually agreed a power-sharing deal in May 2007, a paradoxical outcome that demands some explanation.

Mitchell *et al.* (2009) use electoral and attitudinal data to show that power-sharing between the strongest ethnic parties broadly reflected the desire of the electorate. The Northern Ireland Election Studies in 1998 and 2003 show that despite the fact that many of those who voted UUP and SDLP in 1998 switched their votes to the DUP and Sinn Féin, respectively, in 2003, judging the latter parties to be 'the most effective voice' of nationalists and unionists, the attitudes of the DUP and Sinn Féin voters towards the core elements of the peace process actually converged. Between 1998 and 2003, the opposition of DUP voters to North–South bodies declined by 25 per cent while their support for power-sharing rose by 33 per cent. Among Sinn Féin voters, acceptance of the principle of consent rose by 11 per cent to 66 per cent and support for decommissioning rose from 63 to 85 per cent. Such a softening of attitudes is unexpected, given the recurrent crises of implementation, but is consistent with the moderated platforms of the hard-line parties. That moderation appeared to result from the realisation of the DUP and Sinn Féin that being relentlessly 'anti-system' would limit their electoral growth. At the same time, the parties' burgeoning constituencies were in favour of a pragmatic approach to power-sharing while desiring the kind of strong defence of ethnic identity offered by the DUP and Sinn Féin. In sum:

> Essentially, each community wants its 'strongest voice' to represent it, but sections of each community want this ethnic champion to act in a more cooperative fashion, or at least in a less 'anti-system' or 'rejectionist' manner – since nothing worthwhile can be gained by choosing to 'exit' the power-sharing framework.
>
> (Mitchell *et al.*, 2009: 403)

Once the DUP and Sinn Féin were confident that they were under no threat from intra-bloc rivals, they were able to pursue an accommodation with the other side. The incentives of power-sharing restrained ongoing outbidding and avoided permanent deadlock.

But how do we understand this turn of events in terms of the societal security dilemma, and the logic and emotions that drove it? Was fatalist logic now a thing of the past on both sides, with fear succumbing to trust and exclusive identities reimagined? An optimistic reading would view the reciprocal moves made by the DUP and Sinn Féin in the lead up to devolution as a process through which each sought to disprove the negative image held by the other side. By decommissioning in 2005 and supporting the police in 2007, republicans were precluding unionists from continuing to reject them as irredeemably subversive. By committing firmly to power-sharing, unionists were precluding republicans from continuing to regard them as inevitably bent on domination. Each side was simultaneously enabling the other to abandon fatalism in favour of co-operation and perhaps even trust. They were exercising what Booth and Wheeler (2008: 7) call 'security dilemma sensibility' – recognising their own responsibility for creating the fears of the other and changing their behaviour accordingly.

There were certainly some glimmers of transcender logic abroad, hinting that the prosaic political bargain did indeed represent more than the sum of its parts. On devolution day, McGuinness (2007) spoke explicitly of the need to escape a Self/Other worldview:

> Ireland's greatest living poet, a fellow Derry man, Seamus Heaney, once told a gathering that I attended at Magee University that for too long and too often we speak of the others or the other side and that we need to get to a place of 'throughotherness'. The Office of the First and Deputy First Ministers is a good place to start.

Paisley, previously the great fatalist, also intimated that the day's events were a decisive break with the past: 'I believe that Northern Ireland has come to a time of peace, a time when hate will no longer rule. How good it will be to be part of a wonderful healing in our province' (Paisley, 2007a). Paisley and McGuinness subsequently formed a good personal rapport. Explaining the events of 2007, Paisley mentioned that he actually prayed with McGuinness during the illness of the latter's mother, an experience that he said neither man forgot (quoted in Carruthers, 2013: 52), and when Paisley died in September 2014, the warmth of McGuinness's tribute drew much comment. Paisley's successor as First Minister and DUP leader, Peter Robinson, was thought to have a more frosty relationship with McGuinness, but nevertheless made the following comments on his old enemy:

> I don't think he is the man he was. There is nothing I have seen over the past number of years that I have been working with Martin McGuinness that would lead me to believe that he would ever go back to the kind of life he had before. I believe he is fully

> committed to making the process work … We have a good interaction. There's a fair bit of banter about football and other issues.
>
> (quoted in Mallie, 2012)

There was no doubt that unionists – always less comfortable with the peace process than nationalists – accepted that republicanism had undergone a genuine and significant transformation. For instance, the human factor in peacemaking became a theme in the efforts of Jeffrey Donaldson, the ex-UUP and now DUP MP, who had opposed the Good Friday Agreement, to disseminate lessons from the Northern Irish peace process. In his view, frank and honest sharing of personal experiences was key to developing understanding. 'We've all been on personal journeys', he remarks (interview with Jeffrey Donaldson MP, 8 May 2009).

There was, however, cause for a much less optimistic reading of developments, one that saw the outworking of mutual self-interest rather than mutual empathy. As one newspaper observed, the joint Sinn Féin–DUP press conference in March 2007 that prepared the way for devolution looked 'more like a carve-up of influence and jobs than a genuine desire to share power' (*The Economist*, 2007). This accusation was to become permanently stuck to the DUP- and Sinn Féin-led Executive. The perks of power-sharing and the unattractiveness of the alternatives may have motivated the parties to strike a mutually advantageous deal but there was little understanding between them, little acknowledgement of the mistakes of the past and no incentive to upset their own ethnic support bases. The DUP boasted of scoring a victory over republicanism while Sinn Féin continued to insist that this was a new phase of the struggle towards Irish unity. Mark Durkan, leader of the SDLP in 2007, voiced the unease of many when he asked whether the DUP and Sinn Féin, those who, he charged, had 'given us the worst of our past', were really fit to provide 'the best of our future' (quoted in Millar, 2007). 'Ethnic rage' was giving way to 'ethnic vanity', as Bew (2007: 581) puts it. A telling indicator of the nature of the DUP–Sinn Féin deal was their pact following the St Andrews Agreement of October 2006 regarding the rule for selecting the First and Deputy First Ministers (see Chapter 5). A change from the practice agreed in 1998 meant that both parties could encourage and electorally profit from mutual fear among voters that the other would gain the top job. Moloney (2008: 474) comments on the new rule thus: 'Once again it was a case of the two extremes in Northern Irish politics nurturing and sustaining each other, but this time quite deliberately.'

And most importantly, only some of the ambiguity in the 1998 Agreement had been resolved – the security issues, especially decommissioning and support for the police. The uncertainty over Northern Ireland's constitutional future and the visible expression of the constitutional present remained, to return inevitably in the form of identity conflict over flags, parades and language, plus the increasingly restive elephant in the room – the past. The institutions were for the most part stable, apart from the brinkmanship that preceded the devolution of policing and justice to the Assembly in early 2010. Yet political stability made visible the remaining contradictions in the new politics that American mediators Richard Haass and Megan O'Sullivan attempted to resolve in the autumn of 2013. Disagreement over flags, parades and the past – the issues on the agenda of those talks – encapsulated the societal anxiety that continued to infuse both extremely localised territorial clashes and debates on the constitutional fate of Northern Ireland. The talks failed, and the ugly reality was pointed out by the journalist Malachi O'Doherty (2014) the morning after. It was actually easier for the main parties not to agree than to try to sell a compromise: 'Sinn Féin can say the republican vision is affirmed, that unionism has a laager mentality and still applies a veto that must be challenged … The DUP can say that it has finally put a halt to the erosion of British sovereignty and the flow of concessions to Sinn Féin.' Meanwhile, away from identity politics, the multi-party Executive proved to be ineffective in handling 'non-political' issues, with logjams arising in relation to a range of social and economic policy areas.

In many ways, then, the Northern Ireland experience bears out Snyder and Jervis's (1999: 19) comment on the (at least short-term) limitations of power-sharing as a prescription for the ethnic security dilemma:

> Insofar as power-sharing rests in the residual ability of the groups to act in their own self-defence, it is as likely to recreate the security dilemma as solve it. Power-sharing reifies the contending groups and ensures that all political mobilisation must take place within the framework of the rival segments. Moreover, since power sharing eschews the full partitioning of the polity in favour of continued political and economic integration, it perpetuates the mutual interdependencies and vulnerabilities that heighten the security dilemma.

This chimes with the criticism that power-sharing in Northern Ireland based on a coalition between officially designated communal blocs panders to ethnic entrepreneurs and their narrow and self-interested definitions of 'their' communities, and does not make for effective governance. In this view, explored in Chapter 6, undermining those blocs through protecting individual, rather than group, rights and incentivising centrist leadership is morally and politically preferable.

Yet the proponents of inclusive power-sharing insist that it simply addresses reality – ethnic blocs exist, and demand political expression and protection – and that stabilising, not reifying, groups and their competition is its goal. While the initial stages may appear to be a continuation of prior patterns of conflict, the mere presence of former enemies within the same political institutions is likely to have a moderating effect, first, because those previously excluded are afforded peaceful avenues through which to pursue their agenda, and second, because the experience of contact and common enterprise works against the fear and mistrust built up during the conflict – the emotions and attitudes that helped create such clearly defined oppositional group cultures in the first place. Mark Durkan, one of the Agreement's chief architects, explains the Agreement's potential to move people 'from the whole psychology of politics of making demands against each other to making decisions with each other and we would find ourselves making decisions for each other before we'd realised it' (interview with Mark Durkan MP, 31 August 2012). Accordingly, it is argued that consociational power-sharing structures are 'biodegradable', albeit over a prolonged and indeterminate period of time (McGarry and O'Leary, 2009: 68). Eventually, ethnicity may become less salient and other, cross-cutting political cleavages permit an incremental process towards a more 'normal' system of government and opposition that does not follow the ethnic fault line and in which group protections are obsolete.

Without doubt, that process is uncharted and uncertain. What is certain, however, is that since 1998, the Agreement's potential to catalyse such a process has been hampered by a string of divisive disputes arising from the 'Troubles', combined with the still-fresh memory of that period. The latter has been particularly potent among the political class, much of which lived through the violence and some of which even took part in it. The arrest in May 2014 of Gerry Adams, leader of Sinn Féin, on suspicion of involvement in a forty-year-old IRA murder, is just one reminder of how little removed the 'new' Northern Ireland is from the 'old' one, regardless of Adams' guilt or lack thereof. Morrow (2001: 14) identifies the root of the essentially relational problem that has characterised post-Agreement politics:

> After all the effort spent on resolving the constitutional dispute through the Agreement, the conflict turns out to be driven as much by a need to protect against and avenge the legacy of conflict itself than by the future of the Irish border. In other words, the conflict continues even after the 'reasons' for the conflict have been resolved: conflict ends up being about conflict. For Northern Ireland, this holds out the prospect that a constitutional settlement, no matter how far reaching, will be threatened by the internal common sense that makes trusting a mortal enemy absurd and makes into a potentially fatal mistake any acknowledgment that our team inflicted injury rather than merely suffering it.

Self-fulfilling, self-recreating fatalist logic has fed off the legacy of the 'Troubles' throughout the post-Agreement period. That legacy has repeatedly renewed enmity and provided opportunities for the parties to seek the triumph they were denied by the Agreement – an accord that avoided apportioning blame or victory (see Conclusion). The echoing impacts of the bloodshed disrupted and, for periods, disabled the new institutions whose very purpose was to undermine the antagonism that was preventing them from functioning. And despite political stability since 2007, ethnicity and communal histories and images of the Other have remained factors in Northern Ireland politics due to lingering communal grievances and mistrust. This has reinforced the self-perpetuating nature of the sectarian party system. The existence of distinct identity groups is essential to the main parties' support, and so realities such as the failure of Haass, the continuing and divisive invocation of the past in current political discourse and the DUP and Sinn Féin's reticence over a shared future policy for reducing societal segregation, are no surprise.

However, the physical insecurity that polarised identities during the 'Troubles' has been in continuous, if at times, faltering, decline. The greatest threat to stability has come from 'dissident' republicans, yet those groups' political and military capabilities have been limited and their threat is reported to be waning due to internal feuding and security force penetration (Morris, 2014). As remaining issues are resolved, the dominant ethnic parties will have less material on which to base their 'ethnic tribune' appeals or to 'play the security dilemma card' (a phrase coined by V.P. Gagnon, quoted in Snyder and Jervis, 1999: 26). It follows that a sustained period of peace and political stability will see the evolution of political arrangements, and will further 'de-escalate' identities in the direction of mutual recognition and 'embedded trust' (Booth and Wheeler, 2008: 197), eroding the invisible walls that circumscribe the lives of many people in the North. The wait, however, for a truly new politics in which the Orange–Green divide is obscured by new alliances and issues, may be longer than both consociationalism's supporters and critics would wish.

Conclusion: the post-settlement security dilemma

That implementing peace can be as, if not more, difficult than coming to agreement is well known. Catastrophes like the Rwandan genocide (which followed the Arusha peace accords) and the Second Intifada (which followed the failed Oslo process between Israelis and Palestinians) offer stern warnings of the dangers that can follow negotiated settlements. The role of the security dilemma *after* an agreement is perhaps underplayed in the literature, though it is recognised.

Snyder and Jervis's (1999) observation that power-sharing may recreate the security dilemma has been noted, while one of the themes of the global case studies contained in Walter and Snyder (1999) is that disarmament can create a tense spiral of mutual threat: a 'security dilemma in the reverse' as Walter (1999: 43) calls it. Mac Ginty (2006a: 111) and Paris (2004: 173) also note the salience of the security dilemma in the post-peace accord phase, resulting from the facts that fighting factions are required to relinquish their military defence capabilities, place their faith in untested institutions and co-operate with those who have recently sought to destroy them.

In concluding this chapter on Northern Ireland's post-settlement experience, it is worth taking these observations further by considering whether it may be appropriate to talk specifically about a 'post-settlement security dilemma'. In their general structure, the post- and pre-settlement security dilemmas are the same: a fatalist approach to security, in the context of uncertainty, provoking insecurity in, and reciprocal threats from, another actor. However, drawing on the Northern Ireland case, we can identify six features of this dynamic after an agreement that distinguish it from its pre-settlement operation.

First, the post-settlement security dilemma is *less intense*. At least a proportion of each faction previously engaged in war is now involved in reducing tension and settling disputes, and a certain number of issues have been resolved in the settlement, meaning that threats/reactions are more limited in scope and less serious in nature than the lethal back-and-forth of the hot conflict. Actors may have developed a degree of optimism regarding the intentions of opponents, although the potential for antagonisms to gather force towards a resumption of war is ever-present.

Second, in the post-settlement security dilemma, *the agreement document itself is a critical factor* – one by definition absent in the pre-settlement security dilemma. That text becomes central to political discourse, with parties trading accusations of bad faith, claims of the deal's folly and/or boasts of being the accord's best defender. When interpretations of the agreement differ and expectations of how it should be implemented are not met, perceptions of vulnerability intensify, support may leach from the deal, and parties may become less co-operative on other aspects of implementation.

Third, in the post-settlement security dilemma, *the injunction to disarm, rather than the increased military capacity of the other side, is the greater cause of fear and insecurity*. Group defence infrastructure in place during violent conflict is required to be dismantled – insurgent armies must stand down, weapons must be dumped, police and military must retreat to barracks, security installations must be removed. This creates an immediate physical vulnerability in that the defence force – for so long revered, respected and relied upon – is suddenly absent. It also poses disorienting ontological questions for the parties to the conflict. Does the method of disarmament required by the peace imply defeat? Are conciliatory moves balanced and reciprocal? What are the personal implications for the individuals who invested their lives in these forces and now must adapt to their destruction or downgrading? Furthermore, group vulnerability is caused by the uncertainty over the reliability of new defence structures – a newly formed army or polity, perhaps comprising both groups – and/or distrust in the third-party body overseeing disarmament and demobilisation. Most of all, disarmament causes insecurity because history has taught the groups that building military strength is the only rational response to the other side's identity and political goals.

Fourth, in the post-settlement security dilemma, although actual violence may be at an end, *the legacy of violence is a significant cause of inter-group antagonism*. State and communal violence bequeaths transitional societies with a complex and emotive set of problems that can become the focus of a new Cold War between ethnic groups, problems that include: group disarmament; the possibility of political prisoner releases; the question of prosecutions versus amnesties for ex-combatants; defining the role in society and in politics of former combatants; what to do with land related to the conflict such as that used for prisons or security installations; how to commemorate events that may be a source of pride for one side but pain and humiliation for another; making the security forces acceptable to both sides. Given that each of these issues is steeped in communal memories of hurt and trauma, and often have no obvious politically or morally correct solution, they have considerable potential to frustrate the operation of the political/institutional provisions at the heart of the peace settlement and the warming of inter-group relations.

Fifth, in the post-settlement security dilemma, *identity issues are likely to be particularly conspicuous in inter-group tensions*. Securing group identity of course lies at the core of pre-settlement violence, yet the ending of violence may make identity conflict more visible and vexed, as antagonism is transferred from the battlefield to the realm of symbols, culture, language and religion. The memory of murder and the perfidy of the other side continues to infuse identity/symbolic conflict with intense, almost transcendental, significance. With military advantage no longer attainable, even minor identity issues become proxy wars in the overarching, zero-sum struggle for ethnic advantage.

Sixth, in the post-settlement security dilemma, *the third-party intervener is a crucial factor in how, or whether, a spiral of tension unfolds*, its actions perhaps determining whether the process ends in a stable, functioning polity or bloodbath. The third-party's role as a credible guarantor of the deal is vital to encouraging the parties to buy into it; groups must trust that if the other side breaks a commitment, it will be noticed and punished by the sufficiently empowered third party. Yet managing the fears and expectations of the parties, perhaps in the context of an ambiguous or incomplete peace document, requires the third party to employ delicate political skills. This task may tempt the third-party to make promises it cannot keep or give assurances to one side that are repugnant to the other, and so the agreement's guarantor may actually contribute to destabilising the agreement and its supporters.

These six dimensions of the post-settlement security dilemma highlight salient features of post-Agreement Northern Ireland and are likely to have more general application, potentially informing understanding of the nature of post-settlement politics in other arenas of conflict. Comparative work is beyond the scope of this book, yet this chapter has clearly set out the analytical relevance of security dilemma theory to post-Agreement Northern Ireland. The Agreement was intended to reverse the logic of the security dilemma by addressing groups' fears and locking them in to a framework that would constrain and render predictable their behaviour, yet a persistent strain of fatalist logic, underpinned by the emotional damage inflicted by decades of violent conflict, prevented the Agreement from fulfilling its transformative purpose. Conflicts over security/the legacy of violence, allied to ongoing identity clashes, delayed stable power-sharing devolution until 2007. While the institutions functioned subsequently, due both to the resolution of previously destabilising security issues and the self-interest of the main parties, the clash of identities did not go away.

The concluding chapter returns to the conditions prevailing in post-2007 Northern Ireland and reflects on the prospects for the future. Now, however, we turn to the political parties themselves and examine in detail how they navigated and shaped the post-Agreement terrain we have just covered. The analysis is structured according to the dominant themes in the parties' experiences. As highlighted earlier, Booth and Wheeler (2008) warn in the course of their exposition of the fatalist, mitigator and transcender logics that political actors rarely show consistent commitment to just one logic, and so recommend applying the logics to ideas rather than people. This book follows this advice, though it does not attempt to classify every policy and statement of the parties either; to do so would make for tedious reading. Instead, the book uses the logics more loosely and more occasionally as a way of understanding the different thought processes within parties, and the kinds of goals pursued by parties, particularly with regard to their escalating or de-escalating impacts. We begin with the largest party in 1998, the Ulster Unionist Party.

2

Ulster Unionist Party

Introduction

The withering of the once-unshakable Ulster Unionist Party (UUP) is perhaps the most striking party-political development of the post-Agreement era. In 1998, it was the fourth largest party at Westminster, holding ten seats. From 2010, it had no Westminster representation at all. The party that ruled Northern Ireland for fifty years, as of 2011, had just one seat on the thirteen-member Executive. Also from 2011, it had fewer councillors on Belfast City Council than the perennially small Alliance Party. However, while the numbers show regression, the politics reveals something different. The party that profited from, and partly orchestrated, the UUP's decline, the Democratic Unionist Party (DUP), actually proceeded to follow the very political path beaten by the Ulster Unionists towards cross-community power-sharing. Hence the historic importance of the UUP leadership's decision to support the Agreement in 1998 and the political thinking of one of the most significant figures of the post-1998 period, David Trimble. His approach – at times courageous, at times grudging, frequently awkward – to some extent epitomised unionism's wider wrestle with the Agreement and its demands.

This chapter begins by tracing the UUP's trajectory from political dominance throughout the pre-1972 Stormont years to marginalisation and insecurity during Direct Rule and the peace process. It then examines the UUP's historic and contentious decision to conclude a power-sharing agreement with nationalism and its interpretation of the provisions of the Agreement, before exploring how the party set about pursuing its two central post-Agreement concerns – IRA disarmament and the protection of the British character of Northern Ireland. Lastly, the formidable challenges facing the party following electoral defeat by the DUP and the latter's acceptance of the broad outlines of the Agreement are assessed.

From domination to marginalisation

The UUP was the main political vehicle of unionist opinion for a century. Organised unionism originally emerged in response to the moves to establish Home Rule throughout Ireland in the 1880s, thus setting the template for future unionist politics as most often a reaction to an agenda set by others (Walker, 2004: 5). When Ireland was partitioned, unionists acquiesced in the hope that it would be a remedy for the years of unrest and insecurity caused by Irish nationalists' campaign for all-Ireland autonomy from Britain. The possibility that it would usher in an era of stability led unionists not to oppose the Government of Ireland Act (1920) that divided the island. 'Ulster wants peace', explained unionist leader Edward Carson to the Lord Chancellor, Lord Birkenhead, 'and above all to be removed from the arena of party politics in the Imperial Parliament' (cited in Harbinson, 1973: 30). For fifty years, until London shut down the Stormont parliament in 1972, the Unionist Party sought to secure Protestant physical and identity security by operating a de facto one-party state. Two historians of the party, Walker (2004) and Harbinson (1973), both emphasise two factors, one external and one internal, as shaping the character of hegemonic unionism and blinding it to the reality that its monopolisation of power was unsustainable. The external factor was the threat – at times violent – from nationalism emanating both from within the border of the six counties and from the Irish state. The perceived danger from a disloyal minority was a constant reminder of the imperative of subordinating that community, while Éamon De Valera's anti-British policies and Catholic-flavoured constitution that laid claim to Northern Ireland seemed to render prophetic many unionist pre-partition predictions of the tenor of Dublin rule.

The internal factor was what Harbinson (1973: 171) calls simply a 'lack of vision'. Because unionist strength depended on the electoral success of the party and that party embraced such a wide spectrum of class and opinion, maintaining power required accentuating issues that would unite the Protestant community yet alienate Catholics within Northern Ireland. Protestant supremacy caused considerable intellectual decadence in the unionism of this period: in times of threat, rational arguments for the Union were trumped by the need to coerce; in times of relative security, there was no spur to develop intellectual defences of the Union. Self-criticism and dissent were stifled by the need to preserve unionist solidarity – unionists were in denial that any discrimination against Catholics at all occurred under their regime (see, for example, UUP, 1969). 'Cloaked in the comfort of its own mythology', it was taken as self-evident by unionism that Northern Ireland was British and should be defended as such at all costs (Mitchel, 2003: 87). Characterised in this period by self-confidence, a sense of superiority and complacency, unionism failed to anticipate the cumulative effect of its mode of governance on relations with the minority in its midst.

The upheavals of the late 1960s and early 1970s punctured unionist hubris. Attempts by a relatively liberal unionist prime minister, Terence O'Neill, to address Catholic grievances provoked splits within the party and intense opposition from without in the form of the Paisleyite movement. The declining security situation led to London introducing Direct Rule in 1972, a decision that 'reduced overnight the Unionist Party from a party of government with patronage at its disposal, to a body of incoherent and ineffectual protest'; deprived of political power it stood as 'a symbol of tarnished ethnic honour' (Walker, 2004: 212). The legitimacy and stability of Northern Ireland had been challenged by civil rights campaigns and IRA violence, and yet a more profound questioning of unionist values was to emanate from Britain. In spite of unionists' protestations of Northern Ireland's Britishness and loyalty to the Crown, the years of Direct Rule saw London operate the province as a distinctly irregular part of the United Kingdom. Reforms targeted at redressing long-standing inequality, failure to eradicate the IRA, close co-operation with the Irish Republic and a general lack of empathy with the unionist cause precipitated a new phase in the unionist personality marked by insecurity, a renewed sense of siege, and pessimism. This was a period of stagnation and splits, the most notable challenges to the UUP coming from the short-lived Vanguard Unionist Party and the DUP, both of which opposed the party's faltering support for the Sunningdale power-sharing Government in 1974.

The greatest blow to unionism came in the form of the Anglo-Irish Agreement of 1985. This inter-governmental pact was designed to ease nationalist alienation in the North by giving Dublin a role in governing the region, and it was agreed without reference to unionism. The 1985 Agreement was condemned by unionists as a capitulation to IRA terrorism and as a likely precursor to further British disengagement from Northern Ireland. Yet the ineffectualness of unionist protest, before and after the accord, consisting of civil disobedience, street rallies and the mass resignation of unionist MPs, underlined unionism's marginality and strategic impoverishment. A growing recognition that unionists needed to expand their tactical repertoire beyond protest and nay-saying – approaches epitomised by Ian Paisley and James Molyneaux, the UUP leader – led to the establishment of a pan-unionist task force to examine unionist options in the wake of the Agreement. As the title of the task force's report expressed, unionists – at least some of them – sought 'an end to drift'. The authors recognised unionism's intense sense of insecurity, contending that the Anglo-Irish Agreement of 1985, the terrorism it was placating and Direct Rule from London were resulting in 'a community increasingly confused as to what is and is not acceptable in a democratic society; a community torn between loyalty to the law and established order, and the compelling conclusion that violence and anarchy are the likeliest route to political reward' (McCusker et al., 1987). Nevertheless, the thrust of the document was that the unionist response to the Anglo-Irish Agreement had been a failure, and it proposed recalibrating unionist strategy in the direction of negotiation: 'Negotiation need not be the precursor to "sell out" or "betrayal". Indeed the assumption that Unionists must inevitably be bested in any negotiations can only reflect the judgment of those who have already sold out and accepted defeat' (McCusker et al., 1987). The UUP and DUP leaderships regarded the report as thinly veiled criticism of their approaches and the document had little immediate impact. Yet, although it expressed scant appetite for flexibility or compromise – hardly indicative of a shift towards transcender logic – it did signal a new awareness within unionism of the perils of fatalistically expecting defeat, and the imperative of confidently crafting fresh ways of engaging with opponents.

And crafting new ways of engagement was precisely the concern of the so-called 'new unionists', a group of unionist intellectuals who, from the 1980s, began to address the perceived need for unionism to be re-thought, re-branded and re-asserted. Through their writings they espoused a better articulated, more reasoned ideology aimed at making unionism comprehensible and attractive outside Northern Ireland and reinvigorated and confident within. Open, pluralist and secular, new unionists sought to show a presentable face to the world in place of the ugly features of populist, fundamentalist Paisleyism and the strange rituals of Orangeism. For instance, Arthur Aughey argued that unionism was founded not upon anachronistic tribalism but the appeal of citizenship within a progressive and liberal state. Diverse and multi-layered identities can be accommodated within the pluralist British state in a way impossible in an Irish Republic based on an exclusively Irish national identity. Unionism is a 'rational political idea' that stands in contrast to 'the narrow perversity of the whole idea of the politics of identity' represented by nationalists who demand simplistic self-identification from Ulster unionists (Aughey, 1989: 12–19). The most significant criticism levelled at this view (for more, see Coulter, 1994; O'Dowd, 1998; Porter, 1998) points out that, contrary to intention, it is yet exclusive in that the 'dichotomy between a politics of citizenship and a politics of identity conveniently ignores the fact that the former is also about *identifying* those who "belong" and those who do not'. Full recognition as citizens is contingent upon accepting the legitimacy of the state borders; nationalists withhold such recognition and thus, unionists would say, disqualify themselves from full citizenship rights. The implication is that 'Catholics are entitled to full civil and religious liberties as individuals but not as nationalists' (O'Dowd, 1998: 79).

Thus, new unionist ideas did not depart from the core values of unionism. The real significance of the ideas was their effect on the unionist self-image. Farrington (2006: 46–7) likens the debate to what is known in the community relations field as 'single-identity work', a process that develops confidence within a community as a precursor to engagement with opponents. While they may not have convinced nationalists of the irresistible sense of unionism, new unionist arguments made enough sense to enough unionists to kindle some optimism that they at least had a case that could and should be fought, and this was evident in the approach of David Trimble to the burgeoning peace process. Taking over from Molyneaux in 1995, he was regarded as a hardliner, and was successful in attaining the leadership because of this fact. A veteran of the Vanguard Unionist Party, he had opposed power-sharing in 1974 and had been in close and public association with Paisley during the Drumcree Orange parade stand-off in July 1995. The latter episode led Paisley to claim the mantle of 'kingmaker' in the UUP leadership contest (Moloney, 2008: 342). Yet Trimble was also an articulate intellectual who shared the new unionist concern to stimulate a proactive movement that could engage boldly with opponents, one that was not handicapped by fatalism and the assumption of inevitable failure (Trimble, 2001a: 46). Perhaps the greatest indicator of new-found unionist confidence, and Trimble's determination to engage, was the UUP's decision to remain in the all-party talks upon the entry of Sinn Féin in September 1997.

The Agreement: 'a permanent settlement'

When the Good Friday Agreement was finally concluded in April 1998, it was success on one issue – the consent principle – that won UUP acceptance of the accord. This was the 'stabilising constitutional core' of the Agreement (Patterson, 1998) and it was accepted by the Social Democratic and Labour Party (SDLP), the Irish Government (which agreed to remove its territorial claim) and implicitly by Sinn Féin. Thus Trimble felt confident in declaring to the final plenary of the talks on 10 April 1998: 'I know we rise from the table with the Union stronger than when we first sat here' (Trimble, 2007: 15). Consent's crucial attribute was its finality; it was thought by most unionists to have no dynamic and so was prized as the best antidote to their insecurity (Farrington, 2006: 135). Accordingly, the UUP conceived of the Agreement as a *settlement* to the conflict. As Trimble stated plainly in a speech a week after the Agreement was finalised: 'We have sought and secured a permanent settlement, not a transitional arrangement' (Trimble, 2001a: 11). Whatever republicans said about the Good Friday deal being a stepping stone to a united Ireland, Trimble was convinced that it was in fact 'a disaster for Sinn-Féin-IRA' and would close the curtain on decades of instability for the Protestants of Northern Ireland (p. 7). With the Irish Republic's territorial claim gone, unionists could now develop a cordial and productive relationship with the South through non-threatening and mutually beneficial cross-border institutions.

By declaring the Agreement a settlement, the UUP leaders were claiming that they had achieved that which had eluded unionist politicians for almost a century. In his history of the party, Walker (2004: 62) underscores the continuous theme of 'anger at the Irish question being revisited and reframed, and their desire for permanence competing with the changing political contexts in London (and Dublin)'. Indeed, the question of whether the 1998 Agreement was in truth more likely to be a settlement or a transitional arrangement was at the heart of a debate within unionism eighty years earlier, at the time of the Government of Ireland Bill. The brother of unionist leader James Craig, Charles, reassured those who worried that the partition in prospect would be a process in nationalists' favour rather than a final settlement: 'It has been said that this Bill lends itself to the union of Ulster and the rest of Ireland. I would not be fair to the House if I lent the slightest hope of that union arising within the lifetime of any man in this House. I do not believe it for a moment' (cited in Harbinson, 1973: 30). Trimble made the very same argument. For the UUP of 1998, the Belfast Agreement represented the satisfaction of unionists' historic desire for closure on the Northern Ireland conflict and the stability that such closure would bring.

That stability would be established not only by the Agreement's resolution of the long-standing constitutional controversy but also by the arrival of devolved, democratic government to Northern Ireland. Unionists resented Catholic grievance at Protestant privilege since Direct Rule began in 1972 in large part because they actually detected a governmental bias towards the Catholic community. 'The system was being run for the benefit of nationalism', in Trimble's words (Millar, 2008: 66). The creation of a devolved assembly would be a welcome departure from a type of government that had been regarded by unionists as 'a form of colonial rule which violates the fundamental rights and entitlements of all the people of Northern Ireland' (McCusker *et al.*, 1987: 3). The UUP welcomed the fact that devolution would be run on power-sharing principles; Trimble castigated those unionists who longed for the return of majoritarian government as deluded. Furthermore, since devolution to a Belfast Assembly was to form part of New Labour's wider devolution plan that included Scotland and Wales, Ulster Unionists could be satisfied that the new form of government would be the UK norm, rather than the exception. Indeed, stability was a primary goal of the devolution experiments; by assuaging nationalism, devolution would in theory strengthen and preserve the Union and stave off dissent (Gillespie, 1998).

Evaluating the Agreement, Trimble distinguished these constitutional and institutional aspects, i.e. the principle of consent and the Assembly, North–South and East–West structures, from what he regarded as matters of policy that would be pursued by the British Government with or without a negotiated agreement between the parties (Trimble, 2007: 16). It was these policy matters – prisoner releases, decommissioning, security and equality reform – that caused sections of the UUP and the unionist public most difficulty in supporting the deal at the time and over the course of implementation (Hayes and McAllister 1999; Mac Ginty, 2004). The UUP leadership attempted to steady the nerves of their supporters by presenting pragmatic justifications for these measures. On prisoner releases, Trimble pointed out that even Paisley had intimated during the Brooke talks of the early 1990s that this issue would need to be dealt with as part of a final settlement (Trimble, 2001a: 31) and, indeed, the UUP could look to a precedent in the release of republican prisoners by the unionist Government after the IRA campaign of 1956–62 (Hennessey, 1998: 8). On police reform, Trimble believed that it was better that an international commission of policing experts make recommendations for reform, as the Agreement had it, rather than a nationalist-slanted local body (Millar, 2008: 89–93), although this is a judgement that he subsequently regretted in the light of what the Patten Commission actually produced (Trimble, 2007: 19). While the UUP was happy that the substance of the Patten reforms was inevitable in the event of a normalised security situation, the party condemned, along with unionists across the spectrum, the changing of the RUC name and symbols.

On equality matters, Trimble argued that at least the UUP would be inside the new Agreement structures where it would be in a strong position to influence the specifics of equality and rights reform as well as the policing and prisoner issues (Trimble, 2001a: 9). Finally, regarding decommissioning, the UUP put its faith in Tony Blair to enforce the linkage between the giving up of guns and the participation of paramilitary-linked parties in the Executive (Hennessey, 1998: 7). Trimble admits that the talks team knew the decommissioning section was the Agreement's weak point but he refused to let it sink the whole deal given that they had made what they believed to be momentous gains for unionism in other areas (Millar, 2008: 65–7). In spite of these arguments for assenting to the 'negatives' in the Agreement, these aspects caused a large minority of the UUP (and six of the party's ten MPs) to reject the Agreement and were to make it highly difficult to sell to the unionist people. Jeffrey Donaldson's last-minute walkout from the talks on 10 April became symbolic of unionist unease with the terms of the Agreement; he found prisoner releases, police reform and the weak clause on decommissioning to be unconscionable and believed he could not ask his constituents to accept them (Davidson, 2004). Many others in the party opposed the Agreement for a similar fusion of moral and political concerns – to concede anything to republicans while they remained unremorseful and untrustworthy was wrong and dangerous for democracy and the Union. This analysis was shared by the DUP and is explored at length in Chapter 5.

In the referendum campaign, the UUP campaigned under the slogan 'Yes for the Union'. The theme was of unionist victory and resurgence, and the UUP enumerated unionists' gains, which were centered on the Agreement's recognition of the legitimacy of Northern Ireland: the acceptance of the consent principle; the end of the Anglo-Irish Agreement; the removal of the Republic's territorial claim; accountable cross-border bodies; and the return of Stormont. Harnessing the zero-sum logic of the security dilemma, republican voices were used to corroborate these gains. One UUP referendum campaign advertisement contained quotations from a range of pro- and anti-Agreement republicans and the Dublin press to back up the argument that the Agreement was a victory for the pro-Union side and that the DUP's charge of a triumph for terrorism was spurious. A quote from Mitchel McLaughlin of Sinn Féin verified that the deal legitimised the British state in Ireland and a line from the Dublin-based *Sunday Business Post* predicted that the Agreement would 'copper-fasten partition for many years to come'. The quotations from nationalist Ireland appeared beside a warning in giant letters: 'This is a bad deal for republicans. Do not fall into their trap.' The trap was for unionists to act according to type, say no to the Agreement and provoke even greater change in the governance of Northern Ireland. Labour MP Kate Hoey was quoted as saying 'the IRA wants unionists to vote "No". That is the best reason to vote "Yes" on Friday' (UUP, 1998a).

The UUP was also keen to talk up its potential influence in the post-Agreement dispensation. Not only did the party pledge to work in the Agreement institutions for the protection of unionist interests, but also emphasised (and overplayed) the party's powers to do this. In the referendum campaign, voters were assured that: in the North–South Ministerial Council (NSMC) a unionist must always be present and the party would always have a veto; the party would ensure that the Government adequately acknowledged the sacrifices and attended to the needs of the RUC and victims; 'our flag and culture' would not be undermined; and the UUP would hold Tony Blair and the other parties to their obligations on decommissioning. 'The Union has been strengthened because it is in our hands alone' (UUP, 1998b). Dublin interference was gone, British commitment was renewed. In a message of support for UUP candidates for the Assembly elections of June 1998, Trimble confidently wrote that the decommissioning issue 'must be addressed to our satisfaction' (UUP, 1998c).

Overall, the referendum campaign revealed the UUP leadership's fear of anti-Agreement unionists both inside and outside the UUP, and displayed an attitude of victory and unilateralism that did not bode well for the implementation of the Agreement, which would require, if it were to succeed, large measures of good faith and dialogue. That said, the party at times struck a more transcendent note. 'There are two main religious denominations', Trimble told the Nobel Prize audience in Oslo, 'But there is only one true moral denomination. And it wants peace' (Trimble, 2001a: 65). Trimble explicitly revised the phrase that had summed up past unionist defensiveness and exclusivity; instead of a Protestant parliament for a Protestant people, the Agreement established 'a pluralist parliament for a pluralist people', and he pledged to be 'a pluralist First Minister'. The people of Northern Ireland 'must embrace the future with the enthusiasm it requires and avoid the mistake of walking into the future facing backwards' (Trimble, 1999a). However, the general tone of the party was imperious, emphasising its ability to influence and command the political process, and that imperiousness barely concealed a profound anxiety about the dangers and direction of that process. This was the paradox at the heart of the UUP's triumphalist campaign to sell the Agreement. While the UUP declared that voting 'yes' was a vote for a future within the United Kingdom, the party also was at pains to point out that voting 'no' did not guarantee that prisoners would not be released, did not guarantee that the RUC would remain untouched and did not guarantee decommissioning. Thus, while the Agreement would apparently 'safeguard Ulster's position within the UK', the UUP admitted in almost the same breath that Her Majesty's Government intended to – Agreement or no Agreement – pursue a set of policies that would jeopardise Northern Ireland's position within the United Kingdom, or at least lend legitimacy to those who sought to undermine that position (see, for example, UUP, 1998b). 'Fortunately, the Agreement secures Northern Ireland's future on the basis of the consent principle', declared Trimble, yet he went on to warn: 'But unionists still need to work together to safeguard the Union and our British identity' (Trimble, 2001a: 124).

In the 1998 Assembly election, the UUP won twenty-eight seats; the anti-Agreement DUP and United Kingdom Unionist Party won twenty and five respectively. The party's vote share, 21.3 per cent, was its lowest ever, with the SDLP topping the poll for the first time with 21.9 per cent. The post-Agreement tasks facing the Trimble leadership were clear. Trimble had stated in 1996 that in relation to the multi-party negotiations, 'our fundamental concerns are peace and democracy, in the language of the peace process, they are called consent and decommissioning' (Trimble, 1996). As the UUP's perspective on the Agreement shows, uncertainty surrounded the achievement of both these goals, their treatment in the Agreement being touched by constructive ambiguity. Ironing out that uncertainty would become the UUP's key concern during implementation. While the principle of consent ostensibly secured Northern Ireland's legitimacy, the actual import and application of British sovereignty after the Agreement was unsure. Meanwhile, the major source of political, social and economic instability for unionists over thirty years – republican violence – was yet to be eliminated. While Sinn Féin demanded its place in government, IRA crime and violence continued and decommissioning – which Blair had told unionists should start immediately after the Agreement – did not happen. Thus, the traditional unionist fears of physical threat and cultural decline – fears based both on exclusivist, nationalist desire and on real threats – continued to shape UUP politics, turning some away from the Agreement and constraining the actions of those whose mitigator logic led them to support the accord. Nowhere was this more in evidence than in relation to the set-piece dispute of the post-Agreement years, decommissioning.

Decommissioning and division

The UUP's post-Agreement obsession with (overwhelmingly republican) paramilitary weapons is inexplicable without appreciating the issue as one with deep roots that went back as far as 1993. The British Government's line on republican disarmament had been inconsistent. In general, the peace process was managed on the assumption that Sinn Féin and the IRA were inextricably linked and that, therefore, so too should be their political fates. Sinn Féin's exclusion from the all-party talks until the IRA ceasefire was renewed in the summer of 1997 and the party's brief exclusion from the talks after IRA-linked murders in February 1998 were just two examples of this assumption in action. Yet the Government was concerned about the dangers of pushing too hard on decommissioning and disrupting what it believed to be republicanism's steady move away from violence. The approach of the British – 'moving goalposts' (Morgan, 2000: 443) – led to Trimble's party reluctantly following these policy shifts in the belief that remaining in the talks and assenting to the Government's parameters made decommissioning and the attainment of other unionist goals more likely than would walking away from the process. Despite the party's position that the IRA give up its weapons before Sinn Féin enter talks, its rejection of the January 1996 Mitchell plan for decommissioning to occur in parallel with talks and then, after Sinn Féin did enter the talks, demands that decommissioning occur then, the UUP still signed an agreement in April 1998 with no weapons having been given up. To both Trimble's supporters and detractors, the unfinished business of the process was obvious.

While the Agreement did not explicitly link decommissioning with setting up the Executive, the UUP position that immediate decommissioning was required by the Agreement rested on four pillars. The first was the Northern Ireland Assembly's Pledge of Office. Since the UUP regarded Sinn Féin and the IRA as a single entity, it believed that Sinn Féin representatives could not credibly take the Pledge and declare their commitment to non-violence until their 'private army' disarmed. The Agreement, said Trimble, 'insisted on the use of exclusively peaceful and democratic means – the disarmament of paramilitary groups was merely the corollary of that principle' (Trimble, 2008). The second was the fact that the dates set out in the Agreement for the completion of both prisoner releases and decommissioning were the same: two years after the referenda on the deal, May 2000. Unionists were under the impression that the twin deadlines meant that those provisions were interdependent. Austen Morgan, a lawyer and member of the UUP talks team, wrote that 'it is difficult not to believe' that prisoner releases and decommissioning were tied (Morgan, 2000: 448); Trimble said that 'you really have to be stubborn' not to see the connection (Millar, 2008: 77). In its submission to the Mitchell Review in the autumn of 1999, the UUP classed decommissioning as a 'non-evolutionary' aspect of the Agreement, i.e. one to which there was no impediment to its immediate execution, in contrast to the 'evolutionary aspects' – the constitutional and institutional provisions that required further negotiation and legislation in order to be implemented (UUP, 1999a). The UUP lamented that the British Government pressed ahead with other 'non-evolutionary' aspects such as prisoner releases, reviews into criminal justice and policing, the establishment of the Human Rights and Equality Commissions and security normalisation, despite the fact that no progress was made on decommissioning.

The third was the now infamous eleventh-hour side-letter. Unhappy with the weak linkage between decommissioning and participation in Executive office in the final draft of the Agreement, Trimble received a letter from Blair promising that should the exclusion mechanism prove ineffective in the event of Sinn Féin defaulting on decommissioning, the British Government would intervene. Furthermore, the letter stated that 'the process of decommissioning should start straight away'. There is perhaps a nugget of constructive ambiguity in the use of the word 'should' rather than 'must', though Trimble certainly saw the letter as a commitment by the British to ensuring disarmament began 'straight away'. Trimble has stated of the letter: 'As a paper issued before the actual agreement and not objected to by any of the other parties it is, in international law, an authoritative interpretation of text of the Agreement' (Trimble, 2007: 18). This letter was pivotal in winning the UUP's support for the Agreement, both on 10 April and later in the party's Executive and Council. Other parties were naturally more sceptical about its worth, although Blair did fulfil his promise in the letter to the extent that he suspended the institutions when decommissioning did not follow the creation of the Executive. (Trimble would have preferred the exclusion of Sinn Féin, but in that event the SDLP would not have remained in the Assembly and government would have collapsed (Trimble, 2007: 18)). The fourth pillar was the pledges made by Blair during the referendum campaign that the Government would make prisoner releases and the entry into government of paramilitary-linked parties conditional on:

> an end to bombings, killings and beatings, claimed or unclaimed; an end to targeting and procurement of weapons; progressive abandonment and dismantling of paramilitary structures; actively directing and promoting violence; full co-operation with the Independent Commission on decommissioning to implement the provisions of the agreement; and no other organisations being deliberately used as proxies for violence.
>
> (Blair, 1998)

While the UUP was alone in its interpretation of the decommissioning requirements, the deal gave the party a significant means of leverage over republicans. Under the compellingly simple slogan, 'no guns, no government', the party endeavoured to force decommissioning by making the fulfilment of unionist obligations (the setting up of the institutions) conditional on the fulfilment of republican obligations (decommissioning). Such an approach was anathema to republicans who saw it as a gambit to force defeat on the IRA, nor was it accepted by the SDLP. The British Government, focused on maintaining Sinn Féin's participation, quickly forgot about its pre-referendum pledges (see Dixon, 2013) and so, while implementation of other parts of the Agreement proceeded, an impasse on decommissioning lasted for eighteen months following the signing of the Agreement. Trimble countered calls for the UUP to go ahead and unconditionally set up an Executive by asking why, if the pressure on republicans to disarm was already great, should it be any greater once they were in government? 'If I agreed to buy a house, but kept stalling on coming up with the money, few would advocate giving me the keys in the hope that I would be shamed or inspired into paying up' (Trimble, 1999b).

The Mitchell Review in the autumn of 1999, led by the American chair of the Good Friday talks, George Mitchell, appeared to produce an understanding among the parties on decommissioning, with Trimble agreeing to participate in devolution in return for a commitment from the IRA to nominate a representative to liaise with the Independent International Commission on Decommissioning (IICD). This was the first example of Trimble's pressure-applying brinkmanship, 'jumping first' while calling on his Agreement partners to follow. He believed this course of action was the only way to get devolution *and* decommissioning, and that it was not an abandonment of 'no guns, no government' since the party always had the option of pulling out (Trimble, 1999c). One of his biographers, Henry McDonald (2000: 309), described the strategy as: 'a political and personal version of Pascal's wager. For the seventeenth-century French philosopher, belief in God is a gamble: if you believe and there is an afterlife in heaven, then it was worth the trouble after all; if you believe and there is nothing, you have not lost anything by having faith.' If republicans turned out to be sincere and decommissioned, then Trimble's gamble was vindicated; if no decommissioning took place, unionists, having done their bit, would at least avoid blame for the process collapsing. In the event, Trimble won the support of the Ulster Unionist Council (UUC) (58 per cent) to enter government but with the help of a crutch – a post-dated letter of resignation that would be triggered should there be no movement on decommissioning. He believed the device was 'tacky' and could allow republicans to claim that it just set another precondition, but it was necessary to win over the doubters (Godson, 2004: 519).

No such movement came and Secretary of State for Northern Ireland Peter Mandelson pre-empted Trimble's resignation by suspending the institutions in February 2000. Then, in a St Patrick's Day speech in Washington, Trimble hinted that he would be prepared for a fresh sequence, entering government without arms up-front. The IRA re-engaged with the IICD, allowing Trimble to win 53 per cent in the UUC for a return to the Executive. Arms dumps were inspected but, with no actual destruction of weapons, UUP discontent persisted. At another special meeting in October, the UUC decided to permit the party to remain in power on condition that Trimble exclude Sinn Féin ministers from NSMC meetings. This policy was designed to draw support away from even stricter measures proposed by Donaldson (Godson, 2004: 628–9) but it yielded no results on weapons and was in fact later declared unlawful. Concerned to bolster his position going into the June 2001 Westminster elections, Trimble wrote another letter of resignation in May to be triggered in July.

The resignation took effect and talks on relieving the impasse were held throughout the summer to no avail. The IRA's first substantial act of decommissioning eventually came in late October 2001. The new global anti-terror climate brought about by 9/11 was credited with applying the necessary pressure, although undoubtedly this merely hastened something that republican participation in the peace process had made inevitable (O'Kane, 2007: 100). Trimble nonetheless saw it as a vindication of his 'high-risk political strategy' of creating crises in the institutions to exert maximum pressure on the IRA (Trimble, 2001b). The act of decommissioning prompted the UUP to permit Trimble's return as First Minister. However, unionist impatience with republicans continued and in September 2002 the UUC agreed to withdraw ministers from NSMC meetings and, assuming the IRA did not complete the surrender of weapons, would withdraw from the Executive on 18 January 2003. This was a mélange of two proposals from Trimble and Donaldson (Thornton, 2002a). However, before the unionists could carry through their threat, the discovery by the Police Service of Northern Ireland (PSNI) of a republican spying operation in Stormont in October led to the institutions' collapse. Another choreographed sequence was attempted in October 2003 but failed due to a lack of unionist confidence in what the IICD was permitted by the IRA to report about the extent of the decommissioning that had taken place. This created the polarised backdrop of the November 2003 Assembly election at which the DUP capitalised on the unionist community's loss of faith in the implementation process.

As this narrative shows, the deep divisions within the UUP over decommissioning shaped the leadership's strategy on the issue. Trimble's opponents claimed that in the concoction of each new compulsion tactic the UUP leader had been dragged further onto their ground, forced to take note of the disquiet in the party (for example, Smyth, 2001). The periodic and very public clashes over strategy held in the arena of the UUC gave the impression of a party without clear direction and a party leadership with limited credibility and party management skills. There was dissent within the republican fold too but, as one journalist put it, 'the problem is unionism wears its splits on its sleeve' (McAdam, 2000). Indeed, there was a 'Groundhog Day' feel to the UUP's high-profile crisis meetings in which Trimble narrowly survived; the SDLP's Mark Durkan recalls 'the Novena of Ulster [Unionist] Council meetings where Trimble teetered on the brink. He couldn't pass a brink without teetering on it' (interview with Mark Durkan MP, 30 August 2012). Nesbitt describes the leadership's predicament: 'It was a matter of if we try and stay in [the Executive] we break it – the Council. So we have to sort of withdraw to keep the party, but keep the options open … So it was a very very very – that's three verys – difficult pragmatic position for David Trimble to work through' (interview with former UUP MLA, Dermot Nesbitt, 10 September 2012). Trimble insisted that, whatever the claims of his critics, he never abandoned the 'no guns, no government' policy because his party's presence in the Executive was always conditional on decommissioning happening (Millar, 2008: 75–6). Yet that brought to light the constructive ambiguity of that very slogan. Martin Smyth, the anti-Agreement UUP MP, could argue that 'no guns, no government' was the one policy that united the UUP (Smyth, 2000) yet clearly even such an ostensibly black-and-white dictum left room for interpretation.

Trimble's flexibility was based on two judgements, both of which indicated a degree of self-awareness regarding unionism's entrapment in the security dilemma, and the potential for that entrapment to worsen. The first judgement was that decommissioning had to be pursued in such a way that unionists win the 'blame game' and avoid the appearance of intransigence that would simply weaken unionism (Trimble, 2002). Again and again, he appealed to the party not to regard decommissioning with less significance, but to carve out an approach to the problem that acknowledged the importance of the institutions to public confidence and international opinion. The UUP leader wanted to prove that Northern Ireland was not a failed political entity and that it could be run with ample support from both communities. Trimble's pragmatism entailed recognising that decommissioning was important, indeed vital, but it must not be pursued in such a way that unionism's gains were needlessly thrown away. He implored his party to 'consider the situation coolly' and act on the basis of 'careful quiet, consideration' (Trimble, 2001a: 142). The implication was that his opponents within the party, armed with emotive arguments, were too eager to act without considering the repercussions. In contrast to Trimble's concern for nationalist and international opinion, his UUP critics were more attuned to the growing disaffection within the unionist community (Smyth, 2000, 2001; Donaldson, 2001).

The second reason for Trimble's flexible approach to decommissioning was his firm conviction that republican leaders were genuinely steering their movement away from violence and this process required some sensitivity from unionists. Godson (2004: 627) notes Trimble's desire not to have his 'hands tied' by hard-liner-inspired deadlines and extra preconditions such as those relating to RUC reform. Although convinced of the necessity of maintaining pressure on republicans, Trimble understood that excessive compulsion tactics could be counter-productive by having a negative effect on the ability of Gerry Adams to manage his constituency. This understanding was evident when he wrote in October 1999: 'Let republicans and loyalists do this [dispose of arms], not simply because of pressure but because they realise that it is the best way forward' (Trimble, 1999b). Commenting in September 2002 on his own strategy to date, Trimble argued that it had been carefully calibrated not to destroy the process altogether: 'There was an exit strategy in each case and in each case things worked according to my expectation. It is all very well to say 'set a deadline' … but tearing the house down and waiting to see what turns up isn't the sensible approach' (Trimble quoted in McAdam, 2002). When it was put it to Trimble in that interview that his opponents were saying that the party must return to the bottom line of the 1998 manifesto commitment that it would not sit in government with unreconstructed terrorists, Trimble displayed his taste for constructive ambiguity by pointing to a different interpretation: 'Ah, but the overriding main commitment of that manifesto was to make this [the Agreement] work' (quoted in McAdam, 2002). Elsewhere he said that he never regarded 'the Agreement of April '98 as being Holy Writ' (Millar, 2008: 67).

Were the splits over decommissioning merely tactical, or did they reflect deeper ideological divisions? Trimble preferred to see them as tactical and it was true that less than one in ten members of the UUC believed in 2000 that Sinn Féin should be allowed to participate in devolved government regardless of whether the IRA decommissioned its weapons (Tonge and Evans, 2001: 122). Decommissioning was non-negotiable, it was just a question of how best to bring it about. But how can this be squared with the apparent recklessness of the 'no' camp's eagerness to bring down the institutions given that such an outcome would probably make decommissioning less likely? Was achieving decommissioning really their only interest? Many commentators and nationalist politicians believed that the tactical differences did stem from more profound divisions over the implications of the Agreement for the constitutional conflict and for the security of unionism. For example, Cochrane (2000) speculated that the arms issue was in actual fact 'simply a placebo, masking a wider struggle between Trimble and Donaldson over the political direction of Ulster Unionism'. The suggestion was that the Trimble–Donaldson saga was a conflict between those unionists willing to accept the opportunities and risks of compromise, and those who feared change and preferred the security of Direct Rule.

A survey of the membership of the UUC conducted at the height of UUP division over decommissioning in the autumn of 2000 found that the differences were indeed more than tactical and 'masked more fundamental questions concerning the future of unionism' (Tonge and Evans, 2001: 115). The authors identified two categories of member, 'Orange skeptics' and 'rational civics'. Orange sceptics opposed the Trimble leadership approach, but also held deep misgivings about the security of the Union and the intentions of republicans. They feared the constitutional direction of the Agreement and resented the reform of Northern Ireland. Rational civics supported Trimble, reflecting their more positive assessment of the Agreement as guarantor of the Union's long-term future, and changes within republicanism, notwithstanding the short-term pain imposed by some of the accord's provisions. Orange sceptics valued traditional Protestant and Orange expressions of cultural unionism while rational civics preferred a secular unionism open to pluralism and cultural diversity. This, then, was the clash between the fatalist logic that continued to harbour a desire for the exclusivist, ethno-centric unionist security of the past, and the mitigator logic that believed that sustainable peace and security for unionism was only possible through compromise and risk.

A major factor in the debate was the moral dubiety of sharing power with Sinn Féin. Trimble's main critics, Donaldson and Smyth, were conservative evangelical Christians who were uncomfortable with what they saw as the moral compromise of Trimble's abandonment of principle ('no guns, no government') in favour of foolhardy pragmatism (sequencing involving weak guarantees of reciprocation) while the IRA remained active. Republicans insisted that what mattered was that the guns were silent, yet, as Aughey contends, this argument was disingenuous, first because those guns were not entirely silent – illegal and violent IRA activity continued – and second because unionists feared that 'the political eloquence of the guns had been actually enhanced' (Aughey, 2005: 128). The anxious succession of UUC showdowns was stimulated by a feeling that democracy was being devalued by ongoing incidents of IRA activity and an unsavoury implementation game in which guns were used as 'bargaining chips for more concessions' (Trimble, 2001a: 140).

The catalogue of IRA misdemeanours recited by unionists prior to the Assembly's suspension in 2002 included gunrunning in Florida, the arrest of three republicans apparently training guerrillas in Colombia, a break-in at Castlereagh police station, an intelligence-gathering operation in Stormont, ongoing cross-border smuggling, ongoing punishment attacks and several murders. Smyth's (2000) question: 'How can Sinn Féin/IRA seriously be deemed fit to be in government when they are commissioning rather than decommissioning?' was simple and irrefutable reason in the ears of many unionists. Pragmatism was not appropriate to such a situation: 'we must withdraw [from the Executive] not for appearance's sake but because it is the right thing to do' (Smyth, 2001). Unionists across the spectrum were not slow in recognising the political logic of simmering IRA violence, or indeed the sense of simply holding on to weapons. Trimble noted the likelihood that the republican leadership had settled for

> a new type of subversion. Not a direct threat to the state with bombs and attacks on the security services, but a Mafia state in which ministerial power will be allied with a well-stocked private army able to control public opinion through intimidation in its heartland. The latter possibility appears to fit the facts of continued gun running and ongoing killing, beating and intimidation.
>
> (Trimble, 1999b)

Refusing to hand over weapons constituted the 'politics of latent threat', designed to squeeze more and more concessions out of the British Government and the unionists (Trimble, 2001b). Similarly, Donaldson, lamented that

> the problem is the IRA keep eating all the carrots that the SDLP and the British government offer them and it seems like they've got this conveyor belt of tinned carrots that keeps being put on order for P. O'Neill and their approach is: 'we'll give as little in return as we need to in order to keep the supply of carrots coming.' Unionism had made it clear that this conveyor belt has to stop.
>
> (Quoted in Farrington, 2006: 147)

In spite of Trimble's acknowledgements of the threat, his party critics saw him as being complicit in the subversion: Smyth opined that 'each crisis in this process involves my party making further concessions or lowering its expectations ... it is not logical to keep offering further movement and more carrots in order for them [republicans] to keep their original commitment [to decommission]' (Smyth, 2001).

Not only did the possession and use of IRA weapons compromise the legitimacy of the Agreement institutions in the eyes of unionists, but it also retrospectively challenged the political and moral foundations of the unionist understanding of the conflict. Unionists saw the 'Troubles' as the unleashing of illegitimate violence on the security forces and citizens of a legitimate state. The failure of the British Government to keep its pledge to enforce the decommissioning–devolution linkage and its apparent pandering to republican demands undermined this view and represented a deplorable revision of history. After the Agreement, the terrorists were suddenly terrorists no more, now to be dealt with by enticement, not law and force. Trimble stated that 'The Agreement is nothing if it not about peace. As the Prime Minister said on 14 May 1998, "There must be an end to bombings, beatings, killings, the acquisition of weapons and the progressive dismantling of paramilitary structures"' (Trimble, 2001a: 140). Given that, as Trimble noted, 'we do not have that yet', unionists were led to suspect that perhaps the Agreement was not about peace as they recognised it but – with republicans stalling on decommissioning and the Government acquiescing – the appeasement of terrorists. Unionists' belief that they were the sole occupants of the moral high ground contrasted with the moral equivalence that the British Government at times drew between the republican and unionist positions. Mandelson irked unionists when he described the decommissioning impasse in March 2000 as 'a sort of Mexican stand-off'. To the Ulster Unionists, this ignored the fact that it had been they who had 'jumped first' in November 1999 only to be let down by the IRA, and the subsequent suspension of the Assembly unfairly punished both sides equally (Godson, 2004: 593–4). Jonathan Powell (2008: 210), Tony Blair's Chief of Staff, notes in his book on the peace process that in the wake of the suspension of the Assembly in 2002, 'the process had become badly discredited and morally undermined. It no longer seemed based on principle'. Reviewing the book, Trimble (2008) comments dryly of this line that unfortunately Powell 'failed to make the connection between his (and Blair's) conduct and the outcome'.

With the IRA's weaponry responsible for countless unjustifiable deaths, the compulsion/conditionality strategy was, to unionists, the only moral method of achieving decommissioning. Achieving it any other way, for example through incentives (which appeared to be the policy of the Governments), would imply that the IRA was something other than a guilty party that should be defeated and disarmed. Republicans envisaged otherwise, as Danny Morrison explained: 'I have no doubt that with the full implementation of the Belfast Agreement, including the adoption of the Patten Commission on policing, the IRA in its own way will put its guns beyond use, beyond government, that the truce will turn into a permanent peace and the war will finally be seen to be over' (Morrison, 1999). To many unionists, this was morally unthinkable, whether or not it was rationally correct; 'its own way' was not an option, republicans had to be forced. The morally ideal procedure for the UUP would have been for the government to have enforced the implied linkage in the Agreement between prisoner releases and disarmament. This would have entailed the exchange of symbolic acts of repentance (decommissioning) followed by forgiveness (prisoner releases). According to Trimble: 'The unionist electorate would have seen the giving up of weapons as an explicit statement that the terrorist campaign was over and an implicit statement that it had been wrong' (Trimble, 2007: 17). The mental obstacles blocking the sharing of power with former IRA activists would have been removed from the unionist mind. Or, as Nesbitt comments: 'Decommissioning was an outward sign of an inward change of attitude. That parallels somewhat what John Hume said about the decommissioning of minds' (interview with Dermot Nesbitt, 10 September 2012). This was not to be, however, and the longer republicans stalled the more vacuous their commitment to non-violence appeared to unionists. As Smyth argued in early 2001: 'even if it [decommissioning] did occur, handing over weapons on the basis that one by one your demands have been met hardly demonstrates a firm commitment to exclusively peaceful means' (Smyth, 2001).

The bitter divisions over how to approach decommissioning made it the central electoral issue for unionists in the post-Agreement years, and electoral considerations played a huge role in defining the contours of UUP strategy on this issue. The UUP leadership needed decommissioning to vindicate its positive assessment of the Agreement and its openness to Sinn Féin's inclusion; as long as the IRA avoided disarmament, Trimble's judgement in supporting the Agreement was under question. Sinn Féin's view, however, was that Trimble made a 'negotiating mistake' in demanding decommissioning, asking for something that could not be delivered; thus, the argument that republicans were to blame for Trimble's party problems is 'crap' (interview with Mitchel McLaughlin MLA, 4 October 2012). In any case, the achievement of decommissioning was continually invoked by the UUP as an incentive to keep the party's members and electorate behind the leadership. The 'no guns, no government' policy was initially put forward in the UUP's manifesto for the June 1998 Assembly election as an attempt to reassure wary unionists liable to seduction by the rejectionism and old certainties offered by the DUP. To shore up his position heading into the June 2001 Westminster election, Trimble signed another post-dated resignation letter to be triggered in July if decommissioning did not materialise. That election also saw the party employ a telling publicity image, a clock face displaying a number of party aims beside each number: 'Anglo-Irish Agreement Gone', 'Devolution', 'Decommissioning', etc. The first nine aims were ticked, indicating that these goals had been attained. Among the five yet to be achieved were 'Decommissioning', 'Stable Government' and 'Greater Economic Prosperity'. The caption read: 'It's time to measure the gains: help us to finish the job' (UUP, 2001).

The intention was to portray decommissioning as lying just around the next corner, yet, not only did the strategy appear to fail in that the party lost four of its ten seats in the election, two years later the message was unchanged. Introducing the 2003 Assembly election manifesto, Trimble recounted the arduous journey the party had taken to ensure republicans abandoned violence for good in accordance with the Agreement. Although the IRA had failed to decommission with sufficient transparency to satisfy the UUP in October 2003, Trimble as ever did not admit defeat, but sought more time: 'Nonetheless the job can be completed. We know what is needed … And we know that there is no one else in the unionist community who can do it!' (UUP, 2003). But the results of that election showed that Trimble's efforts to rally the majority of unionism around his pressure-applying tactics had finally run out of steam. While the UUP maintained its vote share, the DUP swallowed up the smaller unionist parties to become, for the first time, the largest unionist party. The trend was spectacularly confirmed in the Westminster election of 2005 when the DUP won nine seats and the UUP was left with just one.

Safeguarding the Union

Alongside the struggle over decommissioning, the UUP fought a costly battle on a different post-Agreement front: against challenges to the unadulterated manifestation of the British constitutional status of Northern Ireland. Trimble stated bluntly on 17 April 1998 that 'these talks were about the principle of consent' (Trimble, 2001a: 11). With the solid anchor of consent in place, he argued, all storms could be weathered. But the UUP's optimism at having secured the principle of consent was tempered by the anxiety that assertive nationalism, armed with the 'green' elements of the Agreement, could nonetheless dilute the meaningfulness of the constitutional position until it was a mere technicality (Aughey, 2005: 123–5). The fact of the Union was enshrined but its nature was 'up for grabs' through commissions of reform and new legislation, institutions and bodies whose effects were yet to be known. Safeguarding the Union by ensuring that the reality of British sovereignty was the guiding principle of implementation became a key battle of the UUP after the Agreement and setbacks in this battle were to be another major source of Protestant disaffection with the Agreement and the Ulster Unionists in the post-Agreement years.

The need to protect Northern Ireland's Britishness, and the ability of the UUP to do so, was a constant theme in UUP discourse throughout implementation. The party maintained its insistence that the Agreement had brought, as Trimble promised it would, the UUP back from the desert to the heart of British political life: 'we deliver modern dynamic representation and maintain parity of services for Northern Ireland ... We do not intend to ever let Ulster Unionism be marginalised' (UUP, 2001: 5). The virtues of devolution were extolled as vindicating the UUP's approach and providing proof that Northern Ireland was not an inevitably flawed polity. 'Devolution worked because Ulster Unionists worked', declared the 2003 manifesto. 'Devolution will work because Ulster Unionists will continue to work' (UUP, 2003). The image of the UUP as a bulwark against the erosion of Northern Ireland's Britishness was propagated continuously, reaching its most blatant in the 2003 Assembly election slogan 'Simply British'. The contrast was often drawn with the DUP which was portrayed as, unlike the Ulster Unionists, unable and unwilling to exercise influence in pursuit of unionist goals due to its opposition to the Agreement and ambivalence towards the political process. For example, in September 2000, Trimble lambasted DUP impotence regarding the crucial issues of flags and policing, claiming major legislative concessions were won solely by the UUP. 'That kind of influence is not accidental', said Trimble, 'but a direct result of the UUP's policy of engagement' (Trimble, 2000a).

But the prominence of this theme was due to the widespread unionist belief, within pro and anti camps, that nationalists were bent on using the Agreement to dilute or destroy the British character of Northern Ireland. As Chapter 1 made clear, the parties did not resolve the matter of how state symbols would be used in the new Northern Ireland due to the significance of symbols to the ongoing identity conflict. The document made clear that Northern Ireland remained part of the United Kingdom but at the same time, sovereignty was to be exercised according to the principles of 'parity of esteem and of just and equal treatment for the identity, ethos and aspiration of both communities' (Agreement, 1998: 2). The Agreement offered little guidance on how or whether parity of esteem for identities would impinge on the visible manifestations of British sovereignty, other than to say that state symbols and emblems should be 'used in a manner which promotes mutual respect rather than division' (p. 20). Disputes arose over the appropriate use of emblems such as Remembrance Day poppies and Easter lilies, but the most politically heated questions concerned the flying of flags from public buildings and the name and badge of the reformed police force. The question was: how could identities be afforded parity of esteem if one or both, as part of their expression, demand privileging by providing the symbols of the state?

The UUP position was simple: the principle of consent that confirmed Northern Ireland's status as part of the United Kingdom logically required that state symbols should be exclusively British in nature. Therefore, unionists were incensed when republicans, during the first period of devolution, claimed that both the Union flag and the Irish tricolour should be flown from public buildings to reflect the Agreement's recognition of the two dominant identities within Northern Ireland. The SDLP advocated the absence of any flags pending cross-party agreement on the issue. Even more contentious, and traumatic, for the unionist community were the proposed policing reforms. Much of the Patten report was uncontroversial but certain sections, most notably the proposed changes to the name and badge of the RUC, caused intense demoralisation within the unionist community.

Trimble exploded; the report was 'an intellectually shoddy document, the product of third-rate academic theorising about the best model for achieving a politically correct police force' (Trimble, 2001a: 130). Citing the section in the Agreement that recognises Northern Ireland's constitutional status as legitimately British, Trimble argued that parties to the Agreement 'cannot, therefore, have any valid objection to the normal and reasonable expression of that legitimacy. The use of a crown in a police badge is a perfectly normal and reasonable expression of that legitimacy; similar to the EIIR on the helmets of mainland police forces' (UUP, 1999b). The UUP leader went on to counter the argument that the imperative of equal treatment of the culture and aspirations of each community contained in the Agreement meant that police symbols should not favour a British identity:

> But this non-discrimination clause does not override the legitimacy of British sovereignty or justify the argument that the institutions of Northern Ireland must reflect two equal nationalisms. There is only one sovereignty in Northern Ireland; there is not joint sovereignty. The recognition of two identities is not the recognition of two allegiances. By recognising Northern Ireland's place within the Kingdom as legitimate, nationalists recognise British sovereignty and recognise that the only valid source of law flows from the enactments of the Queen in Parliament. That recognition is allegiance even if it lacks the emotional commitment that we associate with the term.
> (UUP, 1999b)

Trimble's distinction between 'identities' and 'allegiances' points to the fundamental tension in the politics of symbols: cultural representation versus state representation. Trimble was saying that police emblems should not be concerned with cultural representation or expressions of identity, but solely the character of the state (which was British). But cultural and state representations are not so easily separated. For instance, Bryson and McCartney's (1994: 50) study into symbols in Northern Irish society found that unionists see their Britishness in terms of 'citizenship in the sense of identification with the institutions of the state'. Commenting on the flags issue at the British–Irish Association in 2000, Trimble quoted the diplomat Sir David Goodall: 'The essential element of their identity is precisely the Unionist sense of living on a territory which is part and parcel of the United Kingdom and not the Republic. Talk of respect for unionist identity must include respect for the territorial element and not just its cultural and social carapace' (Trimble, 2001a: 135). Unionist identity and the Union are regarded as co-dependent – a foundational principle of unionism no less espoused by new unionists and Trimble's UUP than any of their predecessors; thus, 'recognition of Britishness in Northern Ireland necessarily requires recognition of the Britishness of Northern Ireland' (McCall, 2006: 313). But if unionists' Britishness demanded to be expressed as the state representation of Northern Ireland, nationalists argued that this subordinated their Irish identity that was supposedly to be on an equal footing with unionists' after the Agreement.

The overlap between Protestant community culture and state culture continued to be evident throughout the UUP's response to Patten as the many 'flaws' were outlined. The party's criticisms rested primarily on the basis that the Commission had not fulfilled its own terms of reference outlined in the Agreement. Many aspects of the report, said the UUP, militated against the document appealing to the Protestant/unionist community and so the Commission had neglected its duty of 'winning widespread community support' (Agreement, 1998: 23). Among those problematic aspects were the recommendation to end the flying of the Union flag from police buildings, 'bias against Protestants' in the recruitment of officers and the lack of recognition of the sacrifice made by police officers. There was a mix of grievances that concerned both the unionist community and the state. Thus the UUP suggested that any reforms that negatively impacted on the unionist community were affronts to the legitimacy of the state, and any reforms that could be interpreted as affronts to the legitimacy of the state were an attack on the unionist community.

In fact, parity of esteem according to the UUP meant the precise opposite to the nationalist understanding. It meant that nationalists, having accepted the constitutional status in the Agreement, should permit the proper expressions of British sovereignty. The party did not believe that this was a partisan interpretation of the principles of the Agreement because the constitutional status was secured for Britain and so this entailed a certain degree of privilege for unionist culture. On the contrary, nationalist opposition to the unionist approach was a breach of the principles of the Agreement: 'They have adopted a tactical position on that [flags and policing]', said Trimble of nationalists. 'Hitherto we have acted in good faith. Perhaps now we should also adopt a tactical approach to the Agreement' (Trimble, 2001a: 142). The strength of feeling within unionism was such that David Burnside, later elected as UUP MP, won support at the March 2000 Annual General Meeting of the UUP for a motion linking policing with the issue of UUP participation in government. To the disquiet of Trimble, the motion pledged the party not to return to the Executive until it had won concessions on the RUC (MacDonald, 2000: 336; Godson, 2004: 598). Eventually, in the package agreed with the British Government at the end of May to allow a return to Stormont, the UUP was relatively successful on both the flags and policing issues. The Union flag was allowed to be flown over government buildings on appointed days of royal significance, with the Secretary of State reserving the right to intervene should disputes between the parties arise. (The UUP accepted the 'designated days' policy, yet was to oppose it over ten years later during the City Hall flag controversy when it vehemently argued for the flag to remain flying every day – see Chapter 6.) The new cross-party Policing Board would be tasked with designing a new police badge that would satisfy all sides, which it succeeded in doing with unexpected ease. The name of the RUC would live on as part of the legal designation of the force – 'PSNI [Police Service of Northern Ireland] (incorporating the RUC)' – although simply 'PSNI' would be used for operational purposes (Godson, 2004: 613–15). Godson's account of the negotiations suggests that Adams, mindful of Trimble's predicament, acquiesced on the question of the police name. Mandelson was also instrumental to the UUP, being 'determined that Unionists had to feel "parity of esteem" if they were to move in a "crab-like way" to inclusivity' (pp. 606–7).

The effect of the challenges to the legitimacy of British symbols was to harden the unionist perception of a general assault on the Protestant community as a result of the 'equality agenda'. Ulster Unionists were generally lukewarm about the peace process's emphasis on equality. It was not a focus of the party during the talks: 'For the Ulster Unionist Party, equality was either an issue that it considered it could not oppose, or did not consider sufficiently important to make a priority' (McCrudden, 2001: 87). Although not necessarily disadvantageous to unionists, the discourse of equality was more often than not looked upon warily, not least because Sinn Féin was its primary generator. Trimble recognised that equality would be an important post-Agreement battleground; equality measures would need to be tempered, but at least his party would be in a good position to exercise influence in this regard because it would be present at the heart of the new political structures (Trimble, 2001a: 9). The equality provisions were in the Agreement largely at the behest of nationalists and republicans and, implicit in their very inclusion in the deal, was the indictment that unionists were responsible for Catholic deprivation. The equality section was full of phrases such as 'human rights', 'anti-discrimination', 'parity of esteem', 'civil rights', 'social inclusion', 'tolerance', 'diversity', 'partnership' and 'mutual respect'. Coupled with the prospect of sharing power with nationalists, these phrases were alien and even threatening to a relatively conservative unionist community that itself felt disadvantaged as a result of Direct Rule. To many unionists, pro- and anti-Agreement, the equality agenda was a denial of their belief that there was no conflict, only terrorism, and was even an amoral attempt to understand the 'causes of terrorism' (Tonge and Evans, 2002: 63; Millar, 2008: 198).

Six months before the Agreement, the UUP's Peter Weir (later to defect to the DUP) expressed a widely held unionist feeling:

> Some nationalists have pursued what they call an equality agenda which is in reality a cover for their demand that every symbol of Britishness is removed from Northern Ireland. This party believes in a true equality agenda where every citizen has the same rights, responsibilities and privileges and where everyone is equal under the law.
>
> (Weir, 1998)

As time went on, there developed the feeling within unionism that implementation followed what was called the 'logic of the Agreement', which meant that the process was driven by the assumption that as the guilty party, unionists had to accept any nationalist-slanted interpretation that was put on the accord. Trimble saw the unacceptability of the Patten report to unionists as a prime example of this lack of mutuality (Trimble, 2001a: 133). Another instance was the make-up of the Human Rights Commission that was condemned as inadequately reflecting the community balance (UUP, 1999a). Other developments, such as the fifty–fifty recruitment system for the police designed to increase Catholic membership and the challenges to the overt signs of Northern Ireland's Britishness were all seen by unionists as part of an affirmative action programme based on the false premise of Protestant advantage. Prisoner releases and high-profile enquiries into killings of nationalists such as those into Bloody Sunday and the Finucane murder seemed to disregard the rights of Protestant victims (Trimble, 2001a: 136). Unionists worried that they were to become the new residents of the Northern Irish 'cold house' that Catholics were in the process of vacating. This sense of unionist loss proved to be remarkably resilient, despite the eventual ascendency of the DUP, and was much articulated and much discussed during the flag protests of 2012–13. By then, 'equality agenda' had fallen out of vogue; the preferred phrase of unionists was 'culture war'.

Thus, despite the compromise at the heart of the Agreement – unionist gain on sovereignty, nationalist gain on the reform of Northern Ireland – there was a crucial difference in nature between each side's achievements in the Agreement that encouraged a unionist perception of imbalance and inequity in implementation. Not only did many unionists' regard the acknowledgement of the constitutional status quo as a fairly modest gain, given that it was what they believed was theirs by right, but they also found themselves having to, time and again, defend that modest gain from nationalist and republican attempts to undermine it through the implementation of equality reforms. The feeling among Protestants that nationalists benefited from the Agreement more than unionists rose from 50 per cent in 1998 to 67 per cent in 2002, while the belief that unionists and nationalists benefited equally dropped from 41 per cent in 1998 to 19 per cent in 2002 (Mac Ginty, 2004: 89). As Patterson and Kaufmann (2007: 255) put it: 'For many Unionists the price extracted for acceptance of an indubitable reality – that a united Ireland would not occur because the IRA had failed to coerce them and no conceivable Irish government would have the capacity or desire to – was an inordinately high one.' The effect of the succession of losses suffered by unionists in the name of equality was to feed the sense of fear and fatalism within the unionist community, and cause Trimble's defining political judgement – that the Agreement would permanently settle the conflict and halt the advances of Irish nationalism – to appear increasingly mistaken.

After Trimble

David Trimble resigned as party leader on 7 May 2005. The day before, he and four other UUP MPs had lost their seats in the Westminster election. In an interview in August 2013, Trimble stated that he regretted not resigning in 2003 when he lost his Assembly seat as this may have averted the electoral disaster of 2005, though he noted that there was a lack of obvious candidates in 2003 (Sweeney, 2013). Given subsequent party decline and uninspiring leadership, and the clear downward trajectory of the UUP, it is doubtful that an earlier resignation would have made a substantive difference. Statements from political leaders in response to Trimble's resignation demonstrated his divisiveness. Pro-Agreement unionists recognised Trimble's contribution to peace, while anti-Agreement unionists said he was out of touch and responsible for the UUP's failures. Blair praised him, saying that without the UUP leader there would have been no Agreement. Durkan also recognised Trimble's centrality at that time, but said that Trimble had failed to go for 'wholehearted implementation' (BBC, 2005a).

This accusation was a common one. Despite Trimble's support for the Agreement, at times expressed in stirring and visionary terms, he was often charged with displaying a lukewarm commitment to the deal and failing to sell it to his party and community. Brian Feeney (1998), a nationalist commentator, asked: 'Has he [Trimble] ever thought that there are so many don't knows in his party because he sounds as if he doesn't know either?' Some regarded Trimble as exemplifying a general absence of a spirit of compromise throughout unionism and the fact that, quite simply, 'unionists were never enthusiastic about the peace process' (interview with Roy Garland, commentator and former UUP member, 4 June 2011). Sinn Féin's Mitchel McLaughlin recognises Trimble's courage in going for the Agreement but adds, 'I also think his little unionist heart struggled with all his head was telling him had to be done' (interview with Mitchel McLaughlin MLA, 4 October 2012). Porter (2003: 222–32) argues that Trimble's 'anti-dialogical' attitude to implementation was out of step with the spirit and principles of the accord. Specifically, the UUP leadership's determination that all acceptable reforms under the Agreement be compatible with a principle of unadulterated British sovereignty (an approach Porter calls 'constitutional overkill') ignored nationalists' justified expectation that the demands of justice and equality, recognised in the Agreement, should guard against such prioritisation. In relation to decommissioning, Porter believes that while pro-Agreement unionists had good cause to require swift and full IRA decommissioning, Trimble's confrontational approach that preferred deadlines and demands to dialogue was counter-productive.

Yet others are more sympathetic. Dermot Nesbitt defends Trimble as follows:

> I know people say, 'Oh Trimble didn't sell it', but where did he not sell it? He put his reputation and leadership on the line. What more do you want, nationalism? A political leader who puts his reputation and leadership on the line. He may not have been the smiley touchey-feely person, but that's a different matter. That's to do with personality.
>
> (Interview with Dermot Nesbitt, 10 September 2012)

Certainly, Trimble's brusque personal style played a role in how he split opinion (see Kerr, 2006: 149), and he was not incapable of ill-judged comments such as the suggestion that republicans needed to be 'house-trained' (Godson, 2004: 616) or that the Irish Republic was a 'pathetic, sectarian, mono-ethnic, monocultural state' (RTÉ, 2002). Godson (2004: 821), Trimble's biographer, asserts that, given the negative aspects of the Agreement, had Trimble lectured unionists on the merits and necessity of the deal as many nationalists and liberal unionists wanted him to, he would have failed to convince. Gentle persuasion and acknowledgement of the Agreement's ambivalent content was a much wiser course to take. Similarly, Dixon (2004) portrays any ambiguity in Trimble's public persona as a result of his need to cater to different audiences, a balancing act forced on him by the fact of his being a political leader nudging an anxious and diverse constituency into new political relationships. Undoubtedly, this must be to the fore in any assessment of Trimble: the drastic constraints placed on him by the threat from anti-Agreement unionism within his party and outside it. Here, it is worth recalling Booth and Wheeler's (2008) comment, mentioned in Chapter 1, that it is unwise to pigeonhole individuals as holding one or other of the logics of insecurity because people's statements/thinking may exhibit one or other of the logics at different times. As has been noted, Trimble's core project of pursuing accommodation with nationalism represented, in the main, the mitigator logic, yet his political situation, plus also perhaps his personal discomfort with the process, caused his policies and statement to oscillate between fatalism and transcendence. In any case, if the greatest vindication is imitation, Trimble's central contribution of co-founding new and consensus-based political structures with nationalism was vindicated by the DUP's acceptance in 2007 of much the same arrangements agreed by the UUP in 1998.

When the DUP overtook the UUP in the 2003 Assembly election, the UUP's relevance to, and influence on, the Agreement's implementation plummeted. The following years saw an ongoing crisis of purpose within the party, manifested in anger at being sidelined in negotiations and in government, major debates concerning party leadership and direction, an ill-fated electoral enterprise with the Conservative Party and high-profile defections. A few months before the 2005 election, the Orange Order voted to end its formal link with the UUP. The Order had occupied a place in the party's structures since the UUP's foundation, providing around a seventh of voting delegates to the party's ruling council. In theory, the split with Orangeism would have the effect of secularising and modernising the party, potentially making the UUP more attractive to liberal unionists, disengaged Protestants and pro-Union Catholics. In actuality, it simply reflected the wider shift of Protestant opinion from the UUP to the DUP, and the Orange Order's preference for the latter party as the most reliable defender of Protestant-unionist interests (McAuley *et al.*, 2011). The DUP's combination of combative unionist advocacy and pragmatism on power-sharing left little political space for another unionist party, and with the Alliance Party encroaching on its liberal flank, the UUP struggled to define itself. All the while, its internal debates, on which the fate of politics in Northern Ireland had so recently depended and which had held such forensic fascination for political observers, were now a subplot to the main drama of the DUP–Sinn Féin courtship.

As power-sharing moved closer and eventually returned after the St Andrews Agreement, the UUP was keen to point out its déjà vu. Paraphrasing Séamus Mallon's famous quip that the 1998 Agreement was 'Sunningdale for slow learners', Trimble's successor, Sir Reg Empey, called St Andrews 'the Belfast Agreement for slow learners' (BBC, 2006b) and lambasted the DUP for pretending that it was not going down essentially the same road that the UUP had travelled in 1998. He told the UUP conference in October 2007:

> The efforts of the Ulster Unionist Party – along with those of other parties, governments and individuals – have been airbrushed out of the shiny new history prepared by the DUP. Ladies and gentlemen, I am sick to the back teeth of the DUP's orgy of self-praise and self-promotion. … Boasting about a 'fair deal' or a 'better deal' doesn't take the same degree of political skill as being able to say that you delivered the deal in the first place!

It was the UUP, said Empey, that created the Assembly and forced republicans to give up their armed campaign, risks from which the DUP was now benefiting. However, Empey admitted that the UUP's divisions had helped the DUP into its ascendant position: 'Our internal war has been a gift to them' (Empey, 2007a). Empey's tenure, which lasted until 2010, saw some notable attempts to reassert the party. With the spotlight off the UUP, Empey set about pushing though further reforms of the party's structures, rules and procedures (Empey, 2007b). In 2006, he caused controversy by attempting to form a grouping within the (suspended) Assembly combining the UUP with the sole Progressive Unionist Party (PUP) member, David Ervine. The PUP, along with the Ulster Democratic Party, had played an important role at the time of the Agreement, their support for the deal providing crucial political cover for Trimble in the face of DUP opposition. However, since then, the party had struggled electorally and the Ulster Volunteer Force (UVF), to which the PUP was loosely linked, had been mired in all manner of illegality (for an analysis of the PUP, see Edwards, 2010). The 'Ulster Unionist Party Assembly Group' was designed to secure entitlement to another seat in the Executive for unionists at the expense of Sinn Féin should d'Hondt be run in the future. However, the alliance came in the wake of a damning report by the Independent Monitoring Commission on the UVF and, given the UUP's years of seeking IRA disarmament, the mooted link-up was met with surprise and criticism, most notably by the UUP's MP, Lady Sylvia Hermon. In the event, the Assembly Group was deemed to contravene the rules by the Assembly Speaker: it did not constitute a political party as was officially understood (BBC, 2006c). Another high-profile attempt to exert itself came in 2010 when the UUP said that it would vote against the devolution of policing and justice powers unless the

Executive reached agreement on the long-running controversy over academic selection. 'If we can't deal with an issue that is currently devolved such as education', said Empey, 'then why is there any reason to think we are fit to take on something as controversial as policing and justice' (quoted in McDonald, 2010). The precondition was not met and the party voted against devolution, though its support was not needed.

Lady Hermon also proved to be out of sync with an even greater gamble by the Empey leadership, the alliance with the Conservative Party that contested the 2009 European and 2010 Westminster polls. During the negotiations that produced the alliance, the formation of a new party had been discussed, reportedly to be named the Northern Ireland Conservative and Unionist Party (NICUP) with David Cameron as leader, but the UUP had been unwilling to put itself out of existence (Walker, 2009). Instead, an electoral agreement was reached in which candidates, agreed by both parties, would stand under the label 'Ulster Conservatives and Unionists – New Force' (UCUNF). Empey trumpeted the electoral pact as good for the Union and, in that favourite theme of Ulster Unionists, said that it would bring them closer to the political heart of the United Kingdom: the alliance would 'allow us to become more fully and demonstrably an equal partner within the UK family … we believe that a pan-UK unionist vehicle is the best way of promoting the values of the union' (quoted in BBC, 2009). However, dissenters emerged from both the UUP and Northern Ireland Conservatives. One of the latter, Jeffrey Peel, claimed that the Conservative Party was being used by the UUP to save it from financial and electoral problems, that conservative values were being compromised by the link and that there was a failure to advance non-sectarian politics in the campaign (Peel, 2010). Sylvia Hermon, who had tended to vote with Labour in the House of Commons, left the party in protest at the link-up, a move that left the new alliance to fight the election with no incumbents.

UCUNF did not win any seats and the UUP's vote share fell from 17.7 per cent in 2005 to 15.2 per cent in 2010. The project was damaged by the unpopularity in Northern Ireland of David Cameron's pledges of spending cuts in the (likely) event that he became prime minister. Controversial too was the decision to support an agreed unionist candidate in Fermanagh–South Tyrone, regarded by some as a sectarian move out of kilter with the liberal unionism supposedly represented by UCUNF; that candidate lost to Sinn Féin by just four votes. Despite not winning seats, the party's vote did not collapse and it can be argued – as UNCUNF candidate Trevor Ringland does – that in the light of the re-alignment within unionism and relatively stable government, it was exactly the kind of experiment that was needed to progress Northern Ireland away from flag-waving politics. Ringland recognises certain handicaps, such as a rushed launch and the name (a 'mouthful'), but states that he and most candidates believed that the party should have continued with UCUNF (interview with Trevor Ringland, 5 March 2014). Empey resigned and his successor, Tom Elliott, did not pursue the alliance.

Elliott, regarded as representing the traditional wing of the party, defeated liberal Basil McCrea in the leadership vote by two to one, although it emerged that a disproportionate number of party voters were from Elliott's home county of Fermanagh. In any event, Elliott appeared unlikely to rejuvenate the party and/or differentiate it from its larger unionist rival. He had stated that he would not attend Gaelic Athletic Association or gay pride events, and, during a speech, had referred to republican hecklers as 'the scum of Sinn Féin'. Mixing medical metaphors, Maurice Hayes wrote in the *Irish Independent* that the choice of Elliott to lead the party was unionism 'retreating into the womb', it had 'settled for a life-support machine' and the party was in 'a near vegetative state'. By rejecting the progressive politics represented by McCrea, the party, said Hayes, showed that it did not understand its predicament: 'The main battle for Ulster Unionists is not, oddly enough, against the DUP but against voter apathy and it will be fought not in the bible-belt but in the leafy suburbs, not in the Orange halls, but in the garden centres' (Hayes, 2010). In short, there were no votes to be gained by looking more like the DUP. The UUP should rather cultivate a progressive, aspirational and inclusive brand of unionism that would have the capacity to entice the large chunk of the population that was pro-Union but did not vote and would never vote for Paisley's party. While this advice made sense, the problem was that much of the UUP was ideologically indistinguishable from the DUP, with little appetite to take the UUP in the kind of direction Hayes was suggesting. Indeed, some believed that the solution to the UUP's lack of political space was to not just imitate the DUP but co-operate and perhaps even merge with the party, and it was the perception that the UUP was 'sleepwalking towards unionist unity' that led to the high-profile defections of Basil McCrea and John McCallister in 2013.

'Unionist unity' was a notion that raised its head periodically since unionism splintered in the early 1970s. UUP MLA David McNarry revealed to the media in January 2012 that exploratory talks had been taking place at the highest level between the two parties for some time, an exposure that led to him being expelled from the party (Purdy, 2012). Stimulants for these talks included the weakness of the UUP, the spectre of Martin McGuinness becoming First Minister if Sinn Féin became the largest party and the DUP's enthusiasm for a single party. In the widely reported 'sleepwalking' speech of October 2012 that foreshadowed the exit from the party of McCrea and McCallister, the latter explained why he believed unionist unity was anathema. First, he saw it as sectarian and regressive; agreed unionist candidates in finely balanced constituencies turned elections into straight tribal headcounts. Second, the DUP was an unfit partner: 'the DUP is a very cold house for civic unionism – for the values of pluralism and liberalism.' Third, unionist unity would lead to stagnant politics at Stormont, precluding opposition and change. Voters would have no choice, unionist unity would stimulate nationalist unity and government would become a permanent alliance of one Orange and one Green bloc. Moving beyond communal designations, d'Hondt and mandatory coalition – measures that were only intended to be temporary means of building confidence – would be impossible. Fourth, unionist unity would not appeal to the new generation of voters with few memories of pre-Agreement Northern Ireland and which was 'not defined by past-divisions' (McCallister, 2012).

This speech turned out to be a proto-manifesto for the party that McCrea and McCallister went on to launch in June 2013, NI21. The ostensible final straw for the pair was the decision by the UUP, now under the leadership of Mike Nesbitt, a well-known former journalist, to agree a candidate with the DUP and Traditional Unionist Voice for the Mid-Ulster Westminster by-election in March 2013. The new party was an interesting experiment in decoupling support for the Union from Protestant tribal baggage. NI21's first chairperson, Tina McKenzie, was the daughter of a convicted IRA member, while the party even used the Irish language in some of its publicity. It supported the designated days policy for the Union flag and took the eye-catching position of opposing the ongoing prosecution of 'Troubles'-related crimes. It was, however, vague on policy and, to a large extent, reinventing the Alliance Party wheel. Here, the main contrast, said NI21, was the fact that Alliance was in the Executive and therefore supporting the moribund system of mandatory coalition that NI21 opposed (McCrea and McCallister, 2013).

The new party was also closely identified with the personalities of McCrea and McCallister, meaning that when that relationship broke down publicly in the week of the party's first electoral test in May 2014, the party's survival was left in doubt. The election was not disastrous; the party received 11,495 votes, though only succeeded in electing one councillor, while McKenzie, the party's European election candidate, received 1.7 per cent of the vote, the same proportion as the Green Party. Nevertheless, after that election and the exposure of the internal rifts, the NI21 brand appeared tarnished, a serious blow given that a core purpose of the party had been to create a fresh and attractive political vehicle for twenty-first-century, post-conflict politics that could engage hitherto lethargic and cynical sectors of the electorate. Undoubtedly, it did so for some people, but the difficulties of achieving further growth were clear.

Conclusion

As Chapter 1 emphasised, fatalist thinking was not the preserve of anti-Agreement forces, neither within unionism nor nationalism, but in fact crossed the pro- and anti-Agreement lines within both ethnic blocs. Perhaps this was most evident in the UUP, which, of all the officially pro-Agreement parties, showed the most equivocal commitment to the accord. The party split on the Agreement, the splits constrained the pro-Good Friday leadership, and the leadership was itself unenthusiastic about much of what the Agreement required of unionism. Even some in the party who supported the Agreement because it secured the principle of consent were fearful of the impact on unionism's ability to retain its cultural vitality and political position. Hence, despite the party's mitigator approach in accepting the Agreement – abandoning the fatalism of unionism's unwillingness to engage with opponents and seeking to accommodate nationalism in order to create a degree of mutual security – the party adopted positions, particularly on decommissioning and symbols, that had the effect of stoking nationalist fears that unionists were in fact un-reconciled to the principle of creating a society characterised by partnership and justice, and which contributed to the post-Agreement security dilemma. Some unionist fears were understandable, given the provocative activities and statements of the IRA, and the emotive peace process issues that had to be confronted. Yet much UUP rhetoric indicated a resilient zero-sum fatalism that desired an exclusively unionist security, railed against the perceived loss of unionist status, and scarcely concealed a hankering for the political and cultural privilege of the past. While Trimble did display a degree of 'security dilemma sensibility' (Booth and Wheeler, 2008: 7) in his approach to implementation, in line with his courageous decision to accept the Agreement, voters decided not to allow him the opportunity to see through what he started.

Blame can be attributed to various actors for the UUP's diminished status: Tony Blair (for breaking pledges on decommissioning and prisoners), Trimble himself (for his approach to implementation), the opposing factions within the UUP (for damaging the party's image and undermining the leadership), and the IRA (for refusing to decommission). But the most significant factor was the DUP's evolution from oppositional outsider to credible and modern vote-winner, willing to make deals but vociferous in defence of identity. This made, and continues to make, a comeback for the UUP based on a clearly distinguished political vision extremely difficult. A de facto ideological unity exists between the two main unionist parties, a similarity that does not, on paper, favour the smaller party. That said, party loyalty, especially in the west of Northern Ireland, and aversion to the DUP will mean that the UUP survives as a viable, if reduced, electoral force. In the natural ebb and flow of democracy, dissatisfaction with the DUP in power could lead to UUP gains in the future, something that may have been behind the modest rise in vote share (0.9 per cent) enjoyed by the UUP in the local elections of 2014.

It is hard to disagree with Empey's charge that by excoriating the UUP for years before and after the Agreement, then deciding to enter government with 'Sinn Féin/IRA', the DUP was an extremely 'slow learner', learning a lesson that the UUP had long before. The DUP would challenge this by indicating the dramatically changed context in 2007 – the IRA had decommissioned and supported the police, moves for which the DUP claim credit. But, as Nesbitt counters, 'we were on a conveyor belt of change', i.e. republicanism was on an irreversible route away from violence that was evident to those willing to see it (interview with Dermot Nesbitt, 10 September 2012). Thus, either the DUP was unable to recognise this, or it did recognise this but opted to first exploit unionist fears and republican intransigence to destroy the UUP before taking power itself. Regardless, two things are certain: first, the damage done to the UUP; and second, the wide acceptance that power-sharing and cross-border co-operation now enjoy within unionism. The UUP's support for the Agreement enabled unionists to become psychologically accustomed to the idea of power-sharing and all-Ireland institutions, and appreciate the significance of securing the principle of consent. For those reasons, the UUP's decision in 1998 will be of enduring significance.

3
Social Democratic and Labour Party

Introduction

In October 2010, former Social Democratic and Labour Party (SDLP) leader John Hume was voted 'Ireland's Greatest' in a public poll conducted by the Irish state broadcaster, RTÉ, beating, among others, Michael Collins and Bono. Previous honours included the Gandhi Peace Prize, the Martin Luther King Award and, of course, the Nobel Peace Prize, which Hume won jointly with David Trimble in 1998. Such accolades highlight a sharp contrast with the fortunes of the party Hume led for twenty-two years; while Hume's place in history is certain, the SDLP has, like the Ulster Unionist Party (UUP), since and indeed before the 1998 Agreement, been in decline. An internal party report obtained by the BBC in 2013 echoed well-known perceptions: the SDLP was 'resting on its laurels', was bereft of prominent figures and, to the public, was largely indistinguishable in policy terms with its dominant rival, Sinn Féin (Walker, 2013a). With the end of the IRA's campaign of violence, Sinn Féin – in a process parallel to the Democratic Unionist Party's (DUP) acquired hegemony within unionism – effectively colonised moderate Northern nationalism at the expense of the SDLP. Yet, also in common with unionist realignment, Sinn Féin triumphed only by following the SDLP's political lead.

This chapter begins by exploring the SDLP's political thinking according to Hume's formulation of the party's aims: reform, reconciliation and reunification. It examines the great extent to which its vision was realised in the Agreement, and how this very fact threatened the post-Agreement vitality of the party. The SDLP's controversial decision not to exclude Sinn Féin from government during the decommissioning impasse is considered, as is how its interpretation of the Agreement manifested itself in its approach to the policing and flags issues. Finally the chapter analyses the political, organisational and financial dimensions of the SDLP's electoral contest with Sinn Féin.

Reform, reconciliation and reunification

The founding of the SDLP in 1970 signalled the political rejuvenation of the Northern Catholic community. After partition, the main vehicle of constitutional nationalism had been the Nationalist Party, the character and activities of which stemmed from the conflicting desires of Northern Catholics to express themselves politically, yet avoid giving legitimacy to the unionist state. It failed to organise properly, frequently abstained from the Stormont parliament and restricted its activities to areas where it could reliably command a majority. As a result, it was open to attack from all sides: 'Unionists accused them of being quasi-revolutionaries, moderate Catholics of not adequately seeking to redress their grievances, and militant republicans vilified them for not having the courage of their convictions to oppose partition by force' (McAllister, 1977: 14; see also Norton, 2014). Ideologically, the Nationalist Party focused on the evil of partition yet improvements in living standards and education led Catholics to see new possibilities for participation in the Northern Ireland state. By the 1960s the party appeared increasingly out of touch with its base, failing to articulate a positive vision and ineffectively opposing unionist rule in Stormont (Maginness, 2002: 33). The necessary injection of fresh thought was provided by a grouping formed in 1965, the National Democratic Party (NDP). Much of the NDP's agenda foreshadowed future SDLP policies and, in 1970, both the Nationalist Party and the NDP were superseded by the SDLP when it was established by a group of Stormont MPs who had been active in the civil rights campaign. The new groupings voiced Catholics' wish to participate fully in the social, political and economic life of Northern Ireland and thus gave de facto recognition to Northern Ireland; the ending of partition was demoted from an immediate demand to a long-term aspiration.

The SDLP's unwieldy name revealed its complex identity. It was united in its opposition to unionism but beyond that splits existed, especially between those who emphasised its nationalist goals and those who prioritised its socialist ethos. The Republican Labour MP at Stormont, Gerry Fitt – at whose behest the word 'labour' had been inserted in the party title – was chosen as the SDLP's first leader, but became increasingly isolated during the 1970s as he perceived in his colleagues an increasing eagerness to press a reunification agenda. He blamed the failure of Sunningdale on his party's impatience for a strong Irish dimension before unionists were ready: power-sharing should have been established first and cross-border matters pursued after a period of stability and trust-building (Ryder, 2006: 289). After Sunningdale, a distinct 'greening' of the party occurred under the influence of figures like John Hume and Séamus Mallon as a response to unionist intransigence on reaching a power-sharing accommodation, something that the SDLP believed had rendered previous, softer approaches ineffectual (Murray and Tonge, 2005: 58–66). From the late 1970s under the leadership of Hume, the SDLP endeavoured to circumvent unionism by influencing the British and Irish to co-operate on developing the role of the Irish Government in Northern matters. This approach bore fruit in the form of the 1983–4 New Ireland Forum and the Anglo-Irish Agreement of 1985. Rather than an end in itself, the party viewed the 1985 Agreement as a precursor to a Northern power-sharing settlement. To that end, Hume engaged in talks with Sinn Féin to explore areas of nationalist commonality and persuade republicans of the futility of violence. The 'Hume–Adams' dialogue is generally regarded as the starting point of the process that culminated in the 1998 Agreement. Hume's stature came to eclipse that of the SDLP; his freelance statesmanship is widely seen as having been pursued at the expense of developing the party (Murray, 1998; Kirby, 2013).

An instructive way of exploring the SDLP's ideology is by unpacking the following summation of the party's aims articulated by Hume:

> Our chosen strategy encompassed reform, reconciliation, and reunification along a path of steady progress, continually narrowing the gap between the reality and the dream, using the political means of dialogue, persuasion, negotiation, accommodation, compromise.
>
> (Hume, 1996: 28)

By first aiming for reform, Hume meant that the SDLP intended to preserve the core vision of the civil rights campaign to achieve equality of treatment for Catholics *within* Northern Ireland. The party was launched on the basis that a united Ireland was not the only solution to nationalist oppression and, in the early days, it was even over-optimistically hoped that the SDLP would attain cross-community support (Murray, 1998: 9). Calls for a Bill of Rights, a Fair Practices Act that would monitor public expenditure and the incorporation of the European Convention on Human Rights (ECHR) into Northern Irish law were prominent in early SDLP proposals and became fixtures in the party's programme (SDLP, 1971, 1972). Equal rights would lead to dialogue instead of repression, respect for diversity instead of cultural alienation. Effectively protecting the civil rights of all would also allay Protestant fears of being coerced into an all-Ireland republic. Another aspect of the SDLP's rights discourse was the demand for 'parity of esteem for [nationalists'] sense of identity and allegiance, expressed in meaningful institutional and other interaction with the rest of the Irish nation' (SDLP, 1997). This was the cherished 'Irish dimension' that was a core demand throughout the SDLP's history.

With the civil and human rights of all parties secure, work could then begin on the second element of Hume's vision, the healing of the broken relationships at the heart of the conflict. The SDLP's concern for reconciliation arose from its oft-repeated conviction that the most important division in Ireland was of its people, not its territory (Hume, 1996). Prioritising people and relationships in the design of political arrangements was, said the SDLP, more appropriate in an era of globalisation, migration and European integration than traditional concepts of indivisible territorial sovereignty. Since the Irish border was as much a reflection of division between people than its cause, the reconciliation of those people had to precede attempts at reunification. The problematic relationships, according to the SDLP analysis, were those between the communities in the North, the two parts of the island of Ireland and the states of the United Kingdom and Republic of Ireland. The SDLP argued that these relationships – 'the framework of the problem' – should become the 'framework of the solution' by each being a component of any peace strategy (Hume, 1996: 29). Thus, the party was keenly aware of the mutual grievance, mistrust and fear that fuelled the cycle of conflict, and the mutual responsibilities for halting that cycle.

The third and final party aim was reunification. The quotation from Hume suggests that reform, reconciliation and reunification were not goals to be pursued simultaneously but rather stages in a process; reform and reconciliation – brought about through an approach of dialogue and accommodation – were means to the end of reunification. However, the party rarely talked about pursuing a united Ireland but rather an 'agreed Ireland', a state of affairs that has in the past defied easy definition. The 'agreed Ireland' concept originated in the mid-1970s, when the SDLP called on the British to move from a position of guaranteeing the Union (and, it was thought, encouraging unionist obstinacy) towards working for reconciliation and agreement on political structures among the traditions in Ireland (McLoughlin, 2010: 85). It remained the party's primary stated goal. According to the 1998 manifesto, an 'agreed Ireland' was 'an Ireland in which the consent of Nationalists and Unionists would be secured for partnership within agreed political institutions based on the highest standards of human rights' (SDLP, 1998a: 1). Given the outcome of the referenda, it was reasonable to assume that the longed-for 'agreed Ireland' was created through the Agreement (McLoughlin, 2010: 183). Indeed, survey research carried out between 1999 and 2002 showed that an overwhelming majority of SDLP members believed that the provisions of the Agreement represented the optimum constitutional solution for Northern Ireland, with a much smaller number opting for a united Ireland (Tonge, 2005: 110). Nevertheless, talk of seeking an agreed Ireland remained. Elsewhere in the 1998 manifesto the SDLP suggested that the new Agreement institutions laid the *foundation* for a new and agreed Ireland (SDLP, 1998a: 4) while John Hume, stepping down as SDLP leader, exhorted the party as it 'continues' to work towards an agreed Ireland (Hume, 2001). Conceivably, these statements were referring to the full implementation of the Agreement, rather than any constitutional change beyond the Agreement. However, in a newspaper article, leading party figure Seán Farren (2002a) expanded the meaning of 'agreed Ireland' by writing that its Irish translation was, in fact, the same as that of 'united Ireland', *Éire aontaithe*:

> *Éire aontaithe* is the SDLP's philosophy and has been from the party's foundation. It was reflected in the party's constitution, drawn up in 1970, which emphasised that Irish unity must be based on the principle of consent. In other words, Irish unity could only be achieved with the consent of the majority of the people living in Northern Ireland.

Here, an agreed Ireland is a united Ireland based on consent – which conflicts directly with the definition given in the 1998 manifesto, that an 'agreed Ireland' merely involved agreed political institutions. Recent statements, however, have cleared up any confusion by explicitly distinguishing 'agreed' and 'united': 'As a nationalist party the SDLP's goal has been not only to secure an Agreed Ireland but to achieve a United Ireland. We delivered on the former with the Good Friday Agreement, and we will deliver on the latter with our strategy for Uniting People' (SDLP, 2011; see also Durkan, 2009).

For their part, unionists certainly thought an agreed Ireland meant a united one; 'agreed Ireland', along with other terms used liberally by Hume such as 'parity of esteem', 'mutuality', 'healing process' and 'post-nationalism', were pejoratively dubbed 'Hume-speak', an impenetrable discourse designed to cloak traditional nationalist intentions to abolish the border. Unionists assumed (correctly) that, whatever the SDLP meant by an agreed Ireland, the party intended it to be a departure from unionists' ideal of the Britishness of Northern Ireland continuing in both ethos and sovereignty (see Cunningham, 1997). The SDLP made clear, in spite of its upholding of the principle of consent, that it regarded the island of Ireland as the legitimate unit of self-determination and that there was only one people on the island of Ireland (in contrast to unionists' conviction that they were a separate people). On this, Hume shared the traditional republican analysis: 'like Theobald Wolfe Tone, the father of Irish republicanism, our vision has been "to substitute for the denomination of Catholic, Protestant and Dissenter the common name of Irishman"' (Hume, 1996: 28). In this way, Hume's thinking had similar limitations to new unionism. Just as new unionists were willing to accord Irish identity the right to cultural expression but not political expression (see Chapter 2), so too did Hume acknowledge unionism as a tradition within the Irish nation but not a separate people with national rights. Hume called on unionists to 'share a piece of earth', 'to pursue and perceive their true interests' and join with the South (Hume, 1996: 57–9).

An agreed Ireland, then, was deliberately ambiguous. It was designed to persuade unionists that they would not be forced into institutional arrangements against their will, yet it reassured nationalists that an internal settlement was not acceptable and it did not rule out attaining a united Ireland as traditionally conceived. Critically, it was this ambiguity that cleared the way for the Agreement: 'Whatever the criticisms of his political discourse – of the ambiguity within it, and the intentions behind it – Hume-speak did offer a flexibility of thought, and thereby helped to create an ideological space within which a political compromise over Northern Ireland could be devised'(McLoughlin, 2010: 228). The downplaying of traditional sovereignty (something unionists railed against in the post-Agreement years), the focus on relationships between the two traditions and mutual consent, all of which were fundamental in Hume's thinking, formed the basis of the Agreement that sought to mitigate, and perhaps allow the transcendence of, the parties' insecurities by balancing the aspirations of unionism and nationalism and permitting exclusive victory for neither.

The Agreement: 'the outstanding achievement of the SDLP'

In his history of the SDLP, Farren (2010: 345) writes of the Agreement that 'ratification [by the SDLP] was a mere formality, since the agreement met all of the necessary criteria specified by the party'. This is an understatement; few, from any political perspective, would deny that the Good Friday accord was very much an SDLP document – in its origins, language, provisions and intent. In the party's own view, the accord was the 'outstanding achievement of the SDLP' (Maginness, 2002: 35) and in its analysis of the document, the SDLP made much of its influence on the various political initiatives that had preceded the Good Friday talks. The Anglo-Irish Agreement was, according to the party, the result of its efforts to persuade the Governments of Britain and Ireland that they had a responsibility to closely co-operate in searching for a resolution to the conflict (SDLP, 1998b; Farren, 2000a: 51). The structure of the 1991–2 Brooke/Mayhew talks was based on the SDLP's three-relationship analysis (Farren, 2000a: 52). SDLP thinking was further validated in the Downing Street Declaration that reiterated the need for reconciliation and new and agreed political arrangements in Ireland and between Britain and Ireland. The party credited its leader with a crucial role in bringing about the ceasefires, while the 1995 Framework Document contained many SDLP proposals on new institutions within Northern Ireland and between North and South (SDLP, 1998b). In sum, the party had good reason to believe that the Good Friday Agreement was a vindication of its ideology and lobbying.

Each element of the SDLP's programme discussed above – reform, reconciliation and reunification – was dealt with to an extent in the Agreement. The party's long-standing concern with the protection of rights was comprehensively addressed by the establishment of a Human Rights Commission and an Equality Commission, the incorporation of the ECHR into Northern Ireland law and the allowance for the drafting of a Bill of Rights for Northern Ireland in the future. The SDLP's assessment of the conflict as consisting of three broken relationships provided the structure of the Good Friday negotiations. The Assembly, the North–South Ministerial Council (NSMC) and the British–Irish Council would be the institutional bandages for the relationships between unionism and nationalism, North and South and Britain and Ireland. Perhaps the most significant healing event for the SDLP was the simultaneous referenda held in May 1998: the party described the polls as 'the most fundamental embodiment of parity of esteem between our traditions' (SDLP, 1998b: 8). Police and justice reform were also measures the SDLP had sought and deemed necessary for the normalisation of community relationships within Northern Ireland.

The perennial nationalist demand that an 'Irish dimension' form part of any settlement was met in the Agreement by the creation of North–South structures through which ministers from the two jurisdictions could work together on matters of mutual concern. This was indeed a recognition of Northern Nationalists' Irish identity, as were the provisions regarding the protection of human and cultural rights and the promotion of the Irish language. As for the SDLP's ultimate goal of a united Ireland, the party was publicly ambiguous about whether the Agreement was a major step in that direction or a final settlement. A survey of party members in 1999 showed that almost 70 per cent believed that the Agreement was a step towards a united Ireland; however, almost 80 per cent agreed that power-sharing with cross-border bodies was the best solution for Northern Ireland (Tonge and Evans, 2002: 62). These figures express some of the ambiguity of purpose also contained in the slippery 'agreed Ireland' idea. While accepting the principle of consent and British sovereignty, nationalists believed that through the Agreement's implementation, the nationalist people and Irish cultural values and norms would be empowered with the result that formal sovereignty may come to matter relatively little (Todd, 1999: 64). In fact, the SDLP, like pro-Agreement republicans, viewed the principle of consent in opposite terms to pro-Agreement unionists. Unionists believed the principle eliminated the possibility of a united Ireland but the SDLP saw it opening up that very possibility since it was a declaration by Britain that it would not stand in the way of unification should the people so desire it (Farren, 2000a: 51).

A key theme in the party's advocacy of the Agreement was the economic boons of restored relationships; improved relationships would lead to greater economic co-operation and prosperity. 'In nations and in regions where relationships are characterised by co-operation, co-ordination and differentiation, success breeds success and everyone thrives. ... We seek for a larger cake rather than a larger slice' (SDLP, 1999a: 5). The conflict had meant economic stagnation in the North, the deterrence of inward investment and the mass emigration of young people. Partnership and equality would allow the talents of both communities to flourish and contribute to a better future for all, creating a society 'deeply imbued with a spirit of equality, social justice and fairness' (p. 1). The three-stranded provisions of the Agreement would institutionalise partnership so that 'barriers can be broken down and a major contribution made to binding up the wounds caused by division and violence' (Farren, 2002b). The NSMC and the implementation bodies would be the main engines for economic progress, involving as they would representatives of both communities in the North and from North and South. Through these new structures, economic policies could be harmonised and the unnatural separate development of the two parts of the island could be arrested (Farren, 2000b).

With the Agreement being, to a great extent, an SDLP wish-list, it had the potential of being a double-edged sword for the party. Now that its vision was, on paper at least, realised, was there a role left for the SDLP in the new dispensation? The party's firm answer was yes, and that role would be what deputy leader Séamus Mallon described as 'custodians of the Agreement' (Mallon, 1998). But the SDLP had to be the custodian in two respects. First, the SDLP had to protect the Agreement from those who may have wished to see it fail. It would do so by emphasising the universalist principles of the Agreement – partnership, dialogue, equality, pluralism – and rebuking the seeking of sectarian advantage. With the policies of the party and the Agreement so intimately linked, the SDLP wished to ensure that the deal would endure and not be sunk by rejectionists on either side or indeed wary supporters pursuing partisan approaches to implementation. The UUP and Sinn Féin were holding notably differing interpretations of how the accord should be implemented and so the SDLP envisaged a role for itself as champion of the Agreement, insisting on full and mutual implementation, encouraging continuing dialogue and warning against renegotiation. 'The approach that gave the Agreement is the approach that will save the Agreement' was the party's conviction (Durkan, 2002). The 'spirit' of the Agreement, i.e. trust, good faith and mutuality, would be emphasised as much as the 'letter'.

In the run-up to the Assembly elections that followed the referenda, the SDLP said that it sought to attain a strong presence in the new institutions 'to make the Agreement work, to ensure its provisions' (SDLP, 1998a: 1). The power of the decommissioning issue to halt implementation, virtually from the outset, made clear to the SDLP the danger of the process revolving a Sinn Féin–UUP axis. Indicating his awareness that the security dilemma had survived the Agreement, Mallon declared that these parties had 'made the vindication of unionism and republicanism their priority, above and beyond their greater responsibility to all of our people' and that his party 'will not allow it [the Agreement] to be misrepresented, to be set aside, or to be used as a party political football' (Mallon, 1998). Indeed, advocating on behalf of the Agreement dominated the SDLP's post-Agreement discourse, as the party sought to remind the public and the parties of the benefits of the Agreement and 'normal' politics, the dangers of failed implementation, the responsibilities of both sides regarding implementation and the lack of a viable alternative to the Agreement and the folly of renegotiation.

Second, the SDLP had to ensure that it would be the custodian of the Agreement in terms of its own, Catholic, community, and not its electoral rival, Sinn Féin. The SDLP would do so by demonstrating the potential of the Agreement to empower the nationalist community. This would involve strong advocacy on issues of interest to that community: equality, rights, inclusive government, police reform and flags and emblems. Strategies regarding these issues would be guided by the Agreement's principles of inclusion and parity of esteem. Yet after the Agreement was signed, the SDLP, with its lack of a clear and ongoing constitutional agenda, contrasted sharply with Sinn Féin, which supported the Agreement whilst remaining stoutly republican in aspiration. That contrast had already been apparent for many years. As Sinn Féin swapped the rhetoric of hardline republicanism for the softer tones of constitutional nationalism, the party increasingly appeared a more youthful and purposeful version of the SDLP, and this showed itself at the polls. Indeed, in the politics of implementation, one of the SDLP's pivotal weaknesses vis-à-vis Sinn Féin was its lack of a politically charged stockpile of weaponry.

The SDLP and decommissioning

Unfortunately, the SDLP's deep desire to overcome obstacles to the Agreement's operation was, for the most part, inversely proportional to its ability to do so. Farren (2006: 115) writes that during the Mitchell Review in autumn 1999 his party's role was 'essentially secondary' and it had 'no lever other than exhortation to offer'. This was to be a recurring theme – the Governments focusing on

Sinn Féin and the largest unionist party with the SDLP vainly seeking inclusion. Later, during attempts to restore devolution in the spring of 2000, the SDLP desired greater involvement in the talks, believing, according to Farren, that input from other pro-Agreement parties could have a positive influence. These calls for inclusion were rebuffed; the UUP and Sinn Féin enjoyed being the focus of attention while the Taoiseach claimed that wider talks would only increase the opportunity for parties to play the 'blame game' (Farren, 2006: 114). After the final suspension in October 2002, the British Government made clear that it preferred to concentrate on reaching agreement between republicans and unionists. When the decommissioning choreography of October 2003 collapsed, Jonathan Powell (2008: 234) recalls that 'Mark Durkan called Tony [Blair] and said, rather smugly, that he "didn't need to say 'I told you so'", having told us we would have nothing but trouble trying to cook up a deal with just Sinn Féin and the UUP and excluding the other parties'. Constructive as wider negotiations may have been, the SDLP's concern at its exclusion was linked by observers to a worry that continuing irrelevance to the process might speed the party's electoral downturn (Thornton, 2002b).

The SDLP's position on decommissioning was based on a belief that the 'letter' of the Agreement was of limited use in approaching the issue. As far as the SDLP could see, there was no 'letter' – the decommissioning section was imprecise. The SDLP certainly did not identify in the Agreement justification for regarding decommissioning as a prerequisite of devolution; Mallon angrily resigned as Deputy First Minister in July 1999 in protest at the UUP's insistence on the precondition. 'They are dishonouring the Agreement', he said of the unionists in his resignation speech. 'They are insulting its principles' (Mallon, 1999). The SDLP did, however, believe that decommissioning and devolution were interdependent. 'You can't have one without the other', wrote Bríd Rogers (2000). Decommissioning was not optional, left to the discretion of the paramilitaries as Sinn Féin claimed. There had been a long-standing expectation that it should happen, that it was a necessary part of the transition to a normalised society. Crucially, it was clearly the expectation of those who had voted 'yes' in the referenda that decommissioning should occur, and therefore the paramilitaries were ignoring the will of the people of Ireland. In October 1998, Mallon proposed a 'double guarantee': the institutions should be set up and if the IRA had not decommissioned by the May 2000 deadline, the SDLP would support Sinn Féin's exclusion; at the same time, if unionists prevaricated on progressing other elements of the Agreement, Sinn Féin could rely on SDLP support. The Governments, however, rejected this idea, preferring to concentrate on talks between the UUP and Sinn Féin (interview with Mark Durkan MP, 30 August 2012).

In spite of the SDLP's relative powerlessness, there were two ways in which it sought to exert influence to sustain the Agreement through the disarmament doldrums. The first was through the 'exhortation' mentioned by Farren above. In keeping with its relationship-focused ideology, this exhortation tended to take the form not of party-political demands or threats, but of calls to exhibit the relational principles that underpinned the Agreement. Take, for example, the following typical SDLP newspaper commentaries on the political situation, Farren writing in the summer of 1999 and Bríd Rogers writing weeks after the first suspension of the institutions in February 2000. For Farren, the Agreement was the only available framework that could allow the relationships at the heart of the conflict to 'develop in a spirit of mutual respect and acceptance' with the potential to break 'history's shackles'. It allowed diverse identities to be asserted in a 'context of equality and parity of esteem'. The parties had to work to create an appropriate 'atmosphere' for future progress. Each partner in the relationship could not just expect the other to concede to it. Responsibilities had to be mutual, a defeatist attitude had to be avoided and the mutual acknowledgement of the concessions each side had made would be 'an important trust building measure' (Farren, 1999).

Rogers explained that there were no simple answers to 'the complex problem arising from our deep divisions and mistrust'. The Agreement was not the solution but the trust and confidence that it had the potential to foster were, 'with each party playing its part along the way in enabling its opponents'. Working in partnership on common ground could break down the barriers between the two sides. The decommissioning issue represented a lack of trust and merely allocating blame was unhelpful. Parties needed to 'learn from mistakes and misjudgements, pick up the pieces and move on. All of us together'. Through 'supporting each other', the common goal of full implementation could be reached. Commitments on all sides to building trust had to be renewed. Rogers concluded by advising republicans and unionists to proceed with decommissioning and devolution respectively (Rogers, 2000). Here was the transcender logic followed by the SDLP, and the party's recognition that the mistrust at the heart of political problems could only be overcome through mutual action and understanding. Where the 'letter' of the Agreement was absent or unclear – and, crucially, the SDLP acknowledged that this was indeed the case – recourse to the 'spirit' should ease the negotiation of obstacles. Trust, mutuality, good faith, respect, partnership – if these attitudes characterised party interaction then there was no reason implementation obstacles should not be overcome.

But a more tangible and controversial way in which the SDLP influenced the decommissioning/devolution affair was through its refusal to co-operate with unionists to expel Sinn Féin from government in spite of no IRA weapons being surrendered or destroyed. This refusal was justified in terms of the inclusivist principles in the Agreement. In common with the Governments, the SDLP believed that previous attempts at power-sharing had failed due to the exclusion of representatives of paramilitaries (Mac Ginty, 1999: 239). Republican participation in the 1990s peace process was seen as instrumental to its success in reaching the 1998 Agreement. Inclusion of the representatives of a large swathe of Northern nationalism was, said the SDLP, key to forming new cross-community relationships (Farren, 1999). For Northern Ireland, a divided society emerging from conflict, the inclusivist dimension of the Good Friday Agreement was essential for forming a consensus that could allow political institutions to work smoothly (Farren, 2002b). To exclude Sinn Féin was to violate the Agreement and the SDLP pledged to resist such attempts: 'As always, we will protect the Agreement and the will of the people' (Rogers, 2001). The party also felt that exclusion would have unpalatable side effects and would escalate tensions:

> Such a decision by the SDLP would have had the effect of postponing indefinitely any prospect of decommissioning at a time when the process had begun, however reluctantly and however long delayed. Secondly, it would also have the effect of two governments implying that the IRA ceasefire no longer held and the dangers that entailed. Thirdly, it would require the SDLP to vote with the DUP, a party that set itself the goal of destroying the GFA; and, fourthly, it would not have placed any sanctions on parties associated with loyalist paramilitaries.
>
> (Farren, 2006: 120)

The SDLP felt that unionist moves to exclude republicans had more to do with the faction fighting within unionism rather than a genuine desire to increase the chances of decommissioning occurring (Graham, 2001). Moreover, from the party's point of view, it was not showing partiality for Sinn Féin for it had been equally and consistently supportive of the inclusion of the DUP, despite the fact that that party did not even support the Agreement (interview with Mark Durkan MP, 30 August 2012). Yet, inevitably, there was an impression that electoral considerations as well as principle were at work in the SDLP's support for Sinn Féin. To have joined the UUP in ousting Sinn Féin threatened punishment at the hands of a nationalist electorate increasingly enamoured with the republican party. Unfortunately, not to do so proved to be equally damaging at the polls as Sinn Féin's acceptability rose relentlessly (Aughey, 2005: 140).

Refusing to penalise Sinn Féin was a deeply contentious stand for the SDLP to take, increasingly so as evidence mounted of an IRA alive and active. As the party stuck to a principle of inclusion at all costs, in the eyes of some it blunted its moral edge. Take, for example, the following scathing critiques in the pages of

Belfast-based *Fortnight* magazine. Liam Kennedy (2003) charged that the SDLP, by refusing to penalise Sinn Féin after years of evasion on disarmament, had 'learned to cohabit with terror'. The rationale that the SDLP had to stay close to republican hardliners to ease their transition to peaceful politics might have made sense in 1997 or 1998, but no more. In any case, no one in the SDLP believed the IRA would ever go back to war. Turning on their head the SDLP's usual claims of risk-taking and history-making, Kennedy wrote: 'While it has called on others to take serious risks for peace, it is not clear that it has taken any serious risks since the signing of the GFA. These have been neatly tilted on to David Trimble ... The SDLP has been content to stay perfectly united, on the sidelines of historical change' (p. 13). Similarly, Alwyn Thomson (2004) pointed out that in spite of the SDLP's obsession with 'protecting the Agreement', the party had set aside a foundational part of the Agreement, namely the commitment to 'exclusively peaceful means'. The result was 'institutional infanticide, electoral homicide and electoral suicide'. The infanticide was on the Assembly. By not expelling Sinn Féin, the SDLP had forced unionists to walk away from power-sharing: 'Having claimed that the Agreement was primarily their baby, they killed it.' The electoral homicide was inflicted on the UUP since Trimble could no longer sell an Agreement that, as the SDLP's actions demonstrated, contained no censure for republican failure to meet the requirements of non-violence. Electoral suicide also resulted since the SDLP effectively erased the distinction between constitutional nationalism and violent republicanism, which had previously been the SDLP's key electoral asset.

Naturally, unionists were frustrated at not being able to form a coalition of moderates with the SDLP (Trimble, 2007). Unionists who suspected that the SDLP was, behind the flowery language, a traditional tribal nationalist party could find confirmation in its dogged concern for Sinn Féin's participation. The SDLP's stance on decommissioning was justified by the desire to preserve a principle – inclusion – that it believed was at the heart of the Good Friday Agreement and needed protection. Undoubtedly that stance simultaneously damaged the Agreement in the eyes of unionists who were preoccupied with the principle not of inclusion, but of non-violence, and perceived that their concerns about decommissioning and criminality were being ignored by a 'pan-nationalist front' intent solely on communal advancement. Even the Alliance Party attacked the SDLP's inaction, charging that if the nationalist rhetoric condemning republican wrongdoing was not backed up by support for substantive penalties, the SDLP 'was letting them off the hook' (*Belfast Telegraph*, 2005). Despite its general concern for the inclusion of Sinn Féin, the British Government also pressed the SDLP to move against the republican party. After the collapse of devolution in October 2002, Durkan made public that Tony Blair had urged his party to exclude Sinn Féin, a request Durkan emphatically declined (Purdy, 2002; see also Powell, 2008: 209). Durkan states that he challenged Blair to guarantee him that in the event of Sinn Féin's exclusion, the British Government would not maintain secret back channels and continue making concessions to republicans, which Blair would not do: 'And I said to him why should I exclude Sinn Féin from the institutions only to find my own party excluded from the real process that'll continue after this' (interview with Mark Durkan MP, 30 August 2012).

Policing, symbols and parity of esteem

Away from the disarmament logjam, the SDLP vigorously pursued a reform agenda in relation to other aspects of the Agreement. The party's critique of the Royal Ulster Constabulary – that it was a partisan force unacceptable to nationalists – was very similar to that of Sinn Féin, yet it was this issue that caused the most significant post-Agreement policy split between the two parties. When, to the ire of nationalists, many of the Patten Commission's recommendations for the new police service did not appear in Secretary of State Mandelson's Policing Bill of May 2000, the SDLP lobbied energetically for amendments as the Bill passed through Parliament. On the Bill becoming law, the SDLP was still not satisfied with it and refused to join the new Policing Board. The key to the SDLP eventually doing so lay in commitments made by the British Government during talks at Weston Park, Staffordshire, in July 2001 that amendments to the legislation would be made, most of which were aimed at increasing the level of accountability and transparency in the new police service. The Secretary of State for Northern Ireland and the Chief Constable's powers over the Policing Board to prevent inquiries or suppress information were reduced while the Police Ombudsman was given enhanced powers of investigation (SDLP, 2002). Meanwhile, Sinn Féin withheld its backing. That the SDLP, the major representative of the Catholic community since the outset of the 'Troubles', came to fully support the new policing arrangements was of immense significance, not only to the wider peace process but also in terms of its own efforts to act as 'custodian' of the Agreement and prove its dedication to making it work. With Sinn Féin remaining outside the new policing structures, it was not difficult for the SDLP to question its commitment to the Agreement and to law and order. Yet, as Chapter 4 notes, Sinn Féin used its withholding of support for the police to its advantage, portraying itself as the least easily satisfied advocate of Catholic interests.

In relation to flags and emblems, Chapter 2 noted the UUP's prioritisation of British sovereignty as the guiding principle. The SDLP strongly opposed this view, advancing a number of arguments against the primacy of British symbols. First, the SDLP challenged the UUP position that 'There is only one sovereignty in Northern Ireland; there is not joint sovereignty. The recognition of two identities [in the Agreement] is not the recognition of two allegiances' (UUP, 1999b). The SDLP countered that identity could not be so easily separated from allegiance since the aspiration to Irish unity was the 'well-spring of our identity … The acceptance of the diversity of allegiance within Northern Ireland is at the heart of the Good Friday Agreement … The SDLP believe that the recognition of diversity of allegiance, once and accommodated, becomes a resolution of conflict rather than a generator of it' (SDLP, 1999b). While the UUP was accepting that the Agreement recognised diverse identities but not diverse allegiances, the SDLP was asserting that the Agreement did in fact accommodate diverse allegiances.

Second, although the SDLP accepted the principle of consent, it pointed out that unionists ignored the fact that there were other principles outlined in the 'Constitutional Issues' section of the Agreement and that 'those principles should be considered in their totality and that each principle should be considered no less important than any other' (SDLP, 2000). The flying of the Union flag, or any flag that represents the identity and aspirations of only one community in Northern Ireland, violated the principles of 'parity of esteem and of just and equal treatment for the identity, ethos and aspirations of both communities' (Agreement, 1998: 2):

> Northern Ireland is a divided society, emerging from many years of conflict. The division has been around issues of national identity, political aspiration and community treatment. In this context, to interpret the constitutional position and principle of consent so as to enable the display of only the Union flag on government buildings on designated days suggests that one national identity, political aspiration and community requirement has a standing legally and practically over those of others.
>
> (SDLP, 2000)

Third, the SDLP believed that the flying of the Union flag alone ignored the Agreement's call for sensitivity in relation to the symbols issue. Fourth, the very existence of the Agreement, said the SDLP, was proof of Northern Ireland's anomalous position within the United Kingdom, meaning that symbolic expression should not simply be, as unionists argued, the same as the practice in the rest of the country. The effect of the principle of consent was to distinguish Northern Ireland's position in the United Kingdom rather than, as unionists claimed, to bring it in line with that of the other regions: 'Uniquely among regions, Northern Ireland has the guaranteed right in law to opt out of the Union should a majority decide this' (SDLP, 2000). There was also the peculiarity of the international treaty between the UK and Irish Governments that was part of the Good Friday Agreement. This treaty reiterated the pledge, contained in the 'Constitutional Issues' section of the Agreement, that the sovereign Government of Northern Ireland should exercise its power with impartiality and in accordance with the principle of parity of esteem (Agreement, 1998: 28).

And fifth, making Northern Ireland more welcoming to nationalists' identity was of practical relevance to whether the new politics in actuality succeeded. For example, in relation to the new police force, Mallon (2000) explained in a BBC interview that the symbols were as important, perhaps more important, in garnering cross-community support than the reforms being enacted:

> Any young man from within the Catholic community, in probably what would have been termed a hard-line nationalist area when he starts to think if he will join the police service, he will not be reading the legislation, he will be judging it on what he sees and if the first thing he sees is a flag that he doesn't particularly adhere to and an emblem that he doesn't particularly adhere to then I pose the question, is he going to be disposed to proceed and join that police service and I think this constitutional argument put forward by the Ulster Unionists simply doesn't stand up.

This was identical to the argument made by the UUP that Patten had failed to fulfil its terms of reference that required the commission to make recommendations on policing that could enable the force to gain cross-community support. Changing the name and emblems of the force, said Trimble, would militate against gaining Protestant support, but not to do so, said the SDLP, would do likewise among Catholics. Overall, the SDLP believed that reaching consensus among the parties in Northern Ireland on how flags and symbols should be used was crucial, and Peter Mandelson's reservation of the right to rule on the issue would solve nothing. The best solution, for the short-term anyhow, was for no flags whatsoever to be flown. Flying no flag was also the party's preferred option in 2012 in relation to the controversy surrounding flag-flying at Belfast City Hall (see Chapter 6), at least in the absence of cross-party agreement. Nevertheless, at that time, the party voted along with Sinn Féin for the Alliance Party compromise motion allowing for flying the flag on designated days, though it was not the nationalist parties' preferred option.

Dilemmas of survival

Throughout its lobbying in relation to the various post-Agreement controversies, the SDLP faced the constant questions of whether and how to distinguish itself from Sinn Féin, a party with which it competed for Catholic votes and to which it increasingly bore resemblance. The predicament was 'whether the promotion of (pan-) nationalist commonalities or post-nationalist politics offers the most promising way forward' (Tonge, 2006: 82). Unfortunately, neither of these options offered a sure route to political growth. As a 2001 report by Democratic Dialogue, a think tank, outlined, Hume's repeated advocacy of 'real' and 'normal' politics offered little prospect of winning the contest with Sinn Féin within the nationalist bloc. Moreover, 'every time the SDLP supports a Sinn Féin policy it risks being seen as acknowledging the republicans' leading role in the Catholic community' (Ruohomaki, 2001). Malachi O'Doherty (2000) put it thus: 'The trap for the SDLP is that they feel obliged to sound like Sinn Féin without marking out the distinction.' This, wrote O'Doherty, was because of the SDLP's worry that selling partnership government as an end in itself without championing communal interests to a similar extent as Sinn Féin would not be enough to maintain its ethnic support base.

The SDLP's problem lay in the fact that Sinn Féin had comprehensively occupied its political space, leaving little room for the SDLP and exposing that party's long-standing organisational and image weaknesses. The SDLP's distinctiveness had appeared to be diminishing before 1998 as John Hume, in the hope of peace, ushered republicans into the political mainstream. A stark and ironic example of this process was the fact that the 1997 Westminster election literature of both Gerry Adams and his SDLP rival Joe Hendron bore a picture of John Hume (Walker, 1997). It was the SDLP contender who was defeated. Embracing the peace process removed the cap on Sinn Féin's support; nevertheless, Sinn Féin's electoral growth before 1998 was driven by new Catholic voters, rather than the poaching of SDLP votes (McAllister, 2004). In the Assembly election of 1998, the SDLP received the highest share of first preference votes of all parties. But in the 2001 Westminster election, Sinn Féin overtook the party, jumping from two to four Westminster seats (21.7 per cent vote share, up from 16.1 per cent in 1997) while the SDLP retained its three (21 per cent vote share, down from 24.1 per cent in 1997).

This was a historic outcome; from its founding until 2001, the SDLP had been the largest nationalist party with around two-thirds of the nationalist vote and usually the second largest party in Northern Ireland behind the UUP. In 2003, the Assembly election confirmed the trend, with Sinn Féin securing twenty-four seats to the SDLP's eighteen, an exact reversal of fortunes from 1998. Subsequently, in 2007 and 2011, Sinn Féin's vote crept upwards, securing twenty-eight, then twenty-nine seats, while the SDLP went down to sixteen then fourteen. The SDLP retained its tally of three Westminster seats but lost more votes in the 2014 local elections. Significantly, surveys conducted after the elections in 1998 and 2003 showed that, contrary to the situation before the Agreement, Sinn Féin's post-Agreement growth was indeed at the expense of the SDLP. Of SDLP voters in 1998, 19 per cent voted for Sinn Féin in 2003 while only 5 per cent of 1998 Sinn Féin voters switched to the SDLP in 2003 (Mitchell et al., 2009: 407).

The electoral results showed that Sinn Féin's combination of support for the peace process with strong advocacy on behalf of traditional nationalist grievances (the police and army, equality, opposition to Orange parades, participation in government) and effective local campaigning easily trumped the SDLP's key selling point – its role in bringing about the Agreement – which was now receding in the nationalist memory. Nevertheless, the SDLP did make some attempt to compete with Sinn Féin on the latter's home turf: support for Irish unity. This was encapsulated in the slogan '100% for the Agreement, 100% for a United Ireland' which was the centrepiece of Durkan's party conference speech in 2002, the predominant message in the party's 2003 and 2005 manifestos and the subject of a major strategy document launched in November 2003 entitled *A United Ireland and the Agreement*. The central proposal was that in the event of a majority of the people of Northern Ireland voting in a referendum for a united Ireland, the institutions of the Agreement should continue to operate. This position was held 'uniquely among parties in the North' and came from a belief that 'all the rights, protections, and inclusion that nationalists sought within Northern Ireland while it is in the United Kingdom, must equally be guaranteed to unionists within a United Ireland' (SDLP, 2003a: 3). This policy, said the SDLP, had a number of advantages. First, it was right in principle since it guaranteed that an egalitarian society was not just for the short term, but that it would endure – whatever the constitutional position – thanks to the Agreement's safeguards. Second, it created the best context in which to win a majority for Irish unity. Voters would know that opting for Irish unity was 'neither a vote against the Agreement nor a vote for constitutional uncertainty' (p. 3). Third, making clear that the Agreement would continue beyond a referendum regardless of the outcome would bolster unionist support for the Agreement in the present. This would be in contrast to the 'antagonistic attitudes and actions of Sinn Féin' that in fact turned unionists off the Agreement (Durkan, 2003).

Indeed, the SDLP claimed to represent 'true republicanism': the party's non-violent credentials and conciliatory persona meant that only it had any chance of successfully persuading a majority for Irish unity (SDLP, 2003b: 6). Understandably, this reassertion of nationalism was interpreted by some as an attempt to 'outgreen' Sinn Féin, though the party denied this:

> I don't think there is any question of the SDLP trying to outgreen Sinn Féin. The reality is that what has happened is that Sinn Féin have been trying to out-SDLP the

SDLP. They have tried to take our polices, our lines, our language, our ideas, our arguments and just come forward with a Sinn Féin remix of them. Yes, that has created difficulties.

(Durkan, quoted in Graham, 2004)

Interestingly, Durkan argues that rather than 'outgreening', the purpose of the proposal that the Agreement would survive within a united Ireland was the very opposite: it was an attempt to show that the Agreement required change of nationalism as well as unionism. The policy indicated

> how our [nationalists'] concept of a united Ireland has actually now been reconditioned by the fact of the Agreement … Just as nationalists have for a long time said there isn't purely an internal settlement in Northern Ireland, there isn't a purely internal settlement in the UK, well this was nationalists maybe realising too in the context of the Agreement, there isn't a purely internal settlement in Ireland either.
> (Interview with Mark Durkan MP, 30 August 2012)

The rationale was that by stressing that the Agreement institutions would survive, even if the sovereign authority changed, talk of Irish unity would become much less disruptive and destabilising to the Agreement that had, crucially, been endorsed by the people North and South. It would also challenge the analysis of dissident republicans who believed that support for the Agreement and a united Ireland were contradictory. However, the extent to which the '100%' message penetrated the nationalist or unionist public consciousnesses is unclear, and levels of support for a united Ireland have remained low.

Another line of attack in the struggle with Sinn Féin was forthright condemnation of republicans' ambivalence towards, and even complicity in, unlawful activity. Durkan mocked the Sinn Féin leadership's rejection of a string of allegations of IRA transgression, asking at his party's conference, 'does anybody actually believe them?' (Durkan, 2002: 5). However, such condemnation was always carefully accompanied by criticism of the unionists' half-hearted commitment to power-sharing, thereby maintaining a 'moral equidistance' from unionists and republicans so as to avoid alienating the nationalist electorate (Aughey, 2005: 140). In later years, after the completion of decommissioning and the resumption of devolution, the issues changed, but the SDLP continued to attempt to mark itself from Sinn Féin by arguing that republicans were still lacking in their commitment to democratic values on a number of fronts. Durkan's successor as leader, Margaret Ritchie, called Sinn Féin a 'centrally controlled authoritarian party', crippled by its own resentment towards Northern Ireland and uninterested in a society shared with unionists. Sinn Féin was 'happy to maintain our current divisions and abnormal segregation. They use and abuse our Irish culture as a political weapon and if scratched are every bit as sectarian as their opposite numbers in loyalism' (Ritchie, 2010a).

Despite the policy and rhetorical manoeuvrings, however, the election figures make clear that the SDLP made no serious progress in regaining its position as Northern Catholics' party of choice. The problem of finding the appropriate political territory on which to fight Sinn Féin was compounded by inter-related organisational, financial and image problems. Sinn Féin's status as an all-Ireland party that had enjoyed electoral successes both north and south of the border made the SDLP look in comparison 'a narrow, sectional, northern nationalist party, accentuating its problems of an ageing membership, low recruitment and loss of electoral (and moral) superiority' (Tonge, 2006: 83). Poor organisation had been a feature of the party stretching back years as energies were directed at the leadership's peace-making efforts. A leaked internal report in April 2000 claimed that the SDLP was middle-aged, middle-class and unfit to meet the Sinn Féin challenge (O'Doherty, 2000). Indeed, the very same claim had been made a decade-and-a-half earlier (Moloney, 1984), and in November 2013 another SDLP-commissioned report was leaked to the BBC that again highlighted the well-known difficulties. Based on focus groups with voters who did not vote for the SDLP but were open to doing so, this report, according to the BBC, outlined that some participants had said that the SDLP was 'the party of the past', while Sinn Féin was seen as 'the party of the future'; the SDLP was viewed as 'having no big figures anymore' while Sinn Féin had 'strong leaders'; and the SDLP 'didn't know if they were British or Irish', while Sinn Féin was seen as 'strongly Irish'. As for SDLP policy differences with Sinn Féin, the research found that the participants could not identify any (Walker, 2013a).

Drawing on interviews with SDLP and Sinn Féin communications staff and journalists, research by Kirby (2013) argues that the SDLP's decline in relation to Sinn Féin was due less to politics than the former's acute lack of money. This in turn led to an inadequate party communication and public relations infrastructure and, accordingly, a limited capacity to influence both journalists and the public. The disparity in finance was caused by both the SDLP's failure to fundraise adequately, particularly in the United States where lucrative opportunities existed, and Sinn Féin's considerable riches gained both legally and illegally (on republican funding, see Rafter, 2005: 188–218). Nevertheless, access to cash was not the only issue: Kirby points out perceptions of stark attitudinal differences between the two parties, with the SDLP complacent about communications and media training and Sinn Féin – largely a result of its experience in armed struggle and the propaganda war – intensely aware of the importance of investing in publicity and exploiting the media. For example, the SDLP employed its first-ever Director of Communications in 1996 and established its first press office in 1997, twenty-five years after Sinn Féin had done the same. Following the Agreement, the SDLP had one full-time communications staff member while Sinn Féin had twelve, both paid and unpaid. The low priority given to communications was symptomatic of broader organisational problems, including the leadership's failure to promote younger members, partly due to its focus on the peace process. In sum, Kirby (2013: 22) concludes that putting the SDLP's electoral woes down to Hume's reaching out to Sinn Féin in the late 1980s and early 1990s 'only serves to cloak or disguise more complex reasons for the party's electoral decline and in fact, seemingly absolves the SDLP of their own internal sins'.

Without doubt, the departure of Mallon and Hume from leadership roles in 2001 left the party without two of its biggest electoral assets and recognisable figures. Garrett Fitzgerald (2003) called the SDLP a 'single generation party', noting that by coming into existence at one crucial historical moment, the abundance of early talent had obscured the need to recruit younger blood for the future. The void left in 2001 was considerable since, as Murray (1998: 257) notes, John Hume's charismatic image and the esteem in which he was held internationally had never been transferred onto his party. In contrast, Gerry Adams' image and persona were closely integrated with those of Sinn Féin. The loss of Hume and Mallon broke the SDLP's connection with the civil rights era and the most prominent exponents of a civil rights agenda were now to be found within Sinn Féin (Murray and Tonge, 2005: 268). The public perception of the SDLP was not helped by relatively frequent leadership changes in the post-Agreement years – as of 2011, four leaders compared to Gerry Adams' thirty-year reign over Sinn Féin. Another personnel problem hit the headlines in September 2013 when Conall McDevitt, a South Belfast MLA, was forced to resign due to media revelations of financial irregularities. McDevitt, relatively youthful at forty-one and a public relations professional, was one of the most articulate voices in the SDLP, a strong media performer and likely future leader. He stood for the leadership in 2011 shortly after entering the Assembly, coming second to South Belfast MP Alasdair McDonnell (BBC, 2013a).

The most striking advantage of Sinn Féin, at least in those critical early years after the Agreement, was the link with the IRA that kept the party in the political limelight during the implementation negotiations. In a candid admission of the cold realities of post-Agreement politics, Tony Blair told an SDLP delegation during difficult implementation talks: 'Your trouble, you've no guns' (quoted in Farren, 2010: 15). The removal of those guns in 2005 positioned Sinn Féin to dominate Northern nationalism indefinitely and, in light of this realignment, two quite radical measures presented themselves after the restoration of devolution in 2007, measures that at least some in the party believed had the potential to reinvigorate the organisation. One was to withdraw from the Executive. Key party figures including Bríd Rogers and Delores Kelly, publicly stated their belief that the party would be better able to distinguish and reassert itself by giving up its one seat on the DUP–Sinn Féin-dominated government (Walker, 2013b). However, given the SDLP's long-standing and dogged commitment to the principle of an inclusive government, it is unsurprising that these calls to withdraw have not been reflected in party policy.

Another, more drastic, course of action favoured by some in the SDLP was to merge with a Southern party. Talk of a merger with Fianna Fáil, the Republic's largest party, had been around since the beginning of the decade, but reached its height in 2007/8 with meetings of senior officials, the Southern party beginning to organise in the North and individuals from both parties making positive noises (*Irish Independent*, 2008). The benefits, it was claimed, would be mutual: the SDLP's electoral problems were clear, while Fianna Fáil saw a move into Northern politics as a boost to its republican credentials. But the dangers, drawbacks and obstacles were many. Some in the party felt that a more natural liaison would be with its left-leaning counterpart in the South, the Irish Labour Party. A link with Fianna Fáil would end decades of SDLP neutrality in relation to the Southern parties, thus reducing its influence in Dublin when Fianna Fáil would inevitably lose power. Most of all, it was far from certain that a fused SDLP–Fianna Fáil would actually achieve the needful: attract votes away from Sinn Féin, especially in the North (Feeney, 2005). Nothing came of the speculation. When Ritchie took over from Durkan as leader of the SDLP in 2010, she shot down the idea, declaring: 'Merger with Fianna Fáil? Not on my watch.' Speaking in April at the Irish Labour Party conference in Galway, she flattered her hosts with talk of shared values, while proceeding to criticise Fianna Fáil's culpability in, and handling of, Ireland's economic crisis (Ritchie, 2010b). This highlighted the reality that an alliance with Fianna Fáil – tainted by an image of greed and recklessness and presiding over an economic meltdown – was a less attractive prospect for the SDLP than it had been a few years previously. For its part, Fianna Fáil has set up branches in Northern Ireland but has not yet contested elections.

Conclusion

'Like the Prodigal Son's brother', is how, according to Durkan, the SDLP can feel in the light of Sinn Féin's ascendancy. 'We've learnt the lesson the hard way that vindication and reward aren't the same thing' (interview with Mark Durkan MP, 30 August 2012). Mallon told an interviewer in 2008 that the St Andrews Agreement was 'hard to watch' and that it was 'a fig leaf to change the name from the Good Friday Agreement to the St. Andrews Agreement' (Purdy, 2008). More than any other party, the SDLP shaped the 1998 Agreement, meaning that subsequent developments, including the DUP's eagerness to disown that deal while de facto accepting it, and the electoral success of republicans who had been responsible for rhetorically and at times physically attacking the SDLP for decades, are historically ironic and undoubtedly, for the SDLP, profoundly galling. As with the UUP, blame for the SDLP's downturn can be variously attributed – to the Governments (for their focus on the extreme parties) or the SDLP leadership (for allowing the party to atrophy). But the greatest factor was Sinn Féin's moderated platform, driven forward by its powerful campaigning machine. In this moderation, Sinn Féin was following an SDLP lead, deliberately imitating and perhaps also unconsciously internalising the moderate party's language, ideas and approach to Irish unity. Indeed, the author witnessed a glaring example of this ideological borrowing/stealing at a private event in late 2013. A high-profile Sinn Féin representative informed the gathering in passing that his party's goal was none other than an 'agreed Ireland' – that centrepiece of distinctly SDLP thinking.

And so, while the SDLP, as a vote-seeking organisation, is likely past its prime, the SDLP's ideas have ongoing significance. The three-stranded approach to talks, the prioritisation of the healing of relationships over Irish unification and the desire to institutionally express new relationships influenced the approach of the Governments, the ideological orientation of Sinn Féin and even the unionist parties that have now broadly accepted, and experienced the wisdom of, these ideas. At the same time, SDLP proposals at times insufficiently appreciated unionist fears and identity, most notably, the Council of Ireland component of the Sunningdale Agreement in 1974 that had greater powers than the all-Ireland elements of the 1998 Agreement; from a unionist point of view, the SDLP was a 'slow learner' too. Nevertheless, with incompatible nationalisms and territorial claims at the core of Irish conflict, the transcender logic that drove Hume's departure from traditional Irish nationalism, his focus on broken relationships and his promotion of European-flavoured ideas concerning the declining significance of borders helped catalyse the transformation of the conflict. This was summed up by his oft-repeated (for good reason) story of how standing on a bridge in Strasbourg and witnessing the peace between Germany and France, a peace embodied in institutional linkages, inspired him that the same was possible in Ireland. Crucial too was the SDLP's dogged adherence to non-violence throughout the 'Troubles' that prevented far greater bloodshed. Unfortunately for the party, a distinguished history has limited purchase in the all-important polling-booth decisions of the public, now or in the future.

4
Sinn Féin

Introduction

In Sinn Féin's 2011 Assembly election manifesto, first on the list of the party's 'key achievements' was the claim that it had 'led the challenge to the imposition of £4 billion cuts to the North's budget by the British government' (Sinn Féin, 2011: 4). This was an interesting boast in the light of the party's several decades of support for a campaign of violence aimed at economically crippling that part of Ireland to which it was referring, prior to the hoped-for eradication of all British influence there. But in the context of Sinn Féin's extraordinary evolution from a propaganda arm of a guerrilla army to a large, modern, constitutional party of government in a UK region, the manifesto claim was just another barely registering indicator of change. More celebrated markers were the handshakes between Martin McGuinness and Queen Elizabeth II in 2011 and 2014. These, like other totemic moves by republicanism, could be interpreted variously: as the establishment honouring an ex-terrorist; as a radical political leader advancing on the peaceful but revolutionary path to liberating Ireland from British control; as a reconciliatory gesture towards unionists; or as a sign of the defeat of republicanism as most people knew it. The ambiguity of such occasions exemplified the complex and contentious nature of Sinn Féin's strategy in relation to the Good Friday Agreement and the wider process of political change.

That strategy after 1998 is the focus of this chapter. It begins with a review of Sinn Féin's roots in the republican tradition, its ideological outlook and its approach to the embryonic peace process. It examines the content of, and rationale for, Sinn Féin's particular interpretation of the Agreement and assesses the party's central claim that the Agreement could be transitional to a united Ireland. Then, Sinn Féin's fixation on promoting equality is described and explained, as is the controversial and shadowy role of the IRA after the Agreement. Lastly, the chapter discusses the most important part of Sinn Féin's post-Agreement strategy: electoral progress.

Breaking the British connection

The contemporary Sinn Féin party can be said to have three lines of ancestry. The first is the republican 'tradition', whose origin is usually traced to 1798, the year of the United Irishmen rebellion. This tradition continues through a succession of movements and individuals that struggled in subsequent years, and usually through physical force, against the British presence in Ireland. It includes Robert Emmet, the Young Ireland movement, the Fenians, Patrick Pearse and the insurrectionists of 1916, the 'old' IRA, the Provisional IRA and Sinn Féin. Although each movement emerged and operated according to specific historical circumstances, republicans view the tradition as essentially a single story, a morality tale in which generations of brave and self-denying Irish men and women have stood to challenge the foreign oppressor while their co-nationals have lurched aimlessly through constitutional politics or languished in selfish materialism. This narrative, republicanism's 'monochrome remembrance of itself' (Patterson, 1997: 9), is called upon to legitimise the actions of republicans in the present. Associated with this tradition are what have been called republican 'metaphysics' (Shanahan, 2009: 40–65) – notions of blood-sacrifice, martyrdom and destiny. Herein lies traditional republicanism's fatalist streak: the belief that force is the natural and necessary response to the British occupation, a response that will indubitably and eventually be successful.

The second line of ancestry begins in 1905 when the first political grouping bearing the name 'Sinn Féin' appeared on the scene of Irish politics, a party formed by the Dublin journalist Arthur Griffith. He did not seek to sever all links with Britain nor espouse violence, but after the 1916 Rising, the Sinn Féin name came to be attached to those who had been involved in the rebellion and it was under that name that a separatist coalition led by Éamon De Valera fought the 1918 Westminster election. Winning an overwhelming majority of Irish seats, the Sinn Féin representatives formed Dáil Éireann, a self-declared provisional government of Ireland. The Irish Republican Army, previously the Irish Volunteers, fought the War of Independence for two years until it was ended with the 1921 Anglo-Irish Treaty. The terms of the Treaty, following the 1920 Government of Ireland Act that saw Ireland partitioned between the six north-eastern counties and the twenty-six others, gave partial autonomy to the twenty-six, still under the British Crown. Sinn Féin and the IRA split between those, under Michael Collins, who believed the Treaty could be a stepping stone to a future, united Irish republic and those, under De Valera, who believed it was a sell-out. Civil war ensued, at the end of which the pro-Treaty forces emerged victorious. In 1926 De Valera and many others left Sinn Féin to form Fianna Fáil and take their seats in the Dublin parliament. Sinn Féin and the IRA survived during the middle decades of the twentieth century as small and peripheral organisations.

The most important date in the emergence of contemporary Sinn Féin is 1969. That year saw a split in Sinn Féin and the IRA producing the 'Provisionals', the Sinn Féin and IRA that were involved in armed struggle hence, and the 'Officials', which were to recede into the background. The cause of the schism was twofold. First, elements in the IRA were unhappy with the movement's increasing emphasis on leftist politics at the expense of armed action. Second, the split was a result of deepening insecurity in the North, with the Northern IRA becoming increasingly militant in the face of loyalist attacks on the Catholic community and unionist indifference to Catholic grievances. That Provisionalism was a product of its time (the late 1960s and early 1970s), place (the urban areas of Belfast and Derry) and circumstances (the exclusion of Catholics under the unionist regime) is important to note, since it dispels the notion of a single self-perpetuating republican tradition. While the Northern IRA leaders may have been steeped in the physical force republican tradition, the droves who rallied to the cause post-1969 were motivated by their desire to defend Catholic areas and their alienation from the British-backed Northern state (McIntyre, 2001). As principally an outlet of communal rage rather than green romanticism, the Provisional IRA 'represented a politics firmly based in daily ties to actual people as well as (more than?) to an imagined community' (English, 2006: 371). As McIntyre (1995, 2001) argues, understanding Provisional republicanism as a force driven first and foremost by seeking the reform of the Northern state and venting the grievances of Northern Catholics, rather than, in spite of the rhetoric, continuing the old task of a united Ireland, reveals how the movement was always susceptible to being (as it eventually was in the 1990s) drawn into a peace process that promised to address those grievances through reform – the major desire of the Catholic community – but not Irish unity.

And Provisionalism's emergence as a response to events rather than as an outworking of ideology explains its political and theoretical impoverishment in its early years. Up until the late 1970s, a preoccupation with conspiratorial organisation and activism meant that republicanism was 'ideologically and strategically primitive' (Bean, 2002: 133). The IRA, and its then subservient political wing Sinn Féin, existed in a 'pre-political world' consumed with a sense of historical grievance and belief in the moral superiority of standing outside – or above – politics and negotiation (Arthur, 2002: 88). Their aim was to force the British to declare their intent to withdraw from Northern Ireland and pave the way for the creation of a federal thirty-two county republic. Beyond being socialist in emphasis and culturally distinct from Britain, the character of the desired united Ireland was never clearly articulated. All this changed at the start of the 1980s when the prison Hunger Strikes of 1980–1 and the election to Westminster of Bobby Sands, one of the strikers, led to the increasing salience of electoral politics within the movement. Those events showed republicans the level of public sympathy within the nationalist community that was there to be harnessed, and henceforth Sinn Féin seriously contested elections alongside the continuing IRA campaign. Through the 'armalite and ballot paper' strategy, republicans sought to combine the best of both worlds, democratic and insurgent, in the service of republican aims. The idea was that growing political strength could gain Sinn Féin a 'republican veto' over political change and prevent an internal Northern Ireland settlement between the moderate elements of unionism and nationalism (Frampton, 2009: 22).

Until the late 1980s republicanism's concern for equality, democracy, rights and culture was secondary to the national question; they existed as 'resonances of separatist nationalist aims, as a part of a republican culture which underlay and gave meaning to the nationalist goals which took the dominant role in the ideology' (Todd, 1999: 56). As Sinn Féin's 1988 document *Towards a Peace Strategy* put it: 'Equality is synonymous with national rights. Partition is in direct contradiction to that' (Sinn Féin, 1988: 10). The Social Democratic and Labour Party's (SDLP) belief in achieving a united Ireland in stages was foolish: 'Stormont is not a stepping-stone to Irish unity' (p. 12). As for unionism, it is 'a child of imperialism', a shallow and artificial creed with the sole function of maintaining British power in Ireland (p. 16). If the British guarantee of Northern Ireland's place in the United Kingdom was removed, unionists would wake up to the fact that a future shared with their Irish countrymen on the rest of the island was in their true interests. However, as republicans entered the 1990s the certainties of this fatalist worldview were to crumble and be replaced with a more accommodating, perplexing and electorally attractive vision.

Changes in the international context have been credited with some role in the republican reassessment: the conciliatory moves by 'sister' revolutionaries in South Africa and Palestine; the end of the Cold War and the credibility that this lent to Britain's claim of holding no selfish strategic interest in the North; the efforts of the United States in boosting Sinn Féin's stature and hinting at the advantages of non-violence by actions such as granting a visa to Gerry Adams in January 1994 (Cox, 2006). Whatever the salience of these factors, the most important cause of republicans' ideological shift was the prolonged success of British strategies to contain the IRA militarily and neutralise Sinn Féin politically. Beginning with the 1985 Anglo-Irish Agreement, the British embarked on the long process of 'eroding the ground where the IRA sank its roots' by addressing the concerns of constitutional nationalism (McIntyre, 1995: 103). At the same time, the penetration of the IRA by British agents constrained the organisation's ability to operate, as did increasingly targeted attacks on the IRA from loyalists. The conflict settled into a costly stalemate and republicans appeared to explore ways out through discussions with the SDLP from 1988. Research by Shirlow *et al.* (2010) among ex-combatants found that many republicans (and loyalists) in fact did not perceive a stalemate – a finding that undermines the 'mutually hurting stalemate' explanation of the origins of the peace process – although a smaller study found a number of republicans to be quite frank that, in their view, the armed campaign was unsustainable (Brewer *et al.*, 2013: 122). In any case, there were no signs that Britain was on the cusp of withdrawing from Northern Ireland, and developments in republican thinking were evident in Sinn Féin's 1992 document, *Towards a Lasting Peace in Ireland*, which offered subtler analysis and more moderate proposals than Sinn Féin had produced previously.

Gone was the long-standing absolutist demand for immediate British withdrawal; it was replaced by a vaguer call for the British and Irish Governments to co-operate in working towards the ending of partition. The unionist community was recognised as a people that needed to be persuaded into a united Ireland – no longer coerced or ignored – in which their rights and identity would be accommodated (Sinn Féin, 1992). In at times war-weary tones, *Towards a Lasting Peace* expressed a general desire to investigate the potential of politics as a means to escape the suffering of armed conflict. As the IRA called a ceasefire in August 1994, Sinn Féin's demand became inclusion in political talks, yet the party knew that those talks were not, as the 1993 Downing Street Declaration made clear, going to negotiate away the principle of consent. Partition would remain for the time being and republicans now turned to precisely the type of gradualism of which they had been so disdainful in the SDLP to realise their goals.

It was not difficult, therefore, to view the ceasefire as representing an abandonment of all that republicans had fought for. The campaign had ended without securing a British declaration of intent to withdraw; on the contrary, republicans were implicitly accepting what had been the unacceptable – the principle of consent and thus the partition of Ireland. This was confirmed in 1997 when Sinn Féin accepted the ground rules to entry into the multi-party talks, the Mitchell Principles, which committed them to non-violence and to abide by any outcome to those talks. Nevertheless, from a republican point of view, a talks process accompanied by the continued growth of Sinn Féin held out a range of favourable possibilities. Unionists may be pushed into a defensive and reactionary corner. Their intransigence could cause relations with the British to deteriorate and talks on a settlement within Northern Ireland to fail. Indeed, republicans were well aware of the destabilising effect that the IRA's ceasefire and Sinn Féin's political growth had on unionism (Frampton, 2009: 105). Critically, there was the potential of the emerging 'pan-nationalist' alliance, comprising republicans, the SDLP,

Dublin and the United States, which could exert pressure on Britain to break the 'unionist veto' (McLoughlin, 2014). In sum, the theory that a weak deal could be transformed by a powerful electoral mandate and pan-nationalist solidarity formed the basis of Sinn Féin's faith in assenting to the Agreement and was the touchstone of how the republican struggle was to continue in the implementation period and beyond.

The Agreement: 'a bridge to the future'

The title of a Sinn Féin document produced in March 1998 when an all-party agreement was in prospect expressed the republican position on any eventual accord: *A Bridge to the Future*. That document admitted that Sinn Féin did not have the political strength to realise its objectives and thus new political arrangements would be treated as transitional to a united Ireland; 'the struggle for this entirely legitimate, democratic and desirable objective will continue beyond May' (Adams, 1998a: 2). That said, the document was firm that 'Any kind of new Stormont or any effort to underpin partition is unacceptable' (p. 2), and while the Agreement that emerged both provided for a new Stormont and underpinned partition, Adams told his party's conference on 18 April 1998 that the deal was a 'basis for advancement'. Republicans must take a strategic and selective approach:

> So Sinn Féin will subscribe to what we view as positive in the Agreement, to those aspects which contribute to moving towards our overall objectives, and it is you, the activists, who with the leadership, shall decide on that. Some of our critics will say: 'You can't do that! You have to buy into it, all or nothing!' But they are wrong.
> (Adams, 1998b: 4)

Despite its failure to meet republican objectives as traditionally formulated, there was much in the Agreement to appeal to republicans. A key factor in winning their support and a key republican demand in the talks was the provision regarding the release of prisoners belonging to paramilitary groups on ceasefire at the time of the Agreement. The 'equality agenda', Sinn Féin's main preoccupation during the talks, was advanced through the enactment of new legislation and the setting up of new bodies to promote and ensure equality in the political, cultural and economic spheres. Human rights standards in the Republic were to be synchronised with those in Northern Ireland. The use, promotion and teaching of the Irish language were to be encouraged and supported financially. All-Ireland linkages that were open to expansion (although under the control of the Assembly in which unionists would have a veto) were established in the form of the North–South Ministerial Council (NSMC) and its affiliated implementation bodies. In the event of the Agreement instituting enduring peace, the British Government committed itself to total security 'normalisation', or 'demilitarisation' as republicans preferred to call it. While British sovereignty remained, republicans argued that it was diluted by the all-Ireland institutions. And instead of cementing Northern Ireland's ties with Britain, McGuinness described the principle of majority consent as 'a clause limiting the life of the Union to the will of a majority in the Northern state … It's a bit like a partner in a relationship saying that the relationship is over, but that s/he is willing to wait until the children have grown up' (McGuinness, 1998: 14).

A delegate to the crucial party conference that followed a week after the signing of the Agreement was quoted in *An Phoblacht/Republican News* as saying: 'For unionists this is as good as it gets, for nationalists it's just a start' (Friel and Lane, 1998). For that bulk of republican opinion that welcomed the Agreement, there was a feeling that, in the jargon, one phase of struggle was coming to an end and another phase just beginning. The 'start' that republicans could discern in the Agreement was of the final leg of the journey towards a thirty-two county Irish republic and, more generally, the beginning of a resurgence of confidence and vitality in their community. A sense of affirmation came with the security and equality reforms that, as McGuinness argued, were at last a repudiation of unionist orthodoxy that 'there was no discrimination but only disadvantage' (McGuinness, 1998: 15). In contrast to the energetic programme of reform sought and secured by nationalists, the unionists' achievement of consent – 'a static condition of principle' – was a fait accompli (Aughey, 2005: 124). Their goal was stability, the republicans', the precise opposite; unionists were back in defence, republicans on the offence. But as the Sinn Féin leadership sought to impress upon the party, the Agreement was not inherently a transitional document. Concerted effort on the part of republicans was required for it to be so:

> It heralds change in the status quo. And it could become a transitional stage towards reunification but only if all those who express an interest in that objective, especially the powerful and influential, move beyond rhetoric to build a real dynamic for national democratic change.
>
> (Adams, 1998b: 4)

> Do we have a level playing field as a result of this phase of negotiations? We clearly do not. What we do have however, is a very visible playing field, with the equality issue up in lights, the clear prospect of change if we have the strength and commitment to hold people to positions outlined.
>
> (McGuinness, 1998: 15)

The Agreement could lead to a united Ireland but 'it will only happen if we make it happen' (McLaughlin, 2002: 45). Realising the Agreement's transitional potential was the primary aim of Sinn Féin, and this required that implementation never stand still. 'The Yes vote in the referendum was a vote for change', said the party's manifesto for the first Assembly election. 'Change' would be wrung out of the Agreement to the maximum degree, the intention being 'to push the Good Friday document to its outer limits and beyond' (Sinn Féin, 1998: 3).

The Adams–McGuinness leadership won overwhelming party backing for the Agreement. This was achieved through a combination of those men's personal standing and charisma, the force of their argument that the Agreement could be transitional, plus an internal party culture that was uninviting to dissent (see Frampton, 2009). Indeed, given the overwhelming pro-Agreement sentiment throughout nationalist Ireland, republican support for the Agreement was required for Sinn Féin's ongoing electoral growth. Frampton (2009: 112) highlights how Adams cleverly and quickly took ownership of the Agreement, styling himself as champion of its full implementation. This supported his efforts to portray the Agreement as a new republican insurgency and abetted Sinn Féin's running side-project of dividing and demoralising unionism. Yet, despite the optimism and apparent clarity of purpose that emanated from republican ranks in mid-1998, the Agreement in fact consolidated the state of uncertainty and contradiction that had characterised republicanism, at least since 1994.

Two unanswered questions loomed large. First, what was to become of the IRA in the light of the Agreement? The post-Agreement role of the IRA is explored below, but suffice it to say that, despite Sinn Féin's acceptance of the Agreement, it was clear that its military wing was, at that time, far from considering retirement. Combined with the party's frequently militant rhetoric, the IRA's continued existence and activity rendered doubtful Sinn Féin's commitment to democracy and, indeed, the wider viability of the new political structures. At the same time, the logic of Sinn Féin's increasing immersion in constitutional politics suggested that the party would have to disentangle itself from militancy sooner or later. The second unanswered question concerned the credibility of the pro-Agreement republican arguments advanced by the Sinn Féin leadership: could the Agreement really bring a united Ireland closer?

In view of these uncertainties, analysts wondered how best to ideologically categorise the Provisional movement in the wake of its endorsement of the Good Friday Agreement. For example, while their descriptions are slightly different, Todd (1999) and Porter (2003) both suggested three possible readings. One was that Sinn Féin had mellowed into a constitutional nationalist party in the mould of the SDLP. It sought only the reform of Northern Ireland in the direction of justice and parity of esteem and had demoted the goal of Irish unity to second place. A second reading was that little real change had taken place; Irish unity continued to be republicanism's primary objective and the movement's acceptance of the Agreement was a mere tactical shift – war by other means. This was the fatalist reading believed by many unionists, certainly those who opposed the Agreement. The third reading, which Todd and Porter correctly thought the most accurate, was that Sinn Féin retained the end of Irish unity but had altered the means to achieve it: for republicans, reforming Northern Ireland was now regarded as the best way of bringing about unity. There was an 'ideological symbiosis' between the universal principles of justice and equality and traditional republican all-Ireland goals (Todd, 1999: 59). Irish unity and the reform of Northern Ireland were now 'interlocking or co-dependent' goals (Porter, 2003: 234).

And yet, as Porter went on to argue, the weaknesses of this strategy were manifest. Official republican theory was that the 'dynamic operation of all-Ireland structures' (McGuinness, 1998: 14) underpinned by closer, all-island economic integration, the empowerment of nationalist culture and identity through the equality agenda, and a growing nationalist population in the North would gradually dissolve the Irish border and detach the six counties from the United Kingdom. In reality, none of these processes would necessarily lead in that direction at all. The all-Ireland structures had a very limited remit and no inherent 'dynamic' of expansion. There was no reason to believe there was an intrinsic link between economic integration and political union. The equality agenda would empower nationalists but it would do so within Northern Ireland. And, while the Northern Catholic population was growing, the number of people desiring a united Ireland remained small. Indeed, in the 2013 Northern Ireland Life and Times Survey, only 15 per cent of respondents thought a united Ireland to be the 'best long term policy' for the North, and just 28 per cent of Catholics (ARK, 2014). The critical ingredient in the transition, said Sinn Féin, would be its own ever-increasing political strength on both sides of the border, and this aspect of the party's programme *was* realistic. But the degree of that electoral growth and how exactly political strength would catalyse tangible constitutional change in Ireland were again unclear (Porter, 2003: 237–40; Bean, 2007: 174–216).

It must be said that events since 1998 have not lent republican arguments any more weight than they had in 1998. The third reading – reform leading to unity – continues to be Sinn Féin's presumably sincerely held understanding of its own strategy, but in the absence of evidence that Sinn Féin actually is bringing an all-Ireland state closer to reality, the first reading looks the most serviceable: Sinn Féin has become a constitutional nationalist party seeking, like the SDLP, to advance the status of Northern Catholics within Northern Ireland, with Irish unity greatly valued but far from reach. That said, Sinn Féin is not impatient, nor unaware that it may be a very long time before its strategy bears fruit. Mitchel McLaughlin explains:

> The Union will be dealt with by an agreed formula which is that at some stage we're going to hold a border referendum and if the verdict of a border referendum is that there's going to be no change to the status quo because we didn't convince enough people, we will accept and respect that outcome. So you're not going to hear us talking about the border referendum for a further seven years because that's the formula that's in the Agreement. And at some stage we believe we are going to win such a referendum. Now if that means we have to wait for a second referendum or we have to wait for a third referendum which would take you into a generation then we will accept and respect the judgement of citizens, of unionists and nationalists, who vote in such a referendum here. So that's our democratic credentials. And we're saying to the unionists, would you accept the outcome if the outcome says there's going to be a united Ireland? And we don't get an answer.
> (Interview with Mitchel McLaughlin MLA, 4 October 2012)

It is interesting to note in passing that, although this view sounds eminently reasonable and unthreatening, it is precisely the perceived inexhaustible patience of republicans, captured in these comments, that some unionists have feared, and continue to fear. According to Gregory Campbell:

> What all the commentators agree about Sinn Féin is that they play the long game … Everybody agrees the long haul is what they're in it for. They don't look at tomorrow or next month or next year. They look at it a generation from now. As they see it, when we're dealing with 800 years, what's the next twenty years? Nothing. That fundamental change that they agreed ten or twelve years ago, they're looking at that as a cog in the wheel towards trying to reassure unionists that things will be better in the new Ireland. We'll not shoot you anymore. As long as everybody bears that in mind, knows that that's what they're about.
> (Interview with Gregory Campbell MP MLA, 7 September 2012)

In any case, in 1998, the idea that the Agreement *could* be transitional to a united Ireland united the vast bulk of the Provisional republican movement. Pro-Agreement unionists, of course, did not believe a transition to Irish unity was probable, nor did republican 'dissidents' – those who had split from the IRA and Sinn Féin in 1997 on the latter's acceptance of the Mitchell principles of non-violence. And it is likely that many mainstream republicans also doubted the arguments but acquiesced out of a sense of their own political weakness and limited options, or exhaustion with war.

However, it was the self-confidence of Sinn Féin that came to be one of the defining features of the post-Agreement period. The party approached the implementation process *as if it would be* transitional to a united Ireland, *as if it were* a vehicle for the achievement of solely nationalist and republican goals. This was 'the abandonment of traditional aims, carried off with considerable swagger' (O'Connor, 2002: 56); Adams 'tells it as if he is confident they will applaud, and they do' (p. 57). It was this swaggering gait that helped Sinn Féin achieve the electoral successes that it did and proved to be an unfailing source of annoyance within unionism. Indeed, in the logic of the security dilemma, anti-Agreement unionists, unable to see past the exterior of republican pleasure at participating in constitutional politics and understanding this as spelling defeat for them, lent credibility to Sinn Féin's arguments and were thus unwitting collaborators in republican reinvention. Yet in republican discourse, the dynamic for change was not most often described as being in the direction of a united Irish republic. Rather, the goal was equality.

Equality: the route to Irish unity

In virtually all aspects of Sinn Féin policy – education, health, housing, employment, culture, policing – equality was the overriding value; it was the party's 'meta-discourse' (McGovern, 2004: 623). Contemporary republicans can justifiably claim, as they do, that equality has been an important pillar of republicanism since the United Irishmen. But prior to the peace process, the predominant concern at all times was the demand for self-determination, popular sovereignty and national independence. To recall the view of equality contained in *Towards a Peace Strategy*: 'Even optimum loyalist tolerance will not permit equality. Equality is synonymous with national rights. Partition is in direct contradiction to that' (Sinn Féin, 1988: 10). On the surface, the Sinn Féin of the peace process appeared to have abandoned that position but a closer examination shows how Sinn Féin continued to equate equality with national rights – the difference was that in the new republican transitional strategy, they would come in a different order. Previously, ending partition was regarded as a prerequisite of equality; now, equality was viewed as the active agent that would gradually erode partition. This was partly based on the traditional republican analysis that partition was designed to prop up Protestant advantage:

> The achievement of equality of treatment for nationalists in the north will erode the very reason for the existence of this statelet. Unionists traditionally support the union

> because it enables them to be top of the heap here. A level playing field will make this impossible and much of unionism will be left without any rational basis.
>
> (Adams, 2003: 300)

Unionist leaders knew this, said Adams, which explained their attempts to prevent the implementation of change under the Agreement (Adams, 2001a). True equality will mean that the chief expression of inequality – the partition of Ireland for the benefit of the unionists, a minority – will have to go, and so for republicans, 'The equality agenda is the way to make the transitional mechanism of the Agreement start its work' (McGovern, 2004: 636). That agenda was to bring Irish/nationalist/Catholic culture, people and political analysis to every sphere of public life in Northern Ireland, and justify it on the basis of the parity of esteem principles in the Agreement. This vision of equality extended beyond individual and cultural equality to *political* equality for Irish nationalism, which, if realised, would end the exclusively British character and status of Northern Ireland. Accordingly, Sinn Féin pledged to 'not rest until we have built a United Ireland of equals' (Sinn Féin, 2007: 3).

Central to the republican worldview was the belief that the relative disadvantage of the Northern Catholic community was a direct result of decades of systematic unionist discrimination, which the British Government had failed to rectify throughout twenty-five years of Direct Rule. The suggestion that a 'level playing field' had been established since the end of Stormont rule in 1972 was patently wrong (Adams, 2001a); for their part, unionists argued that *they* had been disadvantaged during that period. The British Government had of course enacted a series of measures throughout Direct Rule aimed at redressing the disparity between Catholics and Protestants in a number of areas – for example, the Fair Employment Agency (1976), its successor the Fair Employment Commission (1989) and the Policy Appraisal and Fair Treatment (1994) initiative designed to 'equality proof' policy. These measures were partly calculated to stymie public support for Sinn Féin and the IRA and address the more limited demands of moderate nationalism. The Good Friday Agreement advanced this British equality agenda through new legislation and bodies. Sinn Féin's equality programme converged with this essentially British agenda, but entailed harnessing and exploiting it to the maximum benefit of republicans. There is, then, considerable irony in the fact that republicans became such enthusiastic proponents of equality reform within Northern Ireland given that such an agenda had been pursued by the British to undermine them. This was an indicator of the extent to which Sinn Féin had, through involvement in the peace process, been pulled back towards the outlook of mainstream, constitutional nationalism.

The creation of social and economic equality dominated Sinn Féin's post-Agreement election promises: the party pledged to campaign for more powers for the Human Rights and Equality Commissions, targets for the elimination in the employment differential between Protestants and Catholics, more powerful anti-discrimination legislation, targeted economic development for disadvantaged areas and the entrenchment of the highest human rights standards throughout the justice system (Sinn Féin, 2001, 2003). Beyond this, Sinn Féin's equality agenda encompassed a range of concerns that were more distinctly 'green' in character. These included equality of treatment for the Irish language and the right to 'provisions for the expression of nationalist and republican sentiments in the display of monuments and symbols that command civic space in public areas, buildings, towns and city centres in equal measure to those of unionism' (Sinn Féin, 2001).

Flags and symbols were of course among the most contentious aspects of post-Agreement Northern Ireland, and the site of one of the most contentious applications of equality by Sinn Féin. The 2012 Belfast City Hall flag dispute, stimulated by a Sinn Féin-led attempt to remove the Union flag from the building, had a long post-Agreement lineage. During the first period of devolution after 1999, unionists were incensed when Sinn Féin ministers refused to fly the Union flag from their departmental headquarters unless the tricolour appeared alongside. The controversy led to British Secretary of State for Northern Ireland Peter Mandelson's introduction of The Flags (Northern Ireland) Order 2000, which provided for the flying of the Union flag from public buildings on designated days. Sinn Féin challenged this in the courts, arguing that it contravened the Agreement, but the judgment found that designated days was a reasonable compromise position (Bryan and McIntosh, 2007). Sinn Féin also pushed for a display of Easter lilies with an accompanying eulogy in the hall of Stormont in 2001 to commemorate the Easter Rising. After heated debate a compromise was reached that would allow the flowers without the eulogy (McCall, 2006: 312).

On symbols, Sinn Féin shared the SDLP's analysis that the principle of parity of esteem for both unionist and nationalist identities should override the 'normal' expression of British sovereignty. The party's position on flags was that under no circumstances should the Union flag be flown by itself, the Irish tricolour should be given equal prominence and if this could not be agreed upon then no flag should be flown (Brown and Mac Ginty, 2003: 90). That said, the party softened this policy in December 2012 when it voted for the Alliance amendment that would see the flag flown from the City Hall on designated days, although this was not indicative of a general party policy. In 2002, the first Sinn Féin Mayor of Belfast, Alex Maskey, chose to lay a laurel as opposed to a poppy wreath two hours before the official Remembrance Day commemoration at Belfast City Hall, a gesture that, significantly, was variously interpreted – by most as an important concession to unionist sensibilities but by some as yet more provocative 'greening' of public life (McCaffrey, 2003). Máirtín Ó'Muilleoir, Sinn Féin Mayor in 2013–14, who was widely acclaimed for reaching out to all sections of society in Belfast during his tenure, attended the Armistice Day commemoration with his Democratic Unionist Party (DUP) deputy and British Legion officials but was out of the country on Remembrance Sunday (*Belfast Telegraph*, 2013).

The other vexed arena of cultural conflict in which Sinn Féin vigorously involved itself was the parading issue. Republicans have regarded Orange parades simply as 'expressions of unionist domination over nationalists' and marches through nationalist areas as causing residents 'to endure the status of second class citizens' (Sinn Féin, 1996). Sinn Féin's strident advocacy on behalf of residents was consistent with its ideological outlook, yet also had a political pay-off. Contentious unionist parades – which have enjoyed little sympathy at all within the Catholic community – offered Sinn Féin the chance to play the role of engaged street activists, standing for and with the 'besieged' people on the ground, thus assisting the party in its image contest with the less confrontational SDLP. In June 2013, Gerry Kelly, Sinn Féin MLA for North Belfast and Policing Board member, was shown in a widely reported YouTube video being carried for a short distance on the bonnet of a police Land Rover. He was apparently trying to stop the vehicle in search of a sixteen-year-old boy who had been arrested for rioting in relation to a contentious parade (*An Phoblacht*/Sinn Féin TV, 2013). It was a revealing video, not simply because it showed the tensions on the ground or the actions of Kelly and the police. It unwittingly dramatised the contrast between Sinn Féin and the SDLP, for the latter's MLA for the area, Alban Maginness, was in the video too, standing quietly beside Kelly as he angrily remonstrated with the police officer in charge. Both parties were present, both engaged with the situation, yet Sinn Féin was literally shouting louder, providing the more combative and visible advocacy.

Policing was of course a highly charged issue for republicans, and equality was offered as the undergirding principle of Sinn Féin's post-Agreement approach. The party had consistently called for the disbandment of the RUC, viewing it as a political police force incapable of carrying out its duties impartially. As the 'armed wing of unionism' charged with the defence of an illegitimate state, it was 'members of the nationalist community who have overwhelmingly suffered ill-treatment in detention centres, had family members or neighbours killed in disputed circumstances, experienced streets and homes sealed off and attacked in dawn raids, and witnessed children harassed, injured and killed by the RUC' (Sinn Féin, 1999). Disbandment, however, was not what was delivered. The Patten Commission, set up under the Agreement to advise on the creation of a policing service acceptable to both communities, made 175 recommendations of change. Among the highlights were: the setting up of a Policing Board consisting of politicians and civil society representatives that would hold the police service and the Chief Constable to account; new recruitment procedures to ensure sufficient cross-community representation; various measures to improve transparency and the changing of the name and symbols (Independent Commission on Policing for Northern Ireland, 1999). While the reforms did not amount to disbandment, they were more far-reaching than Sinn Féin expected from a British-appointed commission headed by a former Conservative cabinet minister (Maillot, 2005: 69). Sinn Féin praised Patten's emphasis on a human rights culture and community policing, but was concerned that the extent and pace of change would not be great enough (Sinn Féin, 1999).

Like the Agreement itself, the Patten proposals were regarded by Sinn Féin as 'a basis for advancement', a starting point from which to fight for more gains through negotiations. The Policing Bill of May 2000 that would implement the police reforms was regarded by both nationalist parties as being a watered-down version of the Patten recommendations. The Revised Implementation Plan, hammered out at Weston Park in July 2001, was still not enough to satisfy Sinn Féin; the SDLP subsequently gave its support to the police. Outstanding republican demands included the creation of an unarmed police force, the banning of plastic bullets, inquiries into collusion between the security forces and loyalist paramilitaries and, crucially, the devolution of policing and justice powers to the Northern Ireland Assembly (Sinn Féin, 2003). Although there were clear ideological reasons for Sinn Féin to take a hard line on policing, delaying support for the Police Service of Northern Ireland (PSNI) also served to distance the party from the SDLP and contribute to Sinn Féin's tougher image (Frampton, 2009: 128–9). When Sinn Féin eventually voted to support the PSNI in January 2007 as part of the series of moves that led to the restoration of devolution in May of that year, the party's demands were not met, notably the devolution of policing and justice powers; this was largely due to the overwhelming pressure exerted on Sinn Féin in 2005–6 by the British, Irish and American Governments. Nevertheless, Sinn Féin leaders portrayed this historic vote (over 90 per cent in favour) as a tactical move that would advance a united Ireland and as one that would bring equality for republicans in relation to policing (Bowcott, 2007).

Another significant instance of republican recourse to equality was Sinn Féin's defence of its inclusion in the political institutions. Unionist attempts to block republicans from the Executive and the NSMC were condemned by Sinn Féin as slights on the rights and dignity of the party and its voters. According to the party, the Agreement depended upon the delivery of equality and an ending of the unionist veto (McLaughlin, 1999). The suggestion was that the ability of unionists to frustrate the political advance of nationalism by preventing devolution was a fundamental attack on the universal principle of equality, rather than simply a tactic in a more localised dispute – decommissioning. At a press conference following David Trimble's attempts to exclude Sinn Féin ministers from North–South meetings, the issue for Martin McGuinness was not decommissioning but equality. The Ulster Unionist Party (UUP) leader was trying to

> treat Sinn Féin ministers as second class ministers; treat Sinn Féin as a second class party; and treat our electorate as second-class citizens … We will not allow David Trimble or anyone else to treat us as anything other than equals … Be under no illusion whatsoever this is not about decommissioning … this is about people who are refusing to accept equality, refusing power-sharing and the critically important all-Ireland dimension to this process.

McGuinness regarded the UUP's action as evidence of the persistent chauvinism of unionism and he warned that it would drag Northern Ireland 'back to the bad old days' (quoted in Graham, 2000).

How successful was Sinn Féin's equality discourse and campaigning? In terms of actually enhancing equality and rights protections, it is difficult to judge what credit should be given specifically to Sinn Féin given that the equality agenda was supported by the SDLP, British and Irish Governments and others. In terms of bringing a united Ireland closer, it is difficult to identify unambiguous steps forward. The main achievement of the equality discourse was in refashioning Sinn Féin's persona for the peace process era and beyond, and the success of that was evident in its post-Agreement electoral growth. There were four reasons why equality was such a powerful message in this regard. First, it provided a rhetorical arsenal through which to portray the Good Friday Agreement as potentially transitional to a united Ireland, thus assisting in the transition of republicanism from war to peace. Equality provided 'acceptable' ground on which to fight unionism and continue the struggle for Catholic-nationalist rights and for Irish unity. Second, making much of equality served the propaganda function of retrospectively beautifying the IRA's campaign of violence, suggesting that it had been the righteous struggle of a people suffering under the yoke of inequality rather than, as widely viewed, an anti-democratic nationalist insurrection.

Third, it resonated with the outlook of much of the Northern Catholic community. Sinn Féin's demands for equality spoke to the traditional nationalist image of unionism as intrinsically supremacist and fed the nationalist suspicion that unionists wished to perpetuate inequality in their own favour. This was what Aughey called nationalists' 'anxiety of frustration' – the worry that 'unionist politics was defined by an ideological inability to trade supremacy for parity of esteem', that unionists, by their very nature, were compelled to undermine nationalist empowerment with its accompanying loss of unionist privilege (Aughey, 2005: 135). The Sinn Féin discourse of ongoing progress towards equality chimed with the climate within nationalist political culture in which expectations and confidence were rising (Mitchell, 2003; Mac Ginty, 2006a: 135). Fourth, the equality discourse broadened Sinn Féin's appeal by marrying the local and the universal. Equality was presented by Sinn Féin as both an agenda of the Catholic community and as a universal value that everyone – including unionists and socially excluded groups – should get behind. This is not to say that many unionists were won over by Sinn Féin's appeal to equality but to highlight that equality offered a way for Sinn Féin to craft a message that might serve its aims of electoral expansion North and South, and of persuading unionists towards a united Ireland, aims so fundamental to its pursuit of Irish unity.

'Sinn Féin/IRA'

Despite Sinn Féin's enthusiasm for equality, one dimension of the party put it on a very unequal footing vis-à-vis the other main parties: its association with the IRA. The peace process of the 1990s was predicated on the inclusion of the paramilitary-linked parties, with Sinn Féin being by far the most politically significant of these. As a result, 'debating the sincerity of Provisionalism's conversion to constitutional politics has been the central issue of Northern Irish politics for the last seventeen years' (Bean, 2007: 218). The republican movement navigated the hoops and hurdles of the peace process by choreographing a separation between Sinn Féin and the IRA, the intended impression being that the former was a democratically mandated party committed to constitutional politics, while the latter remained an armed revolutionary organisation, watching, not participating in, the political developments. Misleading as this separation was, it did create enough ambiguity for the British and Irish Governments to include Sinn Féin in the peace process in the hope of ending republican violence for good. Unionists, particularly those who opposed the peace process, pilloried the idea that Sinn Féin and the IRA were separate, and showed this disdain through their liberal use of the moniker 'Sinn Féin/IRA'. Yet, gradually, the IRA did reduce its military capability sufficiently to convince unionists – then in the shape of the DUP – that Sinn Féin's path away from violence was genuine and irreversible. In the rest of this section, we explore the political significance of the IRA after 1998, for Sinn Féin and for the implementation of the Agreement.

As we have seen, it was clear in April 1998 that the decommissioning of IRA weapons would be one of the major stumbling blocks to the success of the Agreement. When, during the first ceasefire, the calls began from the British Government that some weapons should be handed in prior to Sinn Féin entering negotiations, republicans rubbished the idea as an artificial barrier thrown up to prevaricate on addressing republican demands. Nonetheless, with the acquiescence of the new Labour Government in London, Sinn Féin was permitted to initially join and eventually conclude the talks without the IRA surrendering any weapons. Despite unionist efforts to include in the Agreement a stipulation that decommissioning must occur before paramilitary-linked parties could sit in the Executive, the issue was fudged, and unionists placed their faith in the British Government to enforce the linkage. The IRA's response to the Agreement raised the temperature of the issue further. 'There appears to be yet another attempt to resurrect the (arms) decommissioning issue as an obstacle to progress', said its statement of 30 April 1998. 'Let us make clear that there will be no decommissioning by the IRA.' Nevertheless, the statement said it was monitoring developments closely and 'We wish Sinn Féin further success in the development of its peace strategy' (BBC, 1998).

Throughout the post-Agreement years, Sinn Féin was emphatic that the decommissioning of weapons was an integral part of the peace process and the creation of a normalised society. The party consistently claimed to be complying with the Agreement's requirement that parties should 'use any influence they may have' to achieve paramilitary disarmament. However, republicans resented the focus on IRA arms and argued that 'taking the gun out of Irish politics' must involve the removal of weapons in the hands of the police and British Army, the loyalists and the 'thousands of licensed guns in the possession of the unionist population' (McLaughlin, 2000). The argument that IRA weapons were of greatest importance because Sinn Féin was the only paramilitary-linked party of sufficient strength to be entitled to Executive seats did not deter Sinn Féin from contesting that it was a non-issue concocted by unionists for their reactionary ends. As McLaughlin (2000) argued, the claim that the IRA should hurry up and disarm and help Trimble out of his party difficulties was spurious since hard-line unionists would simply proclaim their opposition to some other aspect of the Agreement and the process. The silence of republican guns should be enough for unionists; the UUP's tactics of post-dated letters, deadlines and penalising Sinn Féin ministers (see Chapter 2) were gratuitous attempts to force humiliation and defeat on the IRA and were evidence of opposition to the Agreement's entire process of change. Continuing loyalist attacks on Catholics were also held up by Sinn Féin representatives as a significant disincentive for the IRA to disarm.

Indeed, Sinn Féin regularly protested that, rather than pressure or opprobrium, the IRA actually deserved congratulation. The peace process was described by the party as being the result of 'unilateral initiatives' by the IRA – the ceasefires, engaging with the decommissioning commission, actual decommissioning – which each took tremendous bravery and effort. 'There would be no peace process if it were not for the IRA', declared Adams without irony (cited in Maillot, 2005: 85). Understanding was sought for the IRA position and the emotional and symbolic magnitude of the task of decommissioning. Disarmament, said the party, would likely follow the creation of the right 'political conditions' or 'the removal of the causes of conflict'. When the institutions were under unionist threat, the party pointed out that collapsing the process would only make decommissioning far less likely (see, for example, Adams, 2000). McGuinness suggested that the failure of the British Government to fulfil its commitments on police reform and demilitarisation was putting the IRA off engaging with the Independent International Commission on Decommissioning (IICD): 'in this type of conflict resolution process, if one side is resiling on commitments made it is going to create difficulty' (quoted in Graham, 2000). The implication at all times was that the IRA could be enticed to disarm if certain demands – Sinn Féin's – were met.

In this respect, Sinn Féin's outlook on decommissioning was the precise converse of that of the UUP. In fact, that the strategies were identical was spelled out by the UUP's Dermot Nesbitt: 'They say we are introducing a precondition by saying "no guns, no government" but we could say their precondition was "no government, no guns"' (quoted in White, 1999). Chapter 2 noted the UUP's categorisation of Agreement issues as 'evolutionary' – those such as the setting up of the institutions that required implementation in a prolonged, negotiated process – and 'non-evolutionary' – those, including decommissioning, which had no barrier to their immediate implementation. Adams provided a similar but opposing categorisation of his own: there existed in the Agreement 'addressed' and 'resolved' issues. Addressed issues were ones not settled in the negotiations, but which were deferred to be resolved at a later date through agreed mechanisms. These issues included 'human rights, policing, justice, equality in all its dimensions, decommissioning and the demilitarisation of society'. These were all key issues that needed resolution, but for any of them to be made a precondition for the implementation of matters that were resolved – the institutional arrangements – was a violation of the Agreement (Adams, 1999).

The IRA served a twofold political purpose for Sinn Féin: one in relation to the party's opponents and one in relation to its supporters. Regarding opponents, given that Sinn Féin's strategy was centred on permanent negotiation, the IRA was a considerable bargaining asset; indeed, the peace process has been called 'a long-drawn-out auction of the IRA as a going concern' (Bean, 2007: 113). By giving so little at each stage – a commitment to meet the IICD here, a token act of disarmament there – the IRA ensured three things: first, that Sinn Féin returned again and again to the negotiating table to seek and often receive more concessions from the Governments; second, that opinion within unionism was destabilised; and third, that Sinn Féin enjoyed publicity and prominence at the expense of its main rival, the SDLP. Paraphrasing Sinn Féin's previous strategy of the 'tactical use of armed struggle', Frampton (2009: 151) notes that, post-Agreement, it became a case of the 'tactical use of the IRA'. The IRA and its mostly silent arsenal continued to fulfil the function that its violent campaign had for decades – that of 'armed propaganda', designed to keep the constitutional issue in the foreground and remind its opponents that it was a live problem requiring resolution (on this rationale for the armed struggle, see O'Doherty, 1998: 98–9).

In addition to serving a political purpose in relation to opponents, the IRA also fulfilled an ideological role within republicanism. Like the equality discourse, the IRA's lingering presence oiled the republican movement's transition out of violence by lending Sinn Féin its militant credentials and ideological credibility (Bean, 2007: 128). Thus, while Sinn Féin's involvement in negotiations and the devolved institutions indicated change, the IRA's survival indicated continuity, and so as well as intimidating political opponents, the IRA functioned to reassure the republican grass roots as the movement headed further from its prior path and deeper into constitutional politics. The IRA's extended farewell, through its series of contacts with the IICD from 2000 to 2005, helped acclimatise republican supporters to their movement's new modus operandi and showed them that their leadership was not going to sell off the IRA too cheaply, nor permit the appearance of IRA defeat. And in this way, the Sinn Féin–IRA double act helped sustain the republican movement's unity, speaking to both radical and moderate wings of its constituency and neutralising the potential for the emergence of a clearly defined republican alternative (Mac Ginty, 2006a: 132–3). When asked why the IRA did not simply decommission soon after the Agreement, McLaughlin replies:

> It would have destroyed our [Sinn Féin's] credibility. It would have harmed our influence which was significant. If you wanted a peace process, if you wanted to end the conflict, there was no point in destroying or damaging us [the Sinn Féin leadership]. And that's what would have happened. In terms of the grassroots. We had to deliver the IRA and we had to do it on the basis of political products.
> (Interview with Mitchel McLaughlin MLA, 4 October 2012)

This comment captures the overlapping purposes of the IRA and its weapons: as power in negotiations and as comfort to the movement. However, it is important to note that the precise balance of opinion within republicanism is unclear, and thus also *how* necessary the IRA and its weapons were to republican reassurance. For instance, in Jonathan Powell's (2008) account of talks with Sinn Féin, Adams and McGuinness regularly tell the British of the pressure they are under from unhappy elements, and Powell and Blair appear to have accepted this. Yet others, including Moloney (2007: 520–1) and Clancy (2010: 175–9), argue that after the Agreement, rather than having their hands tied, Adams and McGuinness were actually in comfortable control over the movement. This suggests that, at the very least, the spectre of splits was exaggerated by Sinn Féin in order to extract maximum negotiating value from the IRA.

It is worth highlighting some examples of how the party skilfully drew legitimacy for its peace process strategy by framing its activities in terms of the republican historical narrative, a narrative in which violence and the IRA predominated. One example was a speech Adams made on 1 January 2007, at the commemoration of the fiftieth anniversary of a failed IRA attack on Brookeborough police station in which two IRA men died. 'The Brookeborough raid', Adams told the crowd, 'was risky. Struggle of any kind is risky. We should remember that those who want to maximise change must be prepared to take the greatest risk' (Adams, 2007). The words were unremarkable but for their political context: the mounting pressure on Sinn Féin to support the PSNI in the wake of the St Andrews Agreement. Thus, Adams pulled off the feat of enjoining the republican grass roots to get behind the party's likely endorsement of the police by means of lauding the bravery of an IRA attack on the police. In a rhetorical sleight of hand, Adams cloaked the contradictions, revealing to his audience only an ongoing republican story of 'struggle' and 'risk'.

A similar instance was Adams' speech on the occasion of another important move by republicanism, the first act of decommissioning in October 2001. He began by setting his remarks firmly in the republican narrative. The venue was Conway Mill in the heart of West Belfast, which, said Adams, 'bore the brunt of an RUC and B Special led pogrom in 1969 against Catholics across this city … Seven people were killed and thousands of families fled the unionist mobs in what was, at that time, the biggest forced movement of civilians in Western Europe since the end of the last world war'. He also affirmed the traditional republican worldview: 'Irish republicans hold that the British connection is the source of all our political ills. The British government has inflicted and continues to sustain historic wrongs on the people of this island.' But the point of the speech was to prepare the way for the announcement by the IICD that the IRA had put a portion of its weapons beyond use, moving into yet another republican ideological no-go area. The statesmanlike air of the Sinn Féin president also helped airbrush the embarrassing context of the events: the arrest of the three republicans in Colombia and the fresh international consensus against terrorism in the wake of 9/11. The Sinn Féin leadership, said Adams, had 'put the view' to the IRA that this was the time to make a move on weapons to 'save the Good Friday Agreement' (Adams, 2001b). As Arthur commented, the speech was an example of the by then familiar capacity of Sinn Féin to revise and reinvent: the speech 'cast republicans in the role of victims *and* as major players on the international stage ... What could have been interpreted as a humiliating climb-down was sold as a piece of magnanimity' (Arthur, 2002: 84–5).

Regardless of the extent of Adams' and McGuinness's party management challenges, the opacity of Sinn Féin's internal workings – in contrast to unionists' very public deliberations – contributed to unionists' lack of sympathy for the Sinn Féin leadership's task of maintaining republican unity. For many unionists, tugged by fatalism, the 'tactical use of the IRA' was a clear demonstration that the republicanism of the peace process was little different from the republicanism of the 'Troubles'. The idea that the IRA and Sinn Féin were separate was viewed as deliberate deceit; Sinn Féin and the IRA were a single entity, two faces of one coin that should be referred to as 'Sinn Féin/IRA'. The sting in this label was not actually its suggestion that the IRA and Sinn Féin were ideologically one and the same, or even that they had shared membership. Rather, the real intended purpose of 'Sinn Féin/IRA' was to convey the speakers' belief that Sinn Féin and the IRA retained a strategic unity, with each face of republicanism assuming a role – one military, one political – and giving a combined and choreographed performance aimed at furthering the overarching republican objective of destroying Northern Ireland. In this view, Sinn Féin claiming that it was seeking to persuade the IRA of the importance of decommissioning, or the IRA pledging its support for Sinn Féin, was mere play-acting. By referring to 'Sinn Féin/IRA' one rejected the idea that republicanism was on a path towards constitutional politics and that the IRA (terrorists) were separate from, or had been 'converted' into, Sinn Féin (democrats). That did not mean that those who avoided referring to 'Sinn Féin/IRA', such as the Governments, accepted the republican conceit of separate groupings. But they hoped that rhetorically separating the two organisations might encourage their gradual, actual separation.

As Chapter 2 described, the unionist fear was that Sinn Féin sought to use its privilege of having a 'private army' to both prop up its power in nationalist areas through intimidation and boost its leverage in negotiations with the Governments. This fear hardened unionist attitudes and it was far from ungrounded. For example, the first Independent Monitoring Commission (IMC) report in April 2004, a full ten years after the first IRA ceasefire, stated that the group

> maintains itself in a state of readiness, and possesses the range of necessary skills, whereby it could revert to much more widespread violence were the decision taken

that it should do so. In addition to its involvement in other criminal activities, PIRA is engaged in the use of serious violence which we believe is under the control of its most senior leadership, whose members must therefore bear responsibility for it.

(IMC, 2004: 17)

Between 1998 and 2005, the IRA was chief suspect in no fewer than thirty murders (Frampton, 2009: 164). Other activity credibly attributed to the group included spying at Stormont, stealing intelligence from Castlereagh police station, training Colombian 'narcoterrorists', smuggling weapons from Florida and extensive organised criminal activity. The killing of Robert McCartney in 2005 and subsequent cover-up, plus the Northern Bank heist in late 2004, brought the long-standing, mafia-style dimensions of the IRA to world attention. All the while, Sinn Féin and the IRA were known to have interlocking leaderships. According to the IMC, 'Some members, including some senior members, of Sinn Féin are also members, including, in some cases, senior members of PIRA' (IMC, 2004: 34). This was widely believed to include Adams and McGuinness (Moloney, 2007). Furthermore, Sinn Féin continued to commemorate and celebrate republicans' use of violence in recent and more distant history. It was not surprising, then, that Sinn Féin denials of, or excuses for, the IRA's activity had little credibility with unionists.

In July 2005, the IRA announced the formal end of its armed campaign and stated that it was engaging with the IICD to put its arms completely and verifiably beyond use. The statement indicated that the decision had come after an extensive internal consultation process that showed 'very strong support among IRA volunteers for the Sinn Féin peace strategy' and it was taken 'to advance our republican and democratic objectives, including our goal of a united Ireland' (quoted in BBC, 2005b). The context for this was the failure of the talks with the DUP in December 2004 and the Northern Bank robbery and McCartney murder soon after. Following the latter two incidents, the weight of domestic and international expectation fell squarely on republicans rather than unionists; the brazenness of the IRA only appeared to vindicate the DUP in not accepting a deal. A tipping point, always inevitable, had been reached in which the IRA had become more handicap than asset to Sinn Féin's political and electoral progress.

The electoral struggle

Electoral growth was essential to the party's gradualist strategy towards Irish unity. With a strong electoral mandate, Sinn Féin believed it could build a dynamic towards Irish unity with the power to turn a new political dispensation – consisting of arrangements falling far short of all-Ireland sovereignty – into a transitional phase to reunification. Outlining his vision for a transitional phase at the 1998 conference, Gerry Adams implored the party to keep building political strength 'because it is by building that strength that we will build the capacity to move both the British government and the unionists' (Adams, 1998b). As noted above, Sinn Féin was aware of its political weakness at the time of the Agreement. McLaughlin comments: 'I think the idea [of inclusivity] was to imprison us within the process as opposed to make us partners, and our view of that was that fair enough, we just have to get stronger' (interview with Mitchel McLaughlin MLA, 4 October 2012). The IRA had failed to end British rule in Ireland, and a minor political party was not going to do it; hence, the urgency and centrality of vote-winning to the new 'phase of struggle'. Legitimising republican activism on the basis of the party's electoral support was a profound new departure for Sinn Féin. Prior to the peace process, republicans had looked to the old Sinn Féin's victory in the 1918 general election as providing all the legitimacy the armed struggle needed. Now, the 'yes' vote in the Agreement referenda and Sinn Féin's support in the various elections that it contested were described as 'mandates for change', while at the same time, Sinn Féin recognised the imperative of persuading the unionists.

The history of Sinn Féin's electoral expansion is as remarkable as it is well known. By the early 1980s, it was clear to the IRA that its military campaign alone was unlikely to force a British withdrawal, while the election of three Hunger Strikers – one to Westminster and two to the Dáil – demonstrated how public sympathy for the republican cause could be converted into votes. In 1983, Gerry Adams was elected to Westminster. His generation of republican leaders knew that their policy of abstaining from taking seats in elected assemblies stood to curtail the impact of the 'ballot paper and armalite' strategy, and, accordingly, that policy was ended in 1986, precipitating the walkout of some traditionalists who subsequently formed Republican Sinn Féin. Throughout the 1980s and early 1990s, Sinn Féin's vote remained static at around 10 per cent, roughly half of the SDLP vote. This represented the core, 'all-weather' republican constituency, with public revulsion at IRA activities apparently putting a cap on Sinn Féin's electoral support. However, the 1996 election to the Northern Ireland Forum saw Sinn Féin's vote jump to 15.5 per cent, and a further growth in the 1998 Assembly election to 17.6 per cent. As noted before, Sinn Féin's growth was initially driven by attracting new Catholic additions to the electoral register and mobilising previous non-voters, rather than eating into its rival's share (McAllister, 2004). But that trend was not to continue after the Agreement, with the traffic of votes being mostly one way from the SDLP to Sinn Féin. In the 2011 Assembly election, Sinn Féin took 26.9 per cent of the vote to the SDLP's 14.2 per cent.

Reasons for Sinn Féin's success in the electoral struggle with the SDLP were discussed in the previous chapter. Ideologically, Sinn Féin came to closely resemble the SDLP – nationalist, eschewing violence for the most part, championing rights and equality, and often sounding magnanimous towards unionists. This more electable political orientation was combined with a range of organisational, structural and communication advantages over the SDLP, including a large number of dedicated activists and significant sums of money. An analysis of republican communication and public relations activities throughout the 'Troubles' concluded that the Sinn Féin leadership's skills in this domain were key to both its contemporary political successes and internal cohesion (Somerville and Purcell, 2011). Hume, whose contacts with Adams began in 1988, was well aware of the potential boons for Sinn Féin at the expense of his own party in the event of republicans ending violence. Indeed, the condition of the SDLP, with scant internal vitality, poor community organisation and domination by John Hume and his ideas, was described by Patterson (1997: 288) as a 'standing incitement to republicans with a modicum of political sense' to wind down the long war and concentrate on the political strategy. Republicans' belief that indefinite electoral growth was possible was crucial to their calculation that a peaceful strategy was viable.

Importantly, that potential growth was not restricted to six counties. Sinn Féin's participation in the peace process coincided with considerable efforts, and some successes, to grow in the Republic. The fact that it transcended the border was promoted by Sinn Féin as one of its key selling points. The tenets of 'Sinn Féin is the only all-Ireland party' and 'the Good Friday Agreement is an all-Ireland Agreement' often appeared together, the combination being core post-Agreement doctrine (Sinn Féin, 2001, 2003). The SDLP was derided as parochial in comparison: it 'isn't a nationalist party', said Adams, 'it is a "Northern Ireland" party, a social democratic party. There are nationalists in it – good nationalists in it' (cited in Murray and Tonge, 2005: 228). Sinn Féin won its first seat in the Irish Parliament in 1997, scoring 2.5 per cent of the vote. This rose to 6.5 per cent and five seats in 2002. Particularly high expectation – on the part of Sinn Féin and commentators – attended Sinn Féin's likely performance in the general election of 2007, yet instead of a political insurgency, the party actually lost one seat. However, in 2011, Sinn Féin and other left-leaning oppositional candidates benefited from the high turnout and public disgust with the long-ruling Fianna Fáil Government that had presided over economic implosion while being mired in personal and financial scandals (Galligan, 2011). Sinn Féin won 9.9 per cent of the vote and more than trebled its tally of seats to fourteen. This election saw Gerry Adams, who had resigned his West Belfast Westminster seat, politically parachute into the Republic's Louth constituency where he was elected with ease. Further gains for Sinn Féin were seen in the local and European elections in 2014; in the former, the party gained over 100 seats and became the third biggest party in the country at local level.

Growth in the Republic offered Sinn Féin the tantalising prospect of simultaneously being in government North and South. Yet that prospect posed or re-posed a range of uncomfortable moral, historical and political questions for the people and parties of the Republic. In the early 2000s, commentators pointed out the double standard of Bertie Ahern assiduously working to secure Sinn Féin's place in the power-sharing Executive in Northern Ireland, while making clear that the party was not a fit coalition partner for Fianna Fáil should that prospect ever arise (*The Economist*, 2002). Ahern's Minister for Justice in the mid-2000s, Michael McDowell, was a particularly vociferous critic of Sinn Féin's links with the IRA, yet such criticism was interpreted as indicative of the political establishment's fear of Sinn Féin's growth in the Republic (Frampton, 2009: 140). The military parade that marked the ninetieth anniversary of the Rising in 2006 was regarded by some as an attempt by Fianna Fáil to boost its republican image in the face of Sinn Féin's challenge (Bowcott, 2006). Yet this occasion re-energised the lingering questions of whether there really was any difference between the violence of the old IRA during the revolutionary period and that of the Provisional IRA, and whether there was a double standard in revering the former – as much of the Southern political class did – and condemning the latter.

This issue was among the many that arose in an insightful documentary made for Irish television channel TV3 in 2013, entitled *Sinn Féin: Who Are They?* (TV3, 2013). In the programme, Sinn Féin figures as well as an array of Southern, Northern and British politicians and commentators reflected on the past, present and future of Sinn Féin, particularly in the Republic. At the very least, the programme was a stark demonstration of Sinn Féin's ongoing capacity to arouse deep emotions for and against: its supporters praised the party's advocacy on behalf of the poor and its efforts to bring about peace; its critics ridiculed its economic policies, damned its stifling internal culture and accused it of supporting crime and violence both in Northern Ireland and in the Irish state. In any case, the documentary indicated the widespread interest in a party that was expected to be a permanent and growing fixture in the Republic's political landscape; indeed it came in the wake of one of the most striking examples of Sinn Féin's electoral ambitions – Martin McGuinness's bid for the Irish Presidency in 2011. Throughout the campaign questions followed him about his IRA past, leading to the kinds of confrontations between Sinn Féin spokespeople, and journalists and IRA victims, that were commonplace in the North but more remarkable in the Republic. McGuinness proved to be a serious contender, however, attaining 13.7 per cent of the first preference vote and coming third, though far behind the winner, Michael D. Higgins, who received 39.6 per cent. Of course, had McGuinness been successful, he would still have presided over a partitioned Ireland – the twenty-six county entity that his party had once regarded as just as illegitimate as Northern Ireland. Equally, should Sinn Féin ever be in government in both parts of Ireland simultaneously, such a situation would not necessarily propel progress towards Irish unity due to the perennial obstacles of unionist opposition, British sovereignty in the North and apathy in much of nationalist Ireland. These outcomes would be powerfully symbolic but their substantive impacts negligible, while it is worth remembering that, at least since 2008, Sinn Féin's Southern growth has not been driven forward by irredentist feeling but dissatisfaction with the management of the economy.

Nevertheless, electoral expansion remains central to Sinn Féin's political project. Indeed, while there has been much debate about the precise nature of republicanism's evolution throughout the peace process (ideological change, tactical change, minimal change, or defeat?), it can be argued that one way of characterising Sinn Féin's new orientation is to recognise electoral growth as the single, overriding principle guiding the party to which all others are subordinate. As noted, this is a colossal break with the past given that democratic legitimacy or lack thereof was not something that much worried the movement. However, winning votes means moving to where the voters are as much as it means influencing their preferences. For instance, the decision of McGuinness to join President Higgins at a white-tie dinner at Windsor Castle in April 2014, part of Higgins' historic state visit to the United Kingdom, was likely calculated (as with many of the party's mould-breaking moves) to maintain Sinn Féin's electability in the South and ensure it was in step with the zeitgeist of British–Irish reconciliation. This is part of the wider phenomenon of Sinn Féin being pulled back towards the less radical preferences of the nationalist electorate (see Evans and Tonge, 2013). The finding of the SDLP internal report, mentioned in the previous chapter, that voters struggled to distinguish between the SDLP and Sinn Féin on policy, was as much an indication of Sinn Féin's general retreat towards a moderate nationalist outlook as it was an indication of the SDLP's difficulty in defining itself. As Bourke comments, republicanism, by embracing the peace process and the potential of a pan-nationalist alliance, tried to 'build a nationalist consensus in its own image', but found that, in actuality, it was itself that was transformed through contact with other actors (Bourke, 2003: 172).

Conclusion

The fatalism of 'Troubles'-era Sinn Féin was exhibited in its catastrophically flawed political analysis. It was an analysis that was blind to unionist fears and identity, that dismissed and undermined non-violent Catholic agitation, that prioritised violence in part under the spell of previous violent republican movements and that saw Britain as a straightforward colonial oppressor. It was also an analysis given some credence by British security tactics and unionist bigotry. By the 1990s, republicans had come to a very different outlook. They had learned that violence could not achieve their objectives, that building political strength through electoral growth and forging alliances with other actors was both possible and preferable to war, that Britain's interest in Northern Ireland may not have been as 'selfish and strategic' as once thought, that the reality of unionist identity was something they had to at least face even if they did not fully accept its legitimacy, and that some unity of the peoples of Ireland was required before political union. Accordingly, the party embraced the mitigator logic of the Agreement, though Sinn Féin at times expressed both fatalist militancy and transcender generosity due to the perceived need to speak to different audiences and maintain unity.

Republicans would of course reject the idea that their outlook became more realistic and accommodating over time. They would argue that circumstances made possible a peaceful strategy in the 1990s that was not possible in the 1970s: the initial analysis was correct at the time. Moderates of various shades of opinion, especially those in the SDLP, would disagree. In any case, the tragic irony is that the legacy of fear, hatred, self-righteousness and grievance created by the violent and self-sustaining outworking of the IRA's fatalism actually works against the current Sinn Féin strategy of uniting Ireland by peaceful means. That legacy obviously hamstrings outreach to unionists, while current all-Ireland linkages, whether economic, political or grass-roots, must bridge the gulf between North and South that widened and deepened during the 'Troubles' largely as a result of the actions of the IRA.

Since the Provisional IRA closed itself down in 2005, the state of ambiguity and contradiction that characterised republicanism since its entry into electoral politics, and especially since it accepted the 1998 Agreement, has been largely resolved. However, celebration and justification of past violence on the part of Sinn Féin continues. In 2013, a republican parade through Castlederg in County Tyrone, which commemorated IRA members who were killed by their own bomb that was destined for the town, and the naming of a play park in Newry after a Hunger Striker, caused outcry among unionists. In 2011, a political and media storm erupted over the party's appointment of an individual who was convicted for her part in an IRA murder to a high-paying, publicly funded special advisor post at Stormont. At the same time, an incoherent position on political violence has also been revealed in Sinn Féin's approach to dissident republicans. While mainstream republican condemnation of dissidents' violence has been strong, it has been delivered in terms of that violence's strategic futility, rather than its moral vacuity. This critical distinction is not lost on unionists, or indeed, probably, the dissidents themselves, who are well aware of the tenuousness of the argument that there is a moral difference between a murder before 1998 and one after, simply because Sinn Féin decided that political avenues existed for it after 1998. But this is a premise on which the entire Sinn Féin 'peace strategy' relies. Keeping faith with its militant past in these ways is part of Sinn Féin's efforts to embrace constitutionalism while remaining united, in full 'possession' of the republican tradition and avoiding ceding credibility or votes to any other republican grouping. It would be another irony if the party's refusal to take a more principled and critical perspective on violence actually hampers the pursuit of the goal that virtually all in Northern Ireland, including Sinn Féin, support: that the 'Troubles' never be repeated.

5
Democratic Unionist Party

Introduction

On 12 July 2006, Rev. Ian Paisley, leader of the Democratic Unionist Party (DUP), declared before a crowd of supporters that republicans were 'not fit to be in the government of Northern Ireland and it will be over our dead bodies if they ever get there' (BBC, 2006a). Less than a year later, Paisley took his place as co-premier of Northern Ireland along with Sinn Féin's Martin McGuinness. The remark was typical of Paisley – self-aggrandising, rousing yet reassuring, delivered with life-or-death import. What was more telling than what he said was the nonchalant reaction of other players in the peace process. Gerry Adams said Paisley's comment was 'offensive but unsurprising'. Social Democratic and Labour Party (SDLP) leader Mark Durkan said that regardless of what Paisley claimed, self-interest would eventually lead the DUP and Sinn Féin to form a government together – they both had a 'passion for power' (BBC, 2006a). The degree of ingenuousness with which Paisley made the promise is unclear, yet what is clear is that it was evident at the time that his party – for reasons of ambition and political constraint – was moving away from its past of righteous separation and entering a new era of agreement, responsibility and compromise.

Why and how the DUP managed to accomplish this extraordinary turnaround are the key themes of this chapter. It begins by examining the ideological roots of the party within hard-line unionism and conservative Protestantism. It then discusses the DUP's view of the Agreement as disastrous for the Union and for democracy, and the DUP's approach to post-Agreement politics that indicated a more subtle and equivocal strategy than its absolutist rhetoric implied. The methods used by the DUP to oppose the Agreement from within the new institutions and the content of its fatalist critique of post-Agreement politics – as corrupt and weighted against unionism – are discussed. Then the chapter examines the twin phenomena of the DUP's gathering electoral strength and its growing openness to a power-sharing agreement with Sinn Féin, processes that culminated in the St Andrews Agreement of 2006. The nature of that agreement and how it compared with its 1998 predecessor are examined, before a final section that identifies the consequences, for the party and the political process, of the DUP's historic decision to enter government in 2007.

God, Ulster and fundamentalist politics

Paisley, a conservative Protestant preacher from Ballymena, founded the party in 1971 along with a collection of other loyalist activists disaffected with the Ulster Unionist Party (UUP). Paisley had been associated with a number of ultra-loyalist groups, including the Ulster Constitutional Defence Committee, Ulster Protestant Volunteers and Protestant Unionist Party, which had sprung up to counter the liberal and ecumenical tendencies in mainstream unionism, particularly under the leadership of Prime Minister Terence O'Neill. The DUP persisted as a bitter electoral rival to the UUP, out-living similar movements of dissent, most notably the Vanguard Unionist Party. Throughout most of the party's history it won a minority of unionist support, although in the polarised atmosphere of the Hunger Strikes in 1981, the DUP attained a share of the general election vote 0.1 per cent greater than that of the UUP; Paisley regularly topped the poll in European elections. A measure of pan-unionist co-operation emerged in the aftermath of the 1985 Anglo-Irish Agreement but the 1990s peace process led to the DUP and UUP once more parting ways, with the DUP implacably opposed to the UUP's pragmatic belief that negotiations may actually secure the interests of unionism rather than damage them. The UUP's post-Agreement difficulties, plus increasing pragmatism from the DUP, opened the way for the DUP to defeat the UUP in the November 2003 Assembly election. Like Sinn Féin, its position as the main party within the unionist community, for the time being, seems unassailable.

For most of his career, Paisley was the very embodiment of the fatalist logic: assuming the worst about opponents' intentions, recoiling from contact or compromise, intensifying the security dilemma through an aggressive and ethno-centric approach to politics. And that career and that approach are inexplicable without reference to the particular brand of conservative Christianity to which Paisley passionately adhered. Before calling out the faithful from the ranks of the liberalisers in the temporal realm of politics, he had done the same in Ulster's ecclesiastical scene, founding, in 1951, the Free Presbyterian Church of Ulster (FPCU) in response to what he perceived as increasing apostasy and doctrinal infidelity in the mainstream churches. Those churches, formed out of the Reformation and once faithful to the true religion, were regarded by Paisley as abandoning it in favour of liberalism, ecumenism and materialism, and as unfit to meet the challenge from the greatest threat to true and biblical Christianity: the Roman Catholic Church. And like previous anti-Catholic Ulster preachers before him such as Henry Cooke, Thomas Drew and Hugh Hanna, Paisley believed that the Catholic Church's advances should be stymied by halting the political advances of its members (Wallis *et al.*, 1986: 16–17). The following extract encapsulates, in Paisley's own words, his religiously grounded politics:

> There are those who mistakenly analyse the Ulster situation in terms of social and economic factors, in terms of politics or philosophies. These theories and analyses collapse because they ignore, deliberately or otherwise, the main key, and that is the most obvious factor: Protestantism versus popery. The war in Ulster is a war of survival between the opposing forces of Truth and Error, and the principles of the Reformation are as relevant today as they were in Europe in the sixteenth century.
> (*Protestant Telegraph*, 15 June 1974, cited in Cooke, 1996: 134)

Thus, religion contributed to Paisleyism's particularly intense sense of group superiority and differentiation, resulting in, as Mitchel (2003: 204) writes, 'an innovative cocktail of fundamentalism with intense nationalism … This potent mixture functions both to define its identity as separate from all others and to sustain its members' exalted sense of calling in their task of defending Ulster'.

Paisleyism's relationship with the British state was governed by the notion of covenanting – a principle, traceable to the political thought of seventeenth-century Scottish Presbyterians, that makes political obligation conditional on the quality of government (Miller, 1978). In spite of having its roots in antiquity, the covenant idea is not qualitatively different from modern, secular ideas of political obligation (Aughey, 1989: 23; Bruce, 2007: 244). Paisley located the doctrine directly in Scripture; his interpretation of Romans 13:1–5 indicated that political power exercised in a manner not in accordance with the will of God should be resisted (Paisley, 1996: 172–3). Hence the decades of distrust, condemnation and outright opposition to the powers that be, whether unionist or British, with Paisley styling himself as the best judge of the godliness of government policy. Although his cause was predominantly expressed in terms of the familiar symbols and traditions of Ulster loyalism and Orangeism, Smyth (1986: 41) notes that 'the verve with which Paisley communicates his beliefs and policies to his supporters and the watching world has been profoundly influenced by the DUP leader's fundamentalist experience'. Paisley cultivated close connections with fundamentalist preachers, churches and institutions in America who shared his extreme conservatism and separatism, and there exist many theological and ecclesiastical parallels between the Free Presbyterian Church and fundamentalist groups in the United States.

The connections that existed between the FPCU and the DUP extended far beyond each organisation's domination by Paisley. Smyth (1986) outlined the church's influence in the fields of candidate selection, party financing, electioneering and, of course, party ideology, though the influence of the FPCU has waned in the post-1998 period of the party's modernisation and diversification (see Tonge et al., 2014). But one of the most striking aspects of the DUP has been its ability, from its foundation, to attract significant electoral support among unionists who do not share the religious beliefs influential in the party. For this there have been a number of overlapping reasons, the principal one being Paisley's skill at portraying himself as the strongest defender of Britishness in Northern Ireland. Here, Mitchel (2003: 204–10) points to the importance of Paisley's religiosity; it allowed him to trump other expressions of unionism by forging the most powerful and elaborate 'national historic-myth', replete with 'golden ages', tales of peril and deliverance, a pantheon of Protestant heroes and an assortment of Romanising and Gaelicising enemies.

Another explanation of the DUP's popularity was the fact that Paisley, with his humble origins, plain-spoken manner and populist appeals, was attractive to many working-class Protestants who felt little affinity with the wealthy unionist establishment represented by the UUP (Tonge et al., 2014: 14–16). And yet another aspect of the party's appeal was the strong resonance of evangelical Protestant Christianity throughout the unionist community, a phenomenon explored extensively elsewhere (Wright, 1973; Morrow, 1997; Mitchell, 2006; Bruce, 2007; Ganiel, 2008; Brewer et al., 2013). Indeed, it has been argued that evangelicalism is the core of unionist identity: 'It defines the group to which [the loyalist] belongs, it figures large in the history of that group, it legitimates the group's advantages (such as they are), and it radically distinguishes the group from its traditional enemy'(Bruce, 1994: 25). Because of the social significance of evangelicalism throughout the Protestant community, 'it impinges strongly, albeit subtly, on the responses of large numbers of apparently secular Protestants' (p. 30). This thesis has been criticised for underplaying the secular dimensions of unionism (Aughey, 1989: 7–12; Coulter, 1994: 7–8) and overplaying the salience of religion in the conflict (McGarry and O'Leary, 1995). But, while Bruce tones down his unionism-as-evangelicalism theme in his later work on Paisley, he provides a convincing explication of the important and multiple roles religion has played in Paisley's success: as a source of strength and inspiration for Paisley and in creating a unity of purpose for his party; forging an image of trustworthiness and reliability; as an object of nostalgia for a backward-looking unionist population – religious and secular – who are still moved by the language and symbols of evangelical Protestantism; as evidence of being down to earth and in touch with the common people, in contrast to the cosmopolitan elite; and justifying unionist belief in the superiority of their cause and identity over those of Catholics (Bruce, 2007: 246–61; see also Morrow, 1997; Mitchel, 2003). As we will see, these religiously inspired aspects of the DUP's popularity are in evidence in the post-Agreement years as they challenge and ultimately defeat the UUP as the dominant voice of Ulster unionism.

But while it is easy and right to emphasise the absolutist and oppositional character of the DUP throughout most of its history, the fundamentalist aspect should not obscure other traits of the party. Extremist tendencies have always existed within certain boundaries, giving rise to a rather contradictory picture, although one that helps makes sense of the party's post-1998 course towards government. On the one hand, the party unflinchingly opposed any modification in Northern Ireland's governance that might address the political grievances of Catholics, notably the Sunningdale Agreement and the Anglo-Irish Agreement. The activism of Paisley and his followers was inspired to a great extent by their (unusual) interpretation of biblical imperatives, and the DUP's style was generally combative and its rhetoric overblown. Moreover, Paisley's party flirted with extra-legal violence and some loyalist combatants have claimed to have been part-inspired by his inflammatory rhetoric (see Brewer *et al.*, 2013: 63–5). As Chapter 1 noted, Paisley is blamed for contributing to the outbreak of 'the Troubles', ushering into existence the very kind of insecurity of which he was warning.

On the other hand, however, the party confined what, for it, was 'a religiously mandated political agenda to the rules of engagement of a liberal democracy' (Bruce, 2001: 402), and it was not incapable of engaging with others. The DUP at times made electoral pacts with the UUP and, as a consistent supporter of devolution, took part in the Brooke–Mayhew talks of 1991–2, the Good Friday talks prior to Sinn Féin entering and other exploratory contacts during the 'Troubles'. It was this capacity for 'normal' political engagement – encouraged by both the opportunities presented to the party and the parameters within which it was forced to operate – that was to become increasingly dominant in the party's personality after 1998.

The Agreement: 'the mother of all treachery'

Uniquely among the parties included in this study, the DUP opposed the Agreement. In alliance with Bob McCartney's much smaller United Kingdom Unionist Party, the DUP fought a vigourous 'no' campaign in the run-up to the referendum on the deal. Paisley's party had been on the political sidelines since September 1997 when it had left the talks upon Sinn Féin's arrival, and now, in April 1998, the Democratic Unionists' worst fears had been realised: their fellow unionists had concluded a deal that both threatened the Union and appeased terrorists. This accord was, said Paisley, 'worse than the Anglo-Irish Agreement, more treacherous than the Framework Document, and poses far greater dangers to the Union than the Sunningdale Agreement ever did' (Paisley, 1998). Peter Robinson, the then DUP deputy leader, described the document as a 'charter for Dublin rule', an 'anti-peace accord' and 'the mother of all treachery' (Robinson, 1998). The Agreement was an attack on the Union, an attack on the unionist people and an attack on law, order and democracy. As Ian Paisley Junior (1998) wrote in a booklet-length polemic:

> It is correct to claim that the content of the Agreement owes much to a conspiracy hatched against Unionists by a great consistent movement of pan-Nationalism which embraces within it gains made at the expense of law and order, while undermining the democratic process that feeds unjustifiable hatred of all that is British in its expression of identity and claim of loyalty in Ulster within the Union.

Accusations of treachery and conspiracy were accompanied by claims that through a well-funded, media-backed 'yes' referendum campaign, the Northern Ireland Office planned to 'manipulate the public mind, deceive the people, exploit its governmental authority and abuse the electoral process' (Robinson, 1998).

In keeping with the DUP's politico-religious ideology, the party provided a critique of the Belfast Agreement that had both political and moral aspects, although these were not entirely separate. The DUP concurred with Sinn Féin's analysis that the Union was profoundly weakened by the Agreement's constitutional and institutional provisions. A 'yes' vote in the referendum, warned Paisley, was quite simply a vote to 'dismantle the Union' (Paisley, 1998). Constitutional change was thought to be unbalanced; the Government of Ireland Act of 1920 that was the basis of Northern Ireland's legal and legitimate position in the United Kingdom was to be scrapped in exchange for a mere modification of the Irish Republic's illegal and illegitimate territorial claim over Northern Ireland. And the DUP exaggerated the powers of the all-Ireland institutions, inaccurately describing them as 'free-standing'. However, the party correctly pointed out that contrary to UUP claims that the Agreement did away with structures set up under the Anglo-Irish Agreement that gave Dublin a say in Northern Irish policy, the two Governments' consultative forum, the Anglo-Irish Conference, would continue much as before, just under a new name – the British–Irish Intergovernmental Conference. Plus, nationalist parties were to be given a guaranteed place in government and a veto on many key decisions in the new Assembly. The ultimate meaning of these measures was that 'the Northern Ireland carriage has been uncoupled from the British train'; their implementation would lead 'inescapably towards Irish unity' (Robinson, 1998).

The DUP's certainty that the Agreement was bad, if not fatal, for the Union was partly based on its zero-sum view of politics, an enduring characteristic of the Paisleyite movement's fundamentalist mindset (see Bruce, 1986: 265–70). Any deal 'enthusiastically endorsed by Dublin' and 'warmly welcomed by the SDLP' could *only* represent a 'dilution and diminution of the Union' (Paisley, 1998). The moral thrust of the DUP's opposition was directed at the Agreement's 'Troubles'-related measures. At the end of a campaign of violence that unionists understood as targeted squarely against them, republicans appeared to be rewarded in the Agreement with three victories. First, they were granted a place in the Executive without being compelled to give up their illegal weaponry. Second, republican paramilitaries (along with loyalists) were to be set free without paying adequately for their crimes. Third, the Royal Ulster Constabulary (RUC), the force that the DUP believed had defended law and order and prevented the province from slipping into anarchy during the 'Troubles', was to be reformed, or as Paisley put it, 'put on the altar and sacrificed to keep the IRA happy' (Paisley, 1998). The DUP saw a clear moral message in these measures: a degree of legitimacy was retrospectively conferred on the IRA and its campaign while it was implied that the security forces were in some way culpable for the conflict.

Overall, the DUP regarded the peace process as drawing an equivalence between things that should have been regarded as anything but equivalent. The party's condemnation of police reform usually juxtaposed an emasculated RUC with an untouchable IRA. The DUP took a much less optimistic view of the principle of consent that Trimble had claimed as his great negotiating success. Consent made territorial claims equivalent, leaving Northern Ireland's constitutional position a hostage to demographics. The DUP pointed out that key decisions in the Assembly required the parallel consent of both communities but the constitution of Northern Ireland was to be decided merely by 50 per cent plus one (DUP, 2003a: 25). And an unjust equivalence was drawn between political parties; the peace process included Sinn Féin as a normal party with a mandate to be respected, brushing under the carpet its links to an active paramilitary organisation. Later, the DUP would complain of another demonstration of this equivalence when the British Government suspended the institutions, penalising all parties instead of what was in the DUP's eyes clearly the problem party – Sinn Féin.

This moral critique proved to be a 'powerful political marketing device' for the DUP (Tonge, 2006: 75). As we noted, the social salience of conservative

Protestantism meant that many secular unionists inhabited the same 'moral universe' as the evangelicals (Morrow, 1997: 56). The DUP's vigorous opposition to the Agreement, often couched, as we will see, in semi-religious language, was a prime example of what Morrow (1997) observed as fundamentalist Protestantism's function as a source of explanation, interpretation and comforting certainty in times of crisis. In a publication produced by the peace-building organisation ECONI (Evangelical Contribution on Northern Ireland), Thomson (2002) articulates several aspects of Protestant doctrine that he asserts played a significant role in many Protestants regarding parts of the Agreement that were 'soft' on paramilitarism as unconscionable. These included the belief in the God-ordained responsibility of government to punish evildoers, the belief that justice is an essential aspect of the character of God, and the importance of obedience to law and covenants in the Protestant tradition. Add to this Southern's (2005) findings on the religious inspiration of the DUP's approach to Sinn Féin. Evangelicalism lays heavy emphasis on the need for the repentance of the sinner as a prerequisite of God's forgiveness and, with this expression of Christianity so widely held within the DUP, many within the party conceptualised the approach to Sinn Féin in the same way. Because republicans had failed, in spite of turning from the armed struggle strategy, to show sincere remorse, the DUP could not show forgiveness by co-operating with Sinn Féin in government (Southern, 2005: 131–2; see also Moloney, 2008: 493).

As Paisley was well aware, a moral/religious critique of the Agreement would resonate with huge numbers of Protestants, from many church denominations and of varying degrees of piety. The Free Presbyterian Church condemned the Agreement as 'unscriptural, unethical and immoral' and Paisley persuaded other conservative Protestant church leaders outside his denomination to sign a letter rejecting the Agreement in the *Belfast Telegraph* (Moloney, 2008: 492). The front page of the May 1998 edition of the Orange Order's periodical, the *Orange Standard*, declared 'no' in large lettering, adding that the Agreement was a document that 'no Protestant in good conscience could support' (cited in McAuley *et al.*, 2011: 132). In sum, while in some cases it may have concealed or accompanied anti-Catholic sentiment, moral indignation was a genuine and widespread Protestant response to the Agreement. It is reasonable to believe that this response was symptomatic of aspects of Protestant political culture rooted in Protestant theological emphases. And this indignation meant that morality was indeed powerful political ground on which the DUP could fight, increasingly so as the results of the Agreement's moral ambiguity became apparent in the implementation period.

Yet while the party's rhetoric continued to be saturated with moral outrage after the Agreement, the party's high principles were quickly compromised.

Following the deal, the DUP had assured the public that it would not take its place in the Executive due to the presence of Sinn Féin; indeed, Paisley said at the time that he still opposed sharing power with nationalists of any kind since they wished to destroy Northern Ireland (Moloney, 2008: 379). This changed after the referendum and the June 1998 Assembly election. As we explore presently, the party opted to take the two places in the Executive to which it was entitled on the basis of its twenty Assembly seats. A new approach was evident in the DUP manifesto for the Assembly election, a shift away from unequivocal opposition to the Agreement and the hysterical and foreboding tones of the party's 'no' campaign communications. The manifesto depicted a strong and confident party rather looking forward to the future, or at least a party not wanting the future to proceed without it. 'Your Best Guarantee' was the slogan; the accompanying detail showed that that guarantee was not of destroying the Agreement and restoring the status quo but of ensuring that the Agreement worked out in as pro-unionist a manner as possible.

The theme was no longer opposition to the Agreement, but merely holding other parties to their promises. Neither prisoner releases nor Sinn Féin entering government were opposed per se, but were only to occur according to a strict interpretation of Tony Blair's pre-referendum pledges. On policing, the manifesto noted the need for a 'strong RUC' and committed the party to 'oppose attempts to put policing in the hands of paramilitaries', but the DUP said nothing of opposing all reform of the police. The party promised that it would 'not collude with others to set up the embryo of a United Ireland' but did not elaborate on how it would approach the working of the all-Ireland institutions (DUP, 1998). The manifesto therefore displayed a strong element of 'wait and see' as the party sought to accommodate itself to the new dispensation that now, after the referenda, was going ahead with or without it. Instead of declaring war on the new politics, the DUP 'behaved as though their role was to act as an insurance policy against its excesses' (Godson, 2004: 495). While the DUP's eventual decision to enter government with Sinn Féin in 2007 appeared to be a shocking U-turn – and it was – it can equally be argued that the DUP's de facto partial acceptance of the Agreement in 1998, demonstrated most clearly through the taking of its ministerial posts, was the truly significant break with decades of protest politics and street demagoguery, and that the seeds of 2007 were planted then.

Preaching against the Agreement

The party's plan was to keep the new arrangements at arm's length yet prove that the DUP was capable of pragmatism and effective policy delivery. It described this approach as 'constructive opposition' – opposing the Agreement 'at every opportunity' but being present in the Assembly to ensure the DUP's voters were represented (Robinson, 2001a). The party justified the strategy of challenging the Agreement structures from within rather than without by referring to its long-standing enthusiasm for devolution and disdain for the deficiencies of Direct Rule. Robinson (2000) explained his party's strategy as being

> twofold, on one hand, to continue to hold the Belfast Agreement up to examination and expose its corruption while on the other hand taking every possible step to block or limit the damage done through its implementation until the moment its developing all-Ireland, terrorist rewarding edifice, can be swept away.

The DUP could have fulfilled the first aim of critiquing the Agreement and gradually convincing the unionist people of its folly by boycotting the Assembly, its committees and Executive. But, said Robinson, that would have left the party bereft of real power to block or hamper the progress of the Agreement. It would also, of course, have entailed electoral dangers given the decreased visibility of the party in the event of abstention from the institutions, harming its chances of defeating the UUP. And it would have meant that the Executive places to which the party was entitled under the d'Hondt mechanism would have gone to other parties.

While the two DUP ministers discharged their duties effectively, they did not sit in meetings of the Executive due to the presence of Sinn Féin, nor did they attend meetings of the North–South Ministerial Council (NSMC). It was not difficult for the UUP to accuse the DUP of gross hypocrisy; the Democratic Unionists were benefiting from the Agreement that they had condemned the UUP for helping bring about. While the party avoided republicans in the Executive, the DUP did sit with them on Assembly committees. As Trimble (2000b) lectured at his 2000 party conference:

> The hokey-cokey hypocrisy which surrounds their attitude to the Agreement, sums up the DUP. They say they're opposed to the whole lot. But it hasn't stopped them sitting beside Sinn Féin in committee almost 500 times. According to them, the Agreement is heading us into a United Ireland. If so, why are they glued like limpets to their positions. ... They holler about the horrors of the Agreement but nothing will get them out of the Assembly.

Furthermore, the charge was often made that the DUP was being inconsistent in its boycott of Executive meetings since its representatives had associated with Sinn Féin for many years in local government. Gregory Campbell responded to this accusation with the analogy of a restaurant – there was a huge difference between sitting in the same eatery with Martin McGuinness and being forced to share a table with him. Sinn Féin's presence in the Assembly would not push the DUP out – there was a duty to effectively represent voters – but to 'get into bed with them and run the country with them, then that's a completely different story', that would be to legitimise terror (Campbell, 2002).

The DUP's 'constructive opposition' also articulated the widespread sense of grievance in the unionist community that the Agreement was solely concerned with the satisfying of nationalists. The perception of Protestant disadvantage was not confined to any one unionist party – it has already been discussed in Chapter 2 – but the logic of the positions of the UUP and DUP on the Agreement compelled the former to lay greater emphasis on the positives of the deal for the Protestant community while the latter tended to be wholly negative. This was the 'cold house for Protestants' danger of which John Reid, Secretary of State for Northern Ireland, spoke in a widely reported speech; Campbell welcomed the acknowledgement of alienation within his community but argued that the 'cold house' scenario was not, as Reid suggested, a future possibility but a present reality and had been for twenty years (Campbell, 2002). The alienation had multiple sources, according to the DUP. The most conspicuous was the presence of Sinn Féin – a party allied to a private army – in government which immediately created an inequality among the power-sharing parties. Another imbalance in the Agreement was said to be the biased institutional expression of the 'totality of relationships', i.e. the emphasis placed on the NSMC over the relatively inactive British–Irish Council (DUP, 2003a).

But it was in the realm of symbols and culture that the DUP claimed to find the most powerful evidence of anti-Protestant discrimination: 'Everything Gaelic, republican and Irish is promoted while all that is British, unionist or Orange is derided and reviled' (DUP, 2001). On the flags issue, like the Ulster Unionists, the DUP bitterly opposed the suggestion that the flying of the Union flag from public buildings should be banned or restricted. The DUP fervently defended the right to march, and while the marching issue pre-dated the Agreement, continuing curtailment of Orange parades in the years after 1998 reinforced the general perception of being victimised by the peace process. Other claims made by the party included the suggestions that the civil service employed a majority of Catholics, Irish language and culture were being funded and promoted to a far greater extent than Ulster-Scots and Catholic areas and community groups were receiving the lion's share of EU and other funds that existed to support the peace (Campbell, 2002; DUP, 2003a). The Human Rights and Equality Commissions were condemned for being unrepresentative of the Protestant community and were perceived to have 'pushed a pro-nationalist, pro-agreement agenda' (DUP, 2003a: 29). One facet of that agenda concerned an area in which the DUP was highly vocal after the Agreement, the definition and treatment of 'victims'. The prevailing definition of victims, and that held by nationalists, the Commissions and government, included those individuals who, having perpetrated terrorist offences, had also been responsible for creating victims. This definition, said the DUP – typical of the unprincipled ideological environment of contemporary Northern Ireland – needed correction given its immoral and anti-Protestant outworking, i.e. the alienation felt by many victims, the huge amount of funding received by 'non-innocent' victims like ex-prisoner groups and the excessive attention paid to investigating crimes suffered by nationalists at the expense of probing atrocities carried out by the IRA (DUP, 2003b).

The DUP bitterly rejected the Patten proposals on policing reform as more appeasement of the IRA, and the bulk of its ire was directed at the Ulster Unionists who had negotiated the policing section of the Agreement. The DUP talked often of the 'destruction' of the RUC, which no doubt pleased republicans who had pursued the more modest-sounding goal of 'disbandment'. The party shared the common unionist belief that any religious imbalance in the RUC's membership had more to do with the IRA's practice of intimidating Catholics out of serving in the police than the force's particular ethos, and therefore changes to the police's emblems and make-up were based on a false premise. Once police reform was a fait accompli, the fifty/fifty recruitment policy of the Police Service of Northern Ireland (which ended in 2011) persisted as a stark symbol for the DUP of the supposedly discriminatory ethos of post-Agreement Northern Ireland. This policy was 'the most outrageous piece of legislation in Western Europe … The people to blame for the underrepresentation of the Catholic community in the RUC are not the big bad unionists but the IRA' (interview with Gregory Campbell MP MLA, 7 September 2012). Even after the DUP entered government in 2007, the party continued to make very similar arguments about the perceived war of attrition on Protestant culture, as we will see later in this chapter, although the language changed somewhat. The party tried to appropriate the shared future discourse by arguing that nationalists, in opposing the Union flag on Belfast City Hall or certain Orange parades, did not want a shared future or shared public space, and were uninterested in reaching cross-community consensus on these matters.

A closer look at the themes and language through which the DUP expressed its opposition to the Agreement helps illuminate the fatalist logic of the DUP and, indeed, reasons for its post-Agreement attractiveness. The DUP had always had a distinct rhetorical style – oppositional and semi-religious – and the qualified participation of the DUP in the Good Friday institutions was accompanied with a relentless, vigorous and bitter discourse of condemnation in which the endowment of the political conflict with a spiritual import was clearly evident. As Porter (2003) explains, the party's opposition to the Agreement exhibited unionists' tendency of acting out a self-appointed role of 'prophetic witness'. The confrontational language used by unionists 'represents an extension into politics of a cultural-religious style derived from the central role the evangelical sermon plays in their worship' (p. 126). The speaker assumes that she has access to a superior source of authority and accordingly makes moral and political judgements in a way that does not invite discussion or expect to be queried. The language of partnership, mutuality and reconciliation that implied the equal status and legitimacy of the two sides was of no use to a party that insisted on its own moral superiority. To enter into dialogue would be to 'allow the unthinkable, namely that republicans' views may be as valid as unionists', that error may be as valid as truth, that bad may have something to teach good' (p. 127).

Adopting this style, the DUP continually drew attention to, first, the degradation of democracy and morality caused by the Agreement and, second, the corrupt means by which this state of affairs was contrived and concealed. The Agreement was 'based on a false foundation of appeasement to terrorism' (Paisley Junior, 2000). The peace process that had spawned it was a mechanism by which Blair, assisted by the 'defeatist' UUP, could channel concessions to the IRA in the hope that republicans would give up violence: 'The broken pledges of David Trimble and Tony Blair have allowed Sinn Féin/IRA to reap all the benefits of the appeasement process without giving anything in return' (DUP, 2001). In and through the Agreement unjustified concessions were freely flowing to republicans; those complicit in this Agreement lacked the moral fortitude to stand up to the IRA, just as the British Government had throughout the 'Troubles' lacked the resolve to deal decisively with terrorism. The British and the UUP were 'pandering to the Provos and paying its ransom' (Robinson, 1999b). Republicans were denounced as 'evil'; the Agreement was 'iniquitous' and, in the words of one DUP councillor, offered 'only an unchristian compromise like Good Friday years ago when Barabbas was preferred to our Lord' (Gibson, 1998). One of the most telling expressions used by the DUP was its description of 'Sinn Féin/IRA' as 'unrepentant' terrorists. Trimble's preferred equivalent adjective was the less religious 'unreconstructed'. Sinn Féin had 'consistently refused to say sorry', and to fraternise with such people was to condone their crimes and insult their victims (Paisley, 2001).

In any case, said the DUP, appeasement was not working. The signs of continuing IRA activity throughout the implementation period were evidence that appeasement was only emboldening republicans in their interminable search for advantage. The party's 2003 manifesto dedicated a full page to detailing republican misdemeanours. The 'Sinn Féin/IRA' ceasefire was an 'illusionary tactic' and the organisation's means and objectives were the same as they had ever been. Illegal republican activity was listed. That apologists of this behaviour were permitted to occupy ministerial office was an unacceptable distortion of democracy:

'Violence and terrorist activity are on the increase in Northern Ireland because it is accepted that terrorists can be admitted to the democratic process while continuing to pursue the path of terror' (DUP, 2003a: 7). The IRA armed and active, the RUC destroyed, the army's presence diminished: civilised society was left without adequate defence. Other threats to the rule of law included the prospect of a Sinn Féin Policing and Justice minister and Sinn Féin-controlled District Policing Partnerships (DUP, 2003a: 12).

This calamitous situation was, said the DUP, created and sustained by a scaffold of lies. It is difficult to overstate the scope and bitterness of the party's accusations of treachery and deceit; few if any individuals or groups associated with the Agreement avoided the DUP's vitriol. Betrayal was to be expected from the British establishment: 'The mainland parties are double dealers, speaking with forked tongues, behaving with neither honour nor dignity' (Paisley, 2001). Typical examples of DUP views on London politicians included the suggestion that Peter Mandelson employed a 'black craft' of 'deceit and chicanery' (Robinson, 2001a), while Trimble's 'trickery' was aided by 'that reprehensible little Secretary of State John Reid' (Paisley, 2001). The British cared not for the Union but only for the appeasement of the IRA. However, just as a special type of Paisleyite invective was reserved for the apostasy of the Free Presbyterians' spiritual cousins in the Protestant churches, the brunt of the DUP's rhetorical batterings fell on those whom it saw as having abandoned the true unionist faith – the Ulster Unionists.

It was, after all, the 'weakness, incompetence and poor judgement' of the UUP leadership that was responsible for the dire straits in which Northern Ireland found itself (DUP, 2001). The Ulster Unionists were 'war weary', 'tired of the struggle' and 'wanted to sue for whatever terms they could grasp' (Robinson, 2001a). Both the DUP's 2001 and 2003 election manifestos spent considerable time recounting the UUP's 'record of failure' and in his party conference speech in 2001, Paisley chose to 'examine the treachery' of the UUP at length in order to leave in no doubt 'how low it will go to stay in bed with IRA-Sinn Féin'. On prisoner releases, cross-border bodies, RUC reform and decommissioning the UUP had broken its promises – in fact, on decommissioning the UUP had been 'surrendering' since 1994. Moreover, treachery was not something recently learned by the UUP. Paisley reminded his listeners how their party's origins lay in those who 'first raised the standard against [UUP leader] O'Neill's treachery' (Paisley, 2001). On the UUP's 'destruction' of the RUC, Robinson commented, 'The party that disbanded the "B" Specials and the UDR has done it again!' (Robinson, 1999b). The UUP's treacherous potential had always been brought to light in the same fashion – through political turbulence that served to separate out the traitors from the faithful: 'Sadly each and every sell-out initiative has revealed that there are those so-called Unionists who are prepared to slither and slide down the road of deceit and betrayal' (Paisley, 2001).

Much of the DUP's anti-UUP invective fell on Trimble personally. He was 'a liar, a cheat, a hypocrite, a knave, a loathsome reptile which needs to be scotched' (Paisley quoted in Moloney, 2008: 367). To successfully pull off his treachery, Trimble employed all manner of dastardly political tricks. The original scam had been the 'constructive ambiguity' of the Agreement, designed to fool the unionist people and let the IRA avoid the decommissioning test. 'The Ulster Unionist Party betrayed the unionist electorate. Remember how it conned unionists with their slogan "Vote Yes for the Union"?' (DUP, 2003a: 30). Trimble's claims that he scored a victory in the Agreement were a 'smoke screen' to obscure his failure in negotiations, as were the many ostensibly genuine attempts of the UUP to force the decommissioning issue. Trimble, said Paisley, was 'a master of deception'; the first decommissioning act in October 2001 was nothing but 'a stunt of smoke and mirrors' (Paisley, 2001). Robinson carried the 'magic' metaphor further:

> Like a performing magician in a seedy burlesque show attempting by sleight of hand to deflect the eye of his audience, Mr. Trimble causes the Unionist community to concentrate on the issue of decommissioning and Sinn Féin/IRA membership of an Executive, while away from their view he sets up the United Ireland structures that when they develop will take Northern Ireland out of the United Kingdom.
>
> (Robinson, 1999c)

The DUP rubbished the paranormal methods required to reinstate Séamus Mallon as Deputy First Minister immediately prior to the first period of devolution in late 1999 – this consisted of MLAs rendering his prior resignation invalid on the grounds that it was never formally accepted. Nigel Dodds reportedly quipped that Mallon's return reminded him of the unlikely reappearance of the supposedly deceased Bobby Ewing in the television drama *Dallas* – he had been in the shower all along (de Bréadún, 1999). In similar terms, the DUP condemned Trimble and Durkan's 2001 re-election as First Minister and Deputy First Minister – 'First Cheat and Deputy First Cheat' (Robinson, 2001b) – with the help of votes from Alliance and Women's Coalition members who re-designated themselves temporarily as unionists. This election, held after the six-week deadline the missing of which should have strictly triggered fresh elections (see Chapter 6), was another example of the dubious lengths to which pro-Agreement parties were willing to go to prop up their deal.

However, charges of treachery in others were invariably accompanied by assertions of the DUP's integrity, and reasons to be fearful were accompanied by assurances of the saving power of the DUP. Descriptions of the DUP as the only unionists who could be trusted were ubiquitous in the party's public communications. They had never broken their manifesto commitments. They discerned the dangers of the process; they had not been taken in by the deception. The relationship between pro- and anti-Agreement unionists was spoken of virtually like that of the saved and the damned, as if the truth had been revealed to the DUP and the 'yes' unionists were lost and in need of deliverance. 'The first step to a Unionist revival is knowledge. When the people become aware of the nature and extent of the betrayal they shall clear from office those who failed to discharge the key trust that was reposed in them' (Robinson, 1999c). Thus alongside the doom and gloom was an optimism that all might be well once the party had achieved electoral pre-eminence. The power of the DUP's principles was said to be increasingly impacting the hearts and minds of the unionist people: '[pro-Agreement unionists] are deserting the delinquent, bankrupt and tragic Ulster Unionist Party leadership and are turning to the DUP who have provided accurate analysis, sound advice and wise leadership' (Robinson, 2001a). The DUP held not merely political positions, but possessed the truth. This truth must be spread with fitting zeal: 'We must go forth and spread the message in every village, town and city that only by supporting this Party can we halt the slide and end the concession granting process. By God's help and grace we cannot, we will not fail' (Paisley, 2001). When the DUP did achieve electoral hegemony – precisely what its preaching against the Agreement was designed to do – it was portrayed as representing a revival of the fortunes and confidence of the unionist community, in tones not dissimilar to those used by the UUP in the wake of the Agreement back in 1998. 'For the first time in a generation Unionism has a leadership that's working', claimed the 2005 manifesto:

> Just remember what it was like only eighteen months ago when the Ulster Unionist Party was in charge. Republicans won concession after concession while unionism was in retreat. In every negotiation republicans exploited the weakness of the UUP and were allowed to dictate their own terms. Now, all that has changed.
>
> (DUP, 2005)

'The election of the DUP [in 2003] brought clarity', said the 2007 manifesto. 'The days of stunts, gestures, half-measures and fudges were over' (DUP, 2007).

From no deal to new deal

This narrative of immorality, Protestant/unionist loss and DUP fortitude helped vault the DUP into first place within unionism. In the relevant conflict literature, the efforts of the DUP to undermine the UUP by portraying itself to the electorate as the strongest champion of unionist interests are referred to as 'ethnic outbidding'. As we saw in Chapter 1, ethnic party systems are thought to have an inherent tendency towards polarisation. The fact that parties seek votes only from within their ethnic group encourages them to highlight threats to the group and claim to have the best strategy for countering those threats. They compete for the reputation of stoutest defender of the group. Thus, of ethnic outbidding, the DUP's manner of defeating of the UUP appeared to be a textbook case. Indeed, the DUP made it plain that its post-Agreement strategy was to combine opposition to the Agreement from within the Assembly and Executive with a concerted and calculated effort to defeat Trimble's party at the polls. According to Robinson, his party concluded that the only sure way of 'democratically defeating the developing all-Ireland process' was by committing 'all our energy, talents, resources and available time towards the electoral defeat of Trimble and his pro-Agreement party'; other options such as pressurising the UUP's ruling council to abandon the Agreement or winning the support of a majority of unionist Assembly members so as to attain a veto were considered less effective (Robinson, 2000). However, the sources of the DUP's post-Agreement success were more complex than implied by the standard outbidding scenario. There were, in fact, three factors at work: 'the operationalization of outbidding (to outflank an in-group rival), modernization (to maximise electoral gain) and moderation (to allow an agreement to share power with Sinn Féin)' (Gormley-Heenan and Mac Ginty, 2008: 49). The DUP won the intra-unionist contest, not solely by outbidding the UUP, but by combining its ethnic muscle with modern and effective campaigning and organisation, and a more accommodating orientation towards the fundamentals of the Agreement.

To explain, first, the modernisation of the DUP, the framework provided by Gormley-Heenan and Mac Ginty (2008) is useful. Drawing on relevant theory, they outline five strategies of party modernisation and show how these are evident in the post-Agreement evolution of the DUP. The first strategy is to centralise the organisational structure of the party. The DUP (like Sinn Féin) has been a famously disciplined party with strong central control. In the post-Agreement years, its cohesion was all the more conspicuous in the light of the UUP's public fragmentation. The UUP's Dermot Nesbitt recalls: 'The DUP could have a meeting and you wouldn't hear one thing about it. If the UUP had a meeting, the press would know all about it. We leaked like a sieve' (interview with Dermot Nesbitt, 10 September 2012). When Jeffrey Donaldson, Arlene Foster and Norah Beare defected to the DUP at the start of 2004, some observers wondered how they would fare in the new regime; their new DUP colleagues did not have the luxury of transferring party allegiance because they had been required to sign a pledge that they would resign their seats if they chose to leave the party (Thornton, 2004). Similar discipline-enforcing contracts were used by the DUP in other elections.

The second party modernisation strategy is to increase professionalism within the party by engaging media consultants, policy advisors and other technocrats. Indeed, it has been observed that one unsung factor in the DUP's success, modernisation and moderation – not mentioned by Gormley-Heenan and Mac Ginty but highlighted by others – was the influx and influence not simply of new party personnel, but of ex-UUP talent. These included key staffers Richard Bullick, Timothy Cairns and Timothy Johnston (Thornton, 2004; Moloney, 2008: 406–7). The third modernisation strategy is to heighten engagement with the state. This entails greater use of public funds for communications and personnel, and the use of party patronage exercised through the state. Gormley-Heenan and Mac Ginty note the swell of state funding that accompanied electoral growth and three life peerages received by the DUP in 2005, a turnaround for the traditionally anti-establishment party. The fourth strategy is to soften ideological stances with the aim of broadening the party's appeal beyond the party's traditional base; we examine the moderation of the DUP presently. And the fifth strategy is the exploitation of modern technologies and campaigning methods. Throughout the post-Agreement period, the DUP displayed an extremely effective communications strategy, with the party's strong central control and enthusiastic embrace of new media facilitating clear and consistent messages to the public. Again, in this area, the contrast with the divided UUP was stark. Indeed, Powell (2008: 239) noted the DUP's relative technological savvy at a meeting in Downing Street in February 2004 when Peter Robinson set out their proposals for devolution with the aid of PowerPoint – 'a first for the peace process'.

Ideological moderation – along with outbidding and modernisation – was the third plank in the DUP's post-Agreement growth. The DUP's reorientation was encapsulated in the 2003 election slogan, 'It's time for a fair deal' (DUP, 2003a), and in the run-up to that election the party published a policy paper, *Towards a New Agreement* (DUP, 2003c) – remarkably titled given the party's record of opposition to any kind of cross-community accord. It was mentioned above that even in the 1998 Assembly election, the DUP's message was attuned to the reality that the Agreement was going ahead in any case, and a similarly pragmatic platform was also evident in the campaign for the 2001 Westminster election (see Mitchell *et al.*, 2002). However, hints of realistic alternatives to the Agreement prior to 2003 took a back seat to the DUP's relentless critique of the unfolding process of implementation. And of course, the DUP was compelled to adopt a predominantly negative stance in the early years of implementation so as to display consistency with years of pre-1998 rhetoric and policy and avoid losing credibility with the electorate (Farrington, 2006: 176). The question is why, in 2003, was the DUP now talking explicitly about renegotiation instead of rejection? There were three reasons.

One was circumstantial. An Assembly election was taking place, the first since 1998, and it was widely believed that the DUP would win it. The election manifesto spelled out what this would mean:

> This election represents the last and best chance to reverse the failures and decline of recent years ... If David Trimble controls over fifty percent of the unionist seats in the Assembly the Belfast Agreement will continue. If Ian Paisley controls over fifty percent of the unionist seats in the Assembly there will be negotiations for a new Agreement.
>
> (DUP, 2003a: 4)

Hence, the DUP's renegotiation proposals were in preparation for its likely hegemonic position in unionism after the election. Indeed, the DUP had been thirsting for an election for some time. It had been 'cheated' out of the opportunity of boosting its numbers in the Assembly in November 2001 when the late selection of the First and Deputy First Ministers strictly should have triggered fresh elections. On that occasion, Paisley accused John Reid of attempting to preserve the Agreement by 'running scared of the ballot box'. Surely this was an admission that the Good Friday deal had lost unionist consent: 'If Trimble is so confident that this process is paying for Unionists let's have an election' (Paisley, 2001). An even more blatant escape from the polls was made by the British Government when it postponed the elections scheduled for the spring of 2003 for fear that the Agreement would be destroyed if the DUP emerged ascendant. Such a result was even more likely when the public eventually did cast their votes in November of that year, given the failure of the pro-Agreement parties to resolve the decommissioning impasse.

The second reason that the political climate was ripe for the DUP to consider renegotiation in 2003 was that, by that stage, the actual extent to which the Agreement had been implemented was in the party's favour, in two respects. First, the failures of five years of implementation gave the DUP ample evidence to support its charge that the Belfast Agreement was in urgent need of a fundamental overhaul. With the Assembly suspended and Trimble's strategy of compelling the IRA to disarm failing, it was not difficult for Paisley's party to trumpet the shortcomings of the Agreement or argue that a change of leadership in unionism was needed. Second, those provisions of the deal that had been most unpleasant for unionists such as prisoner releases and RUC reform had been irreversibly realised, meaning that the DUP could contemplate a new deal without being tarnished by association with the most unpalatable, and in its view, immoral (but for the purposes of winning cross-community support, essential) components of the peace process. After the November 2003 election, Trimble commented sarcastically that he would 'look forward to the day when he [Paisley] gets the name of the RUC restored and the released IRA prisoners sent back to jail' (quoted in Tonge, 2006: 75). This remark, intended to point out the hollowness of the DUP's promises to reverse the supposed damage done to unionism by the UUP, also conveyed the reality that Paisley was in the agreeable position of being able to negotiate a deal without the hot potatoes of prisoners and police; the risk, and cost, had already been borne by Trimble.

The third and most significant factor in the DUP's change of tack was the fact that the promise of a new deal, as opposed to no deal, accorded with opinion in the unionist community at the time. That the party's 2003 victory was won on the basis of the 'fair deal'/new agreement message confirms this. A 1999 poll showed that 32 per cent of DUP supporters voted 'yes' in the referendum on the Agreement while 50 per cent wanted to see it work (Irwin, 2002: 235). The 2002 Northern Ireland Life and Times Survey indicated that, while Protestants increasingly believed that nationalists benefited disproportionally from the Agreement, there was nonetheless clear support among Protestants for the two key ideas that underpinned the Agreement – consent and power-sharing. In addition, a significant majority of Protestants – 70 per cent – believed the Assembly had achieved a lot or a little (Mac Ginty, 2004: 92–5). The Northern Ireland Election Studies showed that support among DUP voters for power-sharing actually increased from 32 per cent in 1998 to 65 per cent in 2003 (Mitchell *et al.*, 2009: 409). In sum, unionists, although they resented the Belfast Agreement's outworking, had internalised the principle of accommodation, could see no realistic alternative and did not think the Agreement was entirely without merit.

And so voters, and the DUP, somewhere around 2003, found themselves in the same political territory: incentivised by the attraction of power-sharing but undimmed in their determination to assert and protect their group identity. From the DUP leadership's point of view, the 'principled no' position of the upper echelons of the party was modulated to attract those in the 'pragmatic no' camp – anti-Agreement unionists who perhaps accepted the broad outlines of the Agreement but were unhappy with Sinn Féin's unconditional presence in the Executive (Farrington, 2006: 176). From the voters' point of view, the DUP appeared to offer robust defence of unionist identity concerns – more than the UUP – but also a willingness to make the new politics work. As we saw in Chapter 1, this is what prompts Mitchell *et al.* (2009) to characterise the DUP (and Sinn Féin) as an 'ethnic tribune party', tribunes being those in ancient Rome chosen by plebeians to defend their interests in government.

A DUP–Sinn Féin agreement came close in late 2004. Talks at Leeds Castle in Kent in September of that year and subsequent discussions led to the abortive 'Comprehensive Agreement' in December. This consisted of British and Irish Government proposals on a timetable for the restoration of the institutions, but it collapsed largely due to the demand of the DUP for photographs of IRA decommissioning (Powell, 2008: 261). Gregory Campbell reflects that photographs would have been a significant confidence-building measure for unionists, but: 'I think in hindsight, it was setting it [the bar] a bit too high although it would have been great to get … I think it was a viable request but it was obviously a bridge too far for the Shinners' (interview with Gregory Campbell MP MLA, 7 September 2012). At that time, Paisley famously declared his belief that 'the IRA needs to be humiliated and they need to wear their sackcloth and ashes not privately but in public' (quoted in Rowan, 2005: 100). The religious language again highlighted the theological influence on the unionist political mind. Peter Robinson commented: 'I think [the sackcloth and ashes speech] should have been perhaps looked at in more theological terms than political terms. … What he in effect was saying is we need people who have made a real life change. … Sack cloth and ashes and so forth, was very much that, you know, born again feeling' (quoted in Rowan, 2005: 108). Seen this way, Paisley's purpose was not unlike Trimble's conception of the moral significance of decommissioning as 'an explicit statement that the terrorist campaign was over and an implicit statement that it had been wrong' (Trimble, 2007: 17). But to the IRA, 'sackcloth and ashes' confirmed that Paisley's party was intent on forcing the IRA to surrender, something that it was intent on avoiding.

The Northern Bank robbery and murder of Robert McCartney and subsequent cover-up followed close on the heels of the failed agreement, and the DUP went into the May 2005 election with a pledge that a government that included Sinn Féin was 'out of the question'. However, the manifesto said that Sinn Féin could join the Executive in the event of 'complete visible, verifiable decommissioning' and an end to all illegal activity (DUP, 2005: 7). Later that summer, owing to the huge political pressure on Sinn Féin and the IRA on both sides of the Atlantic, the IRA announced that it had finally and fully decommissioned and declared its war at an end. The DUP responded unhappily; there were witnesses – one Protestant and one Catholic clergyman – but no photographs or detailed inventory as it had demanded, not enough, it said, to build confidence in the unionist community. Nonetheless, it was clear that the IRA move had transformed the political context dramatically, potentially paving the way for an unthinkable pact between the DUP and Sinn Féin

The deal that eventually emerged was branded the St Andrew's Agreement, produced after three days of set-piece talks in the eponymous Scottish town in

October 2006. In April, the Governments had set a deadline of 24 November for inter-party consensus on devolution. Given the DUP's hostility to the 1998 Agreement, one might expect its 'renegotiated' deal to be dramatically different from its predecessor. And the name – 'the something Agreement' – implied a document of equal scope to Good Friday. This was not the case. St Andrews was a relatively slight and technical document that did not upset the fundamental architecture and principles of 1998. In fact, the St Andrews Agreement spelled this out; the Governments reaffirmed their commitment to the 1998 Agreement and advised that 'All parties to this agreement need to be wholeheartedly and publicly committed, in good faith and in a spirit of genuine partnership, to the full operation of stable power-sharing Government and the North-South and East-West arrangements' (St Andrews, 2006: 1). The substance of St Andrews entailed corrections to certain procedural problems that had become apparent in the previous experience of devolution, and various DUP and Sinn Féin wish-list items. New rules designed to improve cohesion in the Executive were outlined. An amended Pledge of Office would require ministers to fully participate in the Executive, British–Irish Council and NSMC, and to observe the joint nature of the First and Deputy First Minister posts. In light of the re-designation affair in 2001, Assembly members would not be allowed to change their community designation for the lifetime of an Assembly. The Northern Ireland Act (2000) that – to the anger of Dublin and the nationalists – had empowered the British Government to suspend the Agreement institutions would be repealed. In addition, the Governments pledged to, inter alia: explore how to resolve the question of contentious parades; move towards a Single Equality Act, Bill of Rights and Irish Language Act (desired by nationalists but, at the time of writing, still unrealised); boost the Ulster-Scots language and culture; and let the fifty/fifty police recruitment policy lapse when Patten's target for Catholic officers was reached. There was also the promise of a generous financial package to underpin renewed devolution (St Andrews, 2006).

But perhaps the most striking provision was the change to the election of First Minister and Deputy First Minister. They would no longer require endorsement by a cross-community vote, but the First Minister would be nominated by the largest party in the largest designation and the Deputy First Minister by the largest party in the second largest designation. This change was arguably a regressive move away from the principle of mutual recognition, though a more positive perspective held that the rule change 'allowed power sharing where trust was lacking' (McGarry and O'Leary, 2009: 62). But a further departure was made in negotiations following St Andrews. The DUP secured agreement that if the largest party in the largest designation was not the largest party overall, the latter should choose the First Minister and the Deputy should come from the largest party in the largest designation. Thus, elections would effectively be referenda on who should be First Minister and it suited both largest parties. The DUP could frighten unionists with the possibility of an ex-IRA First Minister, while Sinn Féin could tempt nationalists with the likelihood that only a vote for Sinn Féin, not the SDLP, could secure a nationalist First Minister. As noted in Chapter 1, these changes to OFMDFM selection inspired the widely held and persistent sense that the DUP–Sinn Féin relationship was less power-sharing than power division, with both sides seeking to capitalise on the mutual fears of the security dilemma (see Moloney, 2008: 473–4).

While the British strove to portray the conclusion of the St Andrews conference as an 'agreement', the parties had not agreed to anything. The narrator of the St Andrews document was not all-party talks participants (as in 1998) but the Governments. St Andrews consisted of the Governments' agreed assessment, in light of separate discussions with the DUP and Sinn Féin, of the measures that should satisfy those parties. In fact, the greatest point of contention between the DUP and Sinn Féin remained to be resolved. This was the demand that Sinn Féin give its support to the police, something that Sinn Féin had said would come only after the devolution of policing and justice powers. The DUP had been persuaded, apparently in part by Mitchell Reiss, the US envoy, that republican support for policing should be the crucial acid test of Sinn Féin's suitability for government (Moloney, 2008: 433). The Governments' Introduction to St Andrews noted their belief that 'support for the police and rule of the law should be extended to every part of the community' (St Andrews, 2006: 2). But it remained to be seen which (or if either) side would 'jump first' on this issue. They were given a month to consult on the proposals. If agreement was not forthcoming, the Governments promised/threatened to 'proceed on the basis of the new British–Irish partnership arrangements to implement the Belfast Agreement' (St Andrews, 2006: 4) This was the so-called 'Plan B' – ongoing Direct Rule with an unspecified degree of increased Dublin involvement. After the month of consultation, the DUP indicated its willingness to proceed towards devolution if Sinn Féin could support policing, a condition that it met at its special conference in January 2007. This opened the way for the historic appearance of Adams and Paisley before the cameras on 26 March and the announcement that devolution day would be 8 May.

Fallout

The DUP's official presentation of the process surrounding St Andrews was that it entailed unionists, robustly represented by the DUP, forcing republicans to meet their demands relating to giving up violence unequivocally. Supposedly, this was an entirely consistent and vindicating climax to its years of opposition to the 1998 Agreement. Paisley wrote in the *News Letter* on 31 March: 'We have been adamant that republicans must take the road to peace and democracy, a road which they did not want to go down. ... Monday, March 26, was a day of great victory for the unionist people of Northern Ireland' (Paisley, 2007b). Yet inevitably, many of Paisley's supporters, accustomed to decades of consistent Paisleyite opposition to republicanism and power-sharing, were left disillusioned and bewildered by the turn of events. Tonge *et al.* (2014), Gordon (2010) and Moloney (2008) provide detailed accounts of the internal friction caused within the DUP by St Andrews. While the party's MEP, Jim Allister – who had a fractious personal relationship with Paisley in any case – was the only high-profile defection, some of the party's top figures were more enthusiastic about the deal than others, while grass-roots disaffection was apparent. A BBC poll published on 9 November found that 31.9 per cent of DUP supporters surveyed did not support the deal, with a further 20 per cent undecided (Devenport, 2006). The dissatisfaction of many within the Free Presbyterian Church led to Paisley being effectively ousted as moderator in 2007.

So why did Paisley decide to enter government with Sinn Féin? Three factors have been suggested: a personal change of heart; long-standing ambition; and the threat of a worse outcome for unionists in the absence of a deal. The 'change of heart' thesis points to his serious illness in 2004, and the influence of his wife Eileen, both of which may have persuaded him of the wisdom of leaving a positive legacy for future generations (Moloney, 2008). Moreover, such softening was facilitated by the patently historic changes in republicanism. Ambition and ego are the preferred explanations of opponents like Allister, and are undoubtedly part of the mix (Gordon, 2010: 208). Indeed, it was widely believed that in spite of Paisley appearing to be naturally and irredeemably anti-establishment, the ambition to lead Ulster was always there. He notably remarked to an *Irish Times* journalist soon after being elected to Stormont in 1969 that 'I would not shirk the duty of becoming Prime Minister of Northern Ireland if the circumstances were such that the people of this country felt I was the right man' (quoted in Smyth, 1987: 28). As Cooke comments on this remark, the implication of all that he had been saying until then was 'that he was the only leader capable of restoring Protestantism to its purity and Ulster to its former glory' (Cooke, 1996: 169). The DUP's post-Agreement rhetoric and activity suggested the same thing. Ambition for power was also evident in other DUP figures such as Robinson, who is credited with masterminding the DUP's post-Agreement strategy. Trimble, for one, believed that from as early as 2000, the Robinson strategy was to allow the UUP to take the political risks in setting up the new arrangements in the hope that it would destroy itself in the process, allowing the DUP to clean up electorally before concluding a deal that would secure the DUP power (Godson, 2004: 496; Gordon, 2010: 211).

Compelling as these explanations are, there was nonetheless a clear political context to the DUP's decision to enter government. First, there was Secretary of State Peter Hain's threat that Direct Rule ministers would proceed with water charges and the abolition of academic selection – 'a very effective form of political blackmail' (Powell, 2008: 279). Second, there was the threat of 'Plan B'. Precisely what 'Plan B' would have consisted of, and the extent to which it was simply a tactic used by the Governments to pressurise the DUP, are not clear (see Gordon, 2010: 14–15). According to Mitchel McLaughlin, it was Sinn Féin that persuaded the British to use the spectre of 'Plan B' to move the DUP at this time (interview with Mitchel McLaughlin MLA, 4 October 2012). But what is clear is that the DUP came to a realisation that the UUP leadership had come to a decade earlier: whether they liked it or not, unionists worked within a context laid down by a sovereign UK Government, and the party had no choice but to adapt to the changing circumstances driven by that Government. Persistent opposition to the plans of the British may have been emotionally satisfying but would ultimately only advantage nationalists (Bruce, 2007: 206; see also Millar, 2008: xvi–xvii).

In April 2007, Paisley told an interviewer that had he not assented to the deal it would have been 'curtains for our country' (Caldwell, 2007); Robinson has made a similar admission of the DUP's limited options (Tonge *et al.*, 2014: 48–9). Like Trimble, these men felt the responsibility of leading unionism: if they did not do a deal, there would not be one, and they would be blamed for it. A leaflet, inserted by the DUP in the *Belfast Telegraph* in October 2006, canvassing readers' views of St Andrews read: 'If you want to save the Union and have a devolved democratic government then the changes which the DUP fought for and obtained in this new Agreement, to safeguard your British and democratic rights, must be made' (DUP, 2006: 1). Thus, the DUP's attempts to sell St Andrews contained the same contradictory mix of triumphalism and anxiety that had characterised the UUP's campaign to sell Good Friday. The DUP was saying that in making some compromises in St Andrews the party was saving the Union and defeating its enemies, yet, simultaneously, it was admitting that it had no real choice but to make those compromises.

The DUP's decision to enter government brought the party unprecedented power and influence, and brought Northern Ireland a degree of political stability it had not known for several decades. In the 2007 Assembly election the party won thirty-six seats, which, coupled with Sinn Féin's strong performance, was viewed as an endorsement of the path the parties were taking towards devolution.

The DUP won a further two seats in 2011 and, apart from independent unionist (former UUP) MP Sylvia Hermon, all unionist Westminster seats have, since 2005, been occupied by the DUP. However, while the DUP's dominant position within unionism (and, indeed, as the largest party overall) appears untouchable for the time being, the party's remarkable about-turn on power-sharing with republicans bequeathed a number of problematic legacies for the party itself and for politics in Northern Ireland.

Perhaps the most tangible was the appearance, for the first time ever, of an electoral rival on its right flank – Traditional Unionist Voice. Jim Allister's campaign of opposition to the DUP–Sinn Féin pact crystallised into a new political party in December 2007. Its electoral performance has been modest, yet the new party, having cornered the market in anti-peace process unionism, has punched above its weight in profile and influence. The new party's first major test was the European election in 2009. Allister, who had been elected as MEP for the DUP in 2004, failed to be re-elected but the result – 66,197 votes (13.7 per cent) for Allister and 88,346 (18.2 per cent) for the DUP's new candidate, Diane Dodds – was regarded as a measure of significant grass-roots disillusionment with the DUP. In 2011, Allister won an Assembly seat and in the 2014 local elections, the party's vote share rose from 2 per cent to 4.5 per cent (thirteen council seats) while Allister improved on his performance in the European poll of that year, winning 75,806 votes. Allister established himself as a fierce and regular critic of the DUP–Sinn Féin alliance in the Assembly and became a fixture in the political media, pursuing the party's aim of being 'the brake on Sinn Féin/DUP misrule' (TUV, 2014).

A second consequence of the DUP re-entering the Executive in 2007 was the nature of governance that followed, widely regarded as ineffective and dysfunctional. This was not solely the fault of the DUP; it was a result of the parallel journeys of both the DUP and Sinn Féin that have seen them enter a cross-community government while failing to disavow their 'wrecker' pasts and insisting on playing to their ethnic bases. After something of a honeymoon period for the new Executive, the novelty of seeing Paisley and McGuinness joking together wore off and the failure of the Executive to deliver good government became apparent. A stand-off over the devolution of policing and justice led to the Executive not even meeting for five months in 2008 and, in early 2010, another round of crisis talks that brought power-sharing to the familiar brink of collapse. A range of critical issues proved to be beyond the capacity of the DUP and Sinn Féin to agree, such as what to do with the site of the Maze/Long Kesh prison, a potential Irish Language Act, welfare reform and the reform of post-primary education. Flags, parading and dealing with the past pushed the parties to their traditional battle lines, while an Executive policy on creating a more shared society did not emerge until 2013 due to disagreement (see Chapter 6). To a certain extent, on all these issues, the DUP and Sinn Féin voiced the concerns of their voters, yet these parties also had a clear self-interest in maintaining a politics of ethnic competition to ensure their dominance within each party's respective ethnic bloc.

A third legacy of the DUP's post-Agreement course has been to contribute to the intense sense of alienation from the new Northern Ireland within working-class Protestant communities. This was evident in the DUP's relationship to the 2012–13 flag protests (see Chapter 6). The flag protesters' anger was not caused primarily by the DUP entering government with Sinn Féin but directed at the perceived campaign of republicans to undermine unionist culture in Northern Ireland. Nevertheless, it was clear that the DUP's new relationship with republicans fed into the protesters' broader sense of disenchantment. As reported in Byrne's (2013) research into the outlook of the protesters, they felt disconnected from the unionist parties, that the DUP had 'sold out' and that working-class Protestants did not have a political voice. One protester said: 'They [the unionist parties] can come and stand at the protests and criticise Sinn Féin but the next day they are doing deals with them and sharing power … that's just hypocritical' (Intercomm and Byrne, 2013: 15). Furthermore, there was resentment at the DUP's actions: first, the party had, along with the UUP, distributed the 40,000 leaflets to raise awareness of the issue, then it had condemned the Council decision to restrict the flag, yet when the protests began, the party was perceived as abandoning them.

Thus, at the heart of the flag protests, was a telling paradox. One the one hand, the flag protesters were complaining that they were politically disenfranchised. Yet on the other hand, the political analysis that motivated the protesters (i.e. that British culture was being undermined by the peace process) was shared by the most powerful party in Northern Ireland, the DUP. So why should loyalists feel unrepresented? The reason was that protesters detected duplicity: the unionist parties heated up the issue by distributing the leaflets yet were an integral part of the political establishment that was empowering the enemy – republicans. This was the political whiplash suffered by many in the Protestant-unionist community as a result of the DUP's deal with Sinn Féin. It was no surprise that many in working-class Protestant communities should have internalised a sense of communal loss: the DUP, in its quest for power, had spent years telling people that they *should* feel a sense of loss, that the peace process was specifically designed to orchestrate Protestant decline. Whether or not the DUP believed its own rhetoric, many loyalists did, and became disillusioned. An interesting indication of the lineage connecting the pre-2007 DUP and the disaffected loyalists was the fact that some protesters too young to clearly remember 1998 self-identified as 'anti-Agreement' (Intercomm and Byrne, 2013: 28; see also Bryson, 2013).

Conclusion

The 1998 Agreement precipitated a sustained and vigorous DUP campaign to exploit and enlarge the fears of unionists for their future, with the explicit purpose of draining support from the UUP. In this, the DUP drew strength from the ongoing subversive activity of its Other, republicans, and the traditional unionist predilection towards pessimism, both of which made unionists receptive to the DUP's claims that its perennial warnings against compromise were correct. However, once the UUP was defeated, hunger for power combined with the undeniable changes within republicanism, plus perhaps a Paisley epiphany, led the DUP to agree to enter government with Sinn Féin. Fatalist logic gave way to the mitigator logic of accommodation. Like republicans, the Paisleyites began the 'Troubles' with a disastrously flawed analysis, an analysis that, among other things, exaggerated threats and helped to fulfil its own prophecies of street unrest and political instability. Significantly, there has been some admission of 'learning'. In a BBC documentary on Paisley's life aired in January 2014, the former party leader said that he accepted that Catholics had been discriminated against under the pre-1972 Stormont regime: 'If you vote down democracy you bring in anarchy. It wasn't one man, one vote. I mean, that's no way to run a country. The whole system was wrong' (BBC, 2014a). Robinson has conceded that 'unionists were slow to accept or appreciate that after the fall of the majority rule Parliament at Stormont in 1972, some form of power-sharing was inevitable' (Robinson, 2012a). These are extraordinary admissions given the central role played by Paisley and the DUP in both opposing the reform of the majority-rule system and, later, precipitating the collapse of the Sunningdale power-sharing government.

While the DUP can still be reasonably described as a hard-line unionist party, the persona that the DUP traded on for over three decades – that of persecuted but uncompromising innocent – is no more. Claims that the party represents the 'politics of holiness' (Thomson, 1998) or the 'politics of purity' (Mitchel, 2003), so apt for so long, require revision following the party's entry to the muddy terrain of negotiation, deal-making and governing. In government, the responsibilities of civic leadership have required the DUP to adopt positions that it would unlikely have countenanced before. One minor but instructive example is the fact that Peter Robinson has been strongly supportive of the ongoing and lucrative production of the American television drama *Game of Thrones* in Northern Ireland, despite the fact that many in his party, in times past, would likely have picketed the sets of such an 'immoral' programme. Explicit religious references are rare in the party's rhetoric, although anti-homosexuality, opposition to abortion, creationism and Sabbatarianism have all been evident in DUP policy positions. This has led to charges of a theocracy. But the DUP is nonetheless constrained by the democratic system while, it must be said, the DUP's approach reflects the relative conservatism of much of its constituency.

Alongside the DUP's immersion in the daily detail of governing, a number of affairs and revelations concerning the party have disrupted the air of infallibility that previously surrounded the party. These include the personal and financial scandal that engulfed Iris Robinson in early 2010 and the forced resignation of Ian Paisley Junior from his post as OFMDFM Junior Minister due to allegations of improper dealings with a property developer (see Gordon, 2010). In the aforementioned BBC documentary, Paisley Senior revealed that he had in fact been forced out of his leadership role in the party in 2008, principally by Robinson and Dodds (BBC, 2014a). This revelation – already known but now described with some bitterness by Paisley himself who had previously denied being forced to quit – obliterated the traditional image of the DUP as a happy family, united in purpose. It also indicated the closing of the Paisley era within unionist politics: the DUP was no longer 'Paisley's' party, neither in fact nor in spirit.

As First Minister, Robinson has encouraged integrated education, praised the Gaelic Athletic Association, and argued that unionism must not be tied to any exclusive cultural or religious trappings. For example, in a 2012 speech in Dublin, he argued:

> For unionism to prosper in the decades to come it must be inclusive and not exclusive. I want to see a broad and inclusive unionism that can embrace all shades of those who support Northern Ireland's present constitutional position. Unionism must reach far beyond its traditional base if it is to maximise its potential. That means forming a pro-Union consensus with people from different religious and community backgrounds.
> (Robinson, 2012b)

Such sentiments are indistinguishable from Trimble's thinking back in 1998, that the Union is most secure if nationalists are accommodated within it; though again, as with Trimble, there are limits to how far Robinson will accommodate nationalists if it means affecting the British character of the state. That became evident during the flag protests when the DUP found itself sharing the street protesters' viewpoint. Yet the fact that it was powerless to reverse the decision made by Belfast City Council and was, indeed, in receipt of blame from the protesters for lending republicans respectability at Stormont, showed that the Democratic Unionists, even in power as the largest party, were at the mercy of wider political realities. Its role in and response to the flag protests also showed that despite Robinson's calls for a more confident unionism and an end to its traditional siege mentality, the party was still quite comfortable with the politics of fear, fatalism and flag-waving. While this outlook may reflect that of many of the party's voters, and may offer some temporary solace, it is not an outlook that lends itself to political stability, cross-community trust or reducing the mono-ethnic ethos of the DUP. Yet those are key to Robinson's stated goal of strengthening the Union through greater unionist inclusivity, and, indeed, are in the vested interests of his party that relishes its position at the centre of power so much.

6

Alliance Party of Northern Ireland

Introduction

In March 2014 a candidate for the upcoming European election remarked to a reporter from the nationalist *Irish News* that she believed the partition of Ireland was 'artificial', that a united Ireland would be 'better placed economically, socially and politically' and that she was 'anti-colonial'. The apparently off-the-cuff comments, hardly unusual in Northern Irish political opining, set off a minor media storm because the speaker was Anna Lo, the high-profile, ethnically Chinese Alliance Party MLA. Unionists seized upon the comments as offensive and questioned Alliance's support for the constitutional status quo endorsed in the Agreement. For them, still enraged by Alliance's role in the Belfast City Hall flag decision, and eager to make political capital, Lo revealed what they already knew: that Alliance was not a unionist party and thus safely assumed to be a nationalist party. Lo's party colleagues, however, responded by arguing that a diversity of aspiration was entirely in keeping with the party's cross-community nature and did not undermine its acceptance of the principle of consent. The chief interest in the comments for political observers was the possibility that they would damage the party's support among moderate Protestants, the constituency from which it drew most of its support, and/or may even have been calculated to extend the party's appeal in the Catholic community (on this affair, see BBC, 2014b).

The episode demonstrated how, even sixteen years after the Agreement, an extremely distant potentiality – change in the constitutional status of Northern Ireland – continued to be widely and routinely invoked as the paramount political issue that should determine how people vote. The controversy also neatly dramatised the Alliance Party's perennial challenge: to express and expand its distinctive location in Northern Ireland politics as neither unionist nor nationalist. How the party went about this after the Agreement is the core concern of this chapter. It begins by exploring the party's founding purposes, its outlook on identity and the constitutional question, and its proposals for resolving the conflict. Alliance's position on the Agreement is then set out with a focus on how the party regarded the document as falling short of its own proposals for creating an integrated society. Then the chapter examines Alliance's status as the main holder of the 'other' designation in the Assembly, and assesses the merits of Alliance's grievances that the Agreement penalised 'others' and gave succour to the very identities that had driven the conflict – unionism and nationalism. Other significant themes, including the party's commitment to promoting a shared society, joining the Executive in 2010 and its role in the flag protests of 2012–13, are analysed.

Beyond, and between, Orange and Green

The Alliance Party was yet another product of the political turmoil of the early 1970s that transformed Northern Ireland's party-political configuration. Formed in April 1970, the party emerged from a split in the New Ulster Movement, a liberal unionist pressure group, as a response to the perceived rightward lurch of the Ulster Unionist Party (UUP) and the rise of Paisleyism. The new party supported the demands of the civil rights campaign and its immediate aim was to support the Stormont Government's programme of reform (Pyle, 1970). Alliance's launch document, *Declaration of Intent: A New Political Charter* (Alliance, 1970), expressed the founders' tacit understanding of the fearful dynamics of the security dilemma, deeper into which the region was slipping. The party rejected the political system of de facto one-party unionist rule, 'democratic in form but not in spirit', which had resulted in a 'shapeless community, riven by sectarian fear'. There was an urgent need for a party whose 'primary objective is to heal the bitter divisions in our community'. Four founding principles were outlined: partnership government between unionists and nationalists; support for the constitutional position of Northern Ireland within the United Kingdom; no adherence to any specific economic policy; and firm and impartial enforcement of the rule of law (Alliance, 1970). The party viewed support for power-sharing and the constitutional position as a 'dual compromise' that could 'allay the fundamental fears of both the Catholic and Protestant sections of the community' (Cushnahan, 1979: 2).

However, the party's credibility was immediately questioned by commentators: it was claimed that Alliance consisted only of middle-class people, an accusation that has followed the party ever since. Oliver Napier, who led the party from 1972 until 1984, accepted that there may have been such a bias but said that he wished to 'disprove the myth that the only moderates were from the middle class' (Pyle, 1970). The party did attract some support from former backers of the Northern Ireland Labour Party (Elliott and Flackes, 1999: 157), but nevertheless, party members have traditionally tended to be urban/suburban well-educated professionals (Evans and Tonge, 2001). Alliance's first electoral test was the 1973 local government elections when it won 13.7 per cent of the vote. In the Assembly election the following month the party polled 9.2 per cent and won eight seats, a result that led to Napier and his deputy Bob Cooper taking seats in the short-lived Sunningdale power-sharing Executive. Alliance's most dramatic electoral result (prior to Naomi Long's Westminster victory in East Belfast in 2010) was in 1979 when Napier came within 928 votes of victor, Peter Robinson. In 1981, local election vote share fell from 14.4 per cent (in 1977) to 8.9 per cent, undoubtedly due to the polarising impact of the Hunger Strikes of that year.

Throughout the 1990s Alliance's vote hovered between 6 and 8 per cent and it appeared to suffer from the peace process's focus on securing agreement between the larger parties. In 1998, the party won six seats (6.5 per cent of the vote) and retained them in 2003, although with just 3.6 per cent of the vote. Since 2007, the party's fortunes have been on a modest rise. It won seven seats in 2007 (5.2 per cent) and eight in 2011 (7.7 per cent). In 2010, it won its first Westminster seat in East Belfast. The weakness of Alliance in the west of the province, and in polarised constituencies like North Belfast, is evident in the fact that in the 2001 Westminster election, Alliance did not even run candidates in Fermanagh and South Tyrone, West Tyrone, Mid-Ulster, Newry and Armagh, Upper Bann and North Belfast, a third of Northern Ireland's constituencies. In 2005, the party was absent from five constituencies; in 1997 and 2010, the party was present in all, yet support remained concentrated in Belfast and its hinterland.

Alliance has based its distinct brand of 'bi-confessionalism in a confessional party system' (McAllister and Wilson, 1978) on a number of claims regarding identity. First, the party has stressed that many people in Northern Ireland identify with neither unionism nor nationalism. These include those in 'mixed' marriages, members of ethnic minorities and those who choose a more multi-layered identity. Second, the party argues that many Protestants and Catholics have more in common with people across the communal divide than with each other: 'It is particularly insulting to suggest to many Protestants that they have more in common with Ian Paisley than with any Catholics, and to suggest to many Catholics that they have more in common with Gerry Adams than any Protestants' (Farry and Neeson, 1999: 1225). Third, Alliance has a particular view of the nature of group identity itself:

> We acknowledge that people identify with and belong to religious, ethnic, cultural and regional communities. These however are not permanent or stable, but are open and fluid. People can have open, mixed and multiple identities. They can belong to many groups, have a complex identity, and have loyalties to different structures and levels of government.
>
> (Alliance, 2013a: 14)

Identity is multi-dimensional and can evolve over time, and, in tune with the analysis of the societal security dilemma presented in Chapter 1, Alliance recognises the manner in which insecurity and mutual threat hardens identities and fuels the fatalist logic: 'violence in support of the "two communities" idea has forced generations of people into choices about security which have embedded hatred and condemned others to silence and marginalisation' (p. 13). Fourth, Alliance implies that unionism and nationalism are inherently destabilising. Shared institutions of government require a shared identity and allegiance to function, and so political stability requires the diminution of unionism and nationalism; 'As long as we cling to two mutually exclusive "identities", our conflict is likely to rumble on' (Alliance, 2004: 2).

In support of these claims, the party often points to polling data that indicate the large number of people who say they are neither unionists nor nationalists; in the 2013 Northern Ireland Life and Times Survey, that figure was 46 per cent (ARK, 2014). The party also highlights the high level of public support for integrated education and a more shared society. However, the paradox is that while polls suggest that many people appear to be sympathetic to much of Alliance's vision, very few people vote for it, or ever have. In the Assembly election of 2011, only 13 per cent did not vote for unionist or nationalist parties. Leadership problems, the lack of media appeal of a moderate party, the 'prisoner's dilemma' nature of voting in Northern Ireland, the popularity of the Social Democratic and Labour Party (SDLP) among moderate Catholics, voter apathy, the middle-class base of the party and the nature of the Agreement institutions have all been advanced as explaining Alliance's limited popularity.

While Alliance has rejected unionism and nationalism from its foundation, the question of whether or not Alliance is 'really' a unionist party has followed it throughout its history. There are three reasons for this, one being the party's origins within liberal unionism. A second is the fact that the majority of its votes and membership have come from the Protestant community and have been concentrated in the Greater Belfast area. In a survey of party members, only a fifth identified as Catholic (Evans and Tonge, 2001: 111). The Northern Ireland Life and Times Survey shows that, usually, the proportion of Catholics that support the party is around half the proportion of Protestants. A partial explanation for this bias in support may be the limited attraction of its liberal ideology to a relatively conservative and communitarian Catholic community; Alliance is affiliated to the UK Liberal Democrats and a member of the Liberal International (interview with Duncan Morrow, Alliance council candidate, 20 May 2014). But the third and primary reason is the party's explicit position that the principle of consent should decide the constitutional status of Northern Ireland. *Declaration of Intent* couched the new party's support for the Union in pragmatic, rather than British nationalist, terms: most people in Northern Ireland supported the Union and challenging it was the main cause of the political turmoil of the day. Alliance also vaunted the Union as being in the 'best economical and social interest of all citizens of the state' and for bringing 'British standards of democracy and social justice' (Alliance, 1970), very 'unionist' swipes at the Irish Republic.

What is not clear here is why Alliance should regard the six counties as the unit of self-determination rather than the thirty-two. The party has since tried to address this question by suggesting that the Northern counties have always been set apart from the rest of Ireland. For instance, in its submission to the multi-party talks, Alliance posited that:

> In more reliable history we are informed that when Congal of Ulster was fighting with Domnal of Meath as far back as 637 AD, his support came from his friends in Scotland. This suggests that there has never been a simple unity of the people of Ireland, that the Northern people have long had a sense of separateness, and often felt closer to those who lived across the channel in Scotland, than they did to those in the south-west of the island. ... For this, and many other historical reasons, the people of the North, with their many different origins, religious views, political affiliations, and cultural attachments, have always been seen as forming a community, though without entirely consistent geographical boundaries.
>
> (Alliance, 1997)

This argument is intended to support Alliance's project of building a united community within Northern Ireland, yet it takes no account of the fact that Northern Ireland was created by and for Protestants. *Declaration of Intent* chastises the unionist and nationalist parties 'for whom the clock stopped in 1920' (Alliance, 1970), yet equally, Alliance could be charged with starting its clock in 1920, accepting the six-county entity, and ignoring the sectarian head count, and threat of violence, that led to its foundation. In the membership survey, 27.6 per cent actually agreed that Alliance was a unionist party and only 2.8 per cent agreed that it was a nationalist party, while remaining within the United Kingdom was by far the preferred constitutional option (Evans and Tonge, 2001: 110–11). However, the party has also been accused of being 'really' a nationalist party. David Ford, party leader from 2001, annoyed unionists when he said he was 'agnostic' about the Union (*News Letter*, 2009), while the Belfast City Hall flag affair and Anna Lo's comments were lightning rods for unionist anger that Alliance was a de facto collaborator in a republican agenda.

Clearly, conveying its non-ethnic identity within a deeply divided society and party system has been challenging, with accusations of bias from both sides being occupational hazards of its centrist positioning. But the party continues to insist that it is neither unionist nor nationalist. Duncan Morrow points out that many Protestants in Alliance are there because they are self-consciously *not* unionist and fixated on the national issue:

> [Being in Alliance] was a way to say we don't think the Union is the key issue, the key issue is how we treat each other. Actually, it's a value problem. There's a values issue here which says that nationality is a subordinate issue to how people treat each other ... So therefore we are what seems to be impossible for people to even accept: utterly and absolutely pragmatic about the border. It is not a metaphysical issue for us, it is an issue of how do we best organise this community so that we can best live together. And, as it stands, that means that it is very clear that the majority wish to remain in the United Kingdom at the moment.
> (Interview with Duncan Morrow, 20 May 2014)

Alliance MLA Chris Lyttle mentions the Lo controversy in explaining Alliance's core goal of preventing the constitutional question from pitting people against each other:

> Anna's comment I think has challenged us to clarify what our party position is and I think it's best summed up that we're a 'united Northern Ireland' party as opposed to anything else. But we have people who are unionist, people who are nationalist, people who are neither, and that's what the Good Friday Agreement was about as well, the principle of consent and your entitlement to be British, Irish, both. I think it provides a challenge to society to get back to seeing what it was we actually agreed in 1998 and I think there's a lot of faux anger from some elected representatives in relation to what Anna said, you know.
> (Interview with Chris Lyttle MLA, 4 April 2014)

The Agreement does cast Alliance's position on the Union in a less unionist light. The acceptance of the principle of consent across the political spectrum and in the Republic makes Alliance's support for Northern Ireland's right to decide its constitutional status less distinctively unionist; as Lyttle points out, a diversity of aspiration within the party is not inconsistent with Alliance's acceptance of the constitutional present as set out in the Agreement since this is the kind of Northern Ireland the Agreement envisaged. Furthermore, the party has qualified its support for consent by, like the SDLP, pointing to the declining significance of borders in a European context. Accordingly, the party has proposed that the principle of consent should be allowed to test public support for other constitutional options that may be devised in the future than simply maintaining the Union or joining the Republic (Alliance, 2004: 6).

Alliance's approach to solving Northern Ireland's political problems was to consistently support cross-community power-sharing. It unequivocally condemned the use of violence and took part in the various talks initiatives throughout the 'Troubles'. However, the party's philosophy and activism were less influential on the shape of the peace process that emerged in the 1990s than those of the SDLP. Alliance's vision of achieving a settlement within Northern Ireland underpinned by a common 'Northern' identity proved inadequate to the task of addressing the desire of Catholics to have their Irish identity institutionally recognised and failed to attract large numbers of Catholic voters after the end of the 1970s. As highlighted by Leonard (1999: 37), the Anglo-Irish Agreement posed an 'ideological challenge' to Alliance. The 1985 Agreement, heavily influenced by John Hume, bypassed the Northern parties and recognised Northern Catholics' Irish identity by giving Dublin an advocacy role on their behalf. This affirmation of Catholic nationalist group identity clashed with Alliance's aspiration of a liberal democracy in which individual rights were paramount. North–South linkages had always been limited in Alliance proposals.

As a multi-party Agreement came closer in the 1990s, it was clear that the emerging arrangements were out of step with Alliance's programme. In its submission to the talks, Alliance challenged the apparent thrust of the process towards balancing two identities rather than pursuing a society devoid of ethnic categories: 'setting out two separate sets of mirroring rights, with parity of esteem between only two traditions ... would not be a healing of the divisions but an institutionalising of them'. Alliance went on to outline its vision:

> Instead we should recognise one set of rights that applies to everyone, one community with a number of rich, overlapping strands of culture and tradition, and recognition of an inclusive pluralism of religious and political thought and adherence which does not marginalise the partners and children of mixed marriages, the values of integrated education, and interdenominational religious activities, and political liberals who do not espouse nationalism of one kind or another.
>
> (Alliance, 1997)

What it perceived as the circumscribed, conflict management approach of the peace process, coupled with Alliance's political weakness, posed a dilemma for the party. Should it support a process that was likely to reduce violent conflict but which it believed was inimical to its liberal philosophy? The party took a pragmatic approach. Alliance's ideal was a liberal society in which unionism and nationalism were either gone, or among a number of equally salient and cross-cutting identities. The reality was that unionism and nationalism persisted while Alliance remained a minor force. Thus, the party made its arguments for a post-Orange/Green society while seeking ways to facilitate accommodation between Orange and Green in the hope that warming cross-community relations expanded the constituency of people whose primary allegiance was to Northern Ireland, rather than Britain or the Republic, and furthered the goal of a united society. This explains Alliance's qualified acceptance of the 1998 Agreement and commitment to its implementation. Indeed, although Alliance was, as we will see, highly critical of consociational aspects of the Agreement that it thought illiberal, a rationale of consociationalism as a temporary measure with transformational potential has been articulated by consociationalism's exponents in very similar terms to the Alliance Party (see McGarry and O'Leary, 2009: 68–9). Or, in terms of our conceptual framework, the mitigator logic of the Agreement, embodied in the joint institutions, security reforms and rights protections, might create the conditions in which the security dilemma could be transcended through trust.

In the talks leading to the 1998 Agreement, the party's agenda was based largely on its 1988 proposals for devolution, *Governing with Consent* (Alliance, 1988). The party advocated a power-sharing assembly governed by a voluntary coalition with decisions taken by a weighted majority of 67 per cent (Alliance, 1997). The party supported the creation of North–South structures, due both to their significance for nationalists and their social and economic benefits. The principle of consent and British sovereignty would remain given the continued will of a majority in Northern Ireland, yet this should be balanced by a robust equality agenda consisting of 'measures to overcome the continuing legacies of long-past discrimination … and making the symbolism and ethos of Northern Ireland more neutral' (Farry and Neeson, 1999: 1233). Alliance did not regard decommissioning as a precondition for talks with paramilitary-linked parties; being on ceasefire was a precondition and the party supported the temporary exclusion of the Ulster Democratic Party (in January 1998) and Sinn Féin (in February 1998) when the Ulster Defence Association and Irish Republican Army breached their ceasefires. Alliance, like Sinn Féin, had little influence within the multi-party talks due to the sufficient consensus rule that meant that an accord could be reached with a majority of unionism and nationalism. Thus, the party was forced into a mediatory role at the expense of pursuing its own agenda and it viewed itself as a 'weathervane', an indicator of whether the emerging deal could command the support of both sides (Leonard, 1999: 52).

The Agreement: 'a Band-Aid solution'

Alliance accepted the Agreement in full, yet believed that the deal contained the 'two-communities' assumptions of which the party had warned. Most inimical to Alliance's politics was the requirement of Assembly members to designate themselves 'unionist', 'nationalist' or 'other'. The party believed that embedding political/ethnic labels into the highest level of government in this way, first, offended its liberal values. Second, designations legitimised and accepted the oppositional identities that Alliance ultimately wished to see diminish in favour of a common Northern Irish identity: 'The language of "two communities," even though it is based in dubious assumptions, is given "respectability" through its formal usage in the Agreement' (Farry and Neeson, 1999: 1241). Third, the word 'other' was deemed dismissive; the party would have preferred 'centre'. Fourth, the designations were there for the purpose of facilitating particular cross-community voting arrangements that Alliance argued were unfair. These were set out in the Agreement as follows:

(i) either parallel consent, i.e. a majority of those members present and voting, including a majority of the unionist and nationalist designations present and voting;
(ii) or a weighted majority (60%) of members present and voting, including at least 40% of each of the nationalist and unionist designations present and voting.

(Agreement, 1998: 5)

Such mechanisms meant that the votes of parties designated 'others' were worth less than those of unionists and nationalists; 'To misquote Orwell: all votes are equal, but some are more equal than others' (Ford, 2001a). This relative powerlessness, Alliance thought, could dissuade voters from supporting non-unionist/nationalist parties. Parallel consent also ran the risk of paralysing the Assembly since growth of anti-Agreement forces could make the threshold unobtainable; Alliance would have preferred contentious issues to be decided by an overall weighted majority. The party also objected to the Agreement's provision that the Executive should comprise all parties eligible under the d'Hondt formula rather than being formed by parties who could agree a common platform and could attain a weighted majority of Assembly representatives, i.e. a voluntary coalition. This, warned the party, was another provision that could lead to fragmented, uncoordinated government (Farry and Neeson, 1999; Alliance, 2004). The validity of these criticisms is assessed presently.

With regard to decommissioning, Alliance noted that decommissioning had not taken place in parallel with talks as the Mitchell Report had envisaged; now, with the Agreement in place, the paramilitaries could have no reasonable objections to decommissioning. While the party's 1998 Assembly election manifesto made a broad statement about the importance of the ending of paramilitarism to the building of trust between parties, and that 'Alliance believes that the early release of prisoners and participation in Government must be linked to the dismantling of terrorist organisations' (Alliance, 1998a), the party nevertheless did not regard decommissioning as a precondition for paramilitary-associated parties to hold Executive office. Alliance welcomed the formation of a commission to make recommendations of police reform, viewing as appropriate action to make it more representative of Catholics and women and changes to the name and symbols. However, the party was to oppose the fifty/fifty recruitment policy on the grounds that it was 'contradictory to the ethos of an integrated service, is discriminatory, and in practice unnecessary' (Alliance, 2004: 25). As for the issue of prisoners, Alliance recognised the likely hurt caused to victims but nonetheless deemed the release of paramilitary prisoners necessary for securing the support of paramilitary-linked parties for the Agreement (on all these matters, see Alliance, 1998a; Farry and Neeson, 1999).

Overall, the Alliance Party viewed the Agreement as a transitional mechanism and a means to an end – a not dissimilar conception to that of Sinn Féin. In the case of Alliance, the end was not to be an all-Ireland republic but a liberal, group-blind democracy remaining, for the time being, within the United Kingdom, governed by integrative power-sharing institutions. Although, in Alliance's estimation, the Agreement was more conflict management than conflict resolution – 'a Band-Aid solution' (Farry and Neeson, 1999: 1221) – the Agreement was not thought to preclude the realisation of Alliance's vision and hence the party accepted it. In an internal party discussion document dated August 1997, Stephen Farry attempted to outline an agenda for the party in the event of a multi-party agreement that fell short of the Alliance ideal. He encouraged the party to view power-sharing as temporary 'affirmative action' and an 'honourable compromise rather than a final solution':

> The direct creation and maintenance of a liberal democracy in the current political climate is unlikely to address the ethnic-nationalist demands of unionism and nationalism. ... While the creation of a liberal democracy should be portrayed as the Alliance solution, in reality conflict management techniques, which recognise the persistence of deep divisions in Northern Ireland, will have to be adopted in the short to medium term, until the underlying problems that sustain conflict are sufficiently minimised.
> (Farry, 1997: 26)

Making the post-Agreement period a 'transitional phase' leading to liberal democracy required increased support for the political centre, a stronger sense of shared identity among the public and a reduction of the importance of the constitutional question relative to social and economic issues. This, then, said Farry, should be the party's agenda, and Alliance should position itself as an opposition to the UUP and SDLP, ready to capitalise on dissatisfaction with the main parties. Alliance's political strength would act as a barometer of how ready Northern Ireland was to progress towards a normal democracy (pp. 25–6).

Farry admitted, however, that this was an 'ambitious' programme, and without doubt, in 1998, the party's prospects appeared contradictory. On the one hand, it seemed likely that enduring peace and stability would benefit Alliance. If the Agreement proved to successfully neuter the constitutional issue, and peace held, people might show a greater openness to voting for centre parties and less concern with shoring up their 'tribe'. Unionist and nationalist identities, polarised by years of violence and mistrust, could become more pluralist and tolerant, and the Agreement and its institutions could engender a greater sense of common belonging and destiny, thus expanding the constituency of the 'Northern Irish' and the 'third tradition' to the advantage of Alliance. On the other hand, there were compelling reasons to believe that ethnic voting would continue and perhaps increase after the Agreement. The Agreement accepted unionist and nationalist cultures and aspirations as equally valid, and did not incentivise support for parties outside the two main blocs. Implementation would throw up a range of divisive issues that could feed antagonistic identities, and if the voters were dissatisfied with the performance of the UUP and SDLP on Orange and Green disputes, their support was likely to go to the DUP and Sinn Féin rather than Alliance.

As it happened, Alliance's vote in the 1998 Assembly election was indeed poorer than the party hoped. The party won six seats; eight or nine would have given them a place in the Executive. The party's magazine editorialised that 'sadly it seems that voters still believe that it is possible to make things work by bolstering their own tribe to represent their interests. The results show the enormity of the task of creating a realignment in politics' (*Alliance News*, 1998). In its campaign – despite the fact that it was sceptical of some of the arrangements, and arguably marginal to their operation and the resolution of remaining issues – Alliance actually styled itself as essential to the new politics: 'You can only trust Alliance to make it work', said an election communication. 'We all know that before long, they'll start facing each other down again, and it will all unwind. We need a strong Alliance vote to hold it together' (Alliance, 1998b). However, this pitch to be a bridge-builder and the party's hope that both its own support and a new identity among people would grow looked increasingly irrelevant as post-Agreement politics came to be dominated by struggles within and between the ethnic blocs. In those struggles, every unionist and nationalist vote mattered and the party's 'other' label appeared to sum up its rather awkward placing in the new dispensation.

Being the 'other' party

The tension between Alliance's desire to support the Agreement and its principled rejection of certain of its procedures came to a head in two episodes in 2001, when the party faced a predicament that had been widely predicted: either align with pro-Agreement unionism in support of political stability, or maintain its position of neutrality and jeopardise the Agreement. In the June 2001 Westminster election, Alliance refrained from running in several constituencies in order to assist pro-Agreement unionist candidates. In two cases this move was decisive. Stephen Farry stepped aside in North Down in order to boost the support of pro-Agreement UUP candidate Sylvia Hermon, who was facing a challenge from the anti-Agreement United Kingdom Unionist Party's Bob McCartney. Justifying the decision in the local paper, Farry said that 'people should view a vote for Hermon as not necessarily a vote for Ulster Unionism but for the Agreement' and that opting not to run was a 'one-off' (Farry, 2001). Hermon was elected, as was David Trimble in Upper Bann, who also may have lost without the support of Alliance voters (*Alliance News*, 2001). The decisions not to run spurred the resignation in protest of Alliance deputy leader, Séamus Close.

This electoral strategy foreshadowed a more dramatic contortion of principle later in the year: the affair concerning re-designation in the Assembly in early November 2001. The Assembly had been in limbo since July when Trimble had resigned as First Minister due to the lack of IRA decommissioning and London subsequently suspended the institutions. After a 'significant' act of decommissioning verified by the Independent International Commission on Decommissionng in October, Trimble decided to return to the Assembly and renominate UUP ministers to the Executive. However, restoring devolution faced the hurdle of the joint election, by parallel consent, of Trimble as First Minister and Mark Durkan as Deputy First Minister. This was in doubt, given the fine balance of pro- and anti-Agreement unionist MLAs. The Women's Coalition secured a change in Assembly rules allowing one of its MLAs to immediately re-designate as unionist in order to shore up Trimble's support. But, in the election on 2 November, Trimble and Durkan were defeated by one vote when two of Trimble's own MLAs, Pauline Armitage and Peter Weir, voted with the anti-Agreement DUP. Thus, the pressure was on Alliance MLAs to re-designate as unionist and support Trimble in a re-run of the election (see Purdy, 2005).

The prospect of compromising its neutrality to facilitate an electoral procedure that it had always opposed put Alliance in an invidious position. The party had long warned that parallel consent voting – as well as being 'institutionalised sectarianism' – created a hostage to fortune; it had been designed to protect a nationalist minority but in actuality would likely give undue influence to another 'minority', anti-Agreement unionism, which could prevent overall unionist support for key decisions. Now, the growth of anti-Agreement unionism was forcing Alliance to take sides. Three Alliance MLAs re-designated as unionist – temporarily for seven days – in return for a British Government commitment to hold a review of voting procedures in the Assembly – and Trimble and Durkan were elected on 6 November. Writing in the *Irish Times* on the 5 November, David Ford, the new Alliance leader, said that the situation in which the party found itself 'stank', but 'some of us are reluctantly prepared to hold our noses for a week' (Ford, 2001b). Survey evidence showed subsequently that a majority of party members opposed re-designation (Evans and Tonge, 2003), while two Alliance MLAs refused to do so at the time.

The party endeavoured to portray this episode as a learning opportunity that highlighted the flaws in the Agreement and vindicated its policy preference for weighted majority voting. In the review of Assembly voting that followed the November election, Alliance pointed out that in the first, failed vote, Trimble and Durkan had received 70.6 per cent of MLAs votes: 'In virtually every other legislative body in the world, a 70% vote would be more than sufficient to elect a Prime Minister/form a Government. But not in Northern Ireland' (Alliance, 2001: 1). However, the voting system remained. In fact, the St Andrew's Agreement entrenched the practice of designations by forbidding re-designation within the term of an Assembly (St Andrews, 2006). Instead of undermining the communal designations, the episode highlighted both the vulnerability of the Agreement and the difficult position of the Alliance Party. The procedural fiddling to allow speedy re-designations and Secretary of State for Northern Ireland John Reid's decision to ignore a deadline on 3 November to call an Assembly election in order to facilitate the reprised vote gave much ammunition to those who believed the Agreement lacked cross-community legitimacy and that the supporters of the deal were bereft of principle. Indeed, the election of Trimble and Durkan precipitated the so-called 'Brawl in the Hall' when scuffles broke out in Stormont's Great Hall between pro- and anti-Trimble unionists (Purdy, 2005).

Protecting the Agreement had required the greatest compromise of Alliance's non-aligned, liberal principles yet: officially declaring itself unionist, albeit temporarily. And, in light of this episode, the party's vision of the Agreement establishing a transitional period in which the centre could grow appeared more and more implausible, given the centrifugal forces at work. Indeed, some saw the re-designation affair as an indicator of the increasing decline of the party, notwithstanding Alliance's promise that it would not be repeated. In the view of Evans and Tonge (2003), growth of anti-Agreement opinion would likely again demand that Alliance support the pro-Agreement UUP, thus alienating Catholic Alliance members and undermining the party's *raison d'être*, and the UUP/SDLP would replace Alliance as the centre ground in Northern Ireland politics. Mitchell (2002: 41) recommended that, to stymie decline, the party's best option in the face of the tribal electorate was to market itself as a non-sectarian unionist party.

The course of political events meant that Alliance did not face serious pressure to re-designate again. The Assembly was suspended in October 2002 and, on its return in 2007 after the Sinn Féin–DUP deal, contained a secure pro-power-sharing majority on both sides. Suspension, which was due to alleged spying by Sinn Féin, meant that Alliance's policy of voluntary coalition gained credibility (and put the party oddly in sync with the DUP, which also sought a resumption of devolution minus Sinn Féin). Voluntary coalition was not now simply philosophically preferable or potentially more efficient than mandatory coalition, but also offered a real path out of the deadlock. In an *Irish News* article, Ford explained that:

> Our proposals were not developed to exclude Sinn Féin but to provide for more effective cross-community government. It is entirely possible for Sinn Féin to be part of such arrangements, provided that it can meet the same standards of democracy, human rights and the rule of law as any other parties. However, where any party does not have the confidence of others, the system removes any veto and allows movement.
>
> (Ford, 2005)

There was not, said Ford, enough trust and confidence for the mandatory coalition system to operate, and he went on to blame the SDLP and the two Governments for being excessively wedded to inclusivity. The SDLP 'is taking pressure off Sinn Féin by refusing to even consider a voluntary coalition'; Tony Blair 'appears to have decided to do nothing to upset Sinn Féin, regardless of the consequences for the rest of this community' (Ford, 2005). Continuing IRA violence gave a moral charge to Alliance's call for moving on without Sinn Féin, and in its rhetoric Alliance attempted to take the moral high ground from the SDLP, which would not consider such a way forward.

However, Alliance's unceasing calls for voluntary coalition and an end to communal designations fell on deaf ears throughout the post-Agreement period;

the Governments would not countenance either, preferring to hold out for an accommodation between unionism – first the UUP, then, from 2003, the DUP – and republicans. To those efforts, the 'other' party was surplus to requirements. Alliance nevertheless argued that communal designations and voting were not simply unfair to 'others', but responsible for the polarisation within unionism and nationalism and the concomitant impasse. After the November 2003 elections, Farry wrote that the 'swing to the extremes' was entirely predictable:

> The principle cause of this result is the institutionalised sectarianism within the Agreement. Rather than trying to create a new political culture in which all parties seek to work in the common interest, the Agreement has entrenched a system of intra-ethnic competition within two separate Unionist and Nationalist polities. The extremes on either side have been able to exploit the 'them' and 'us' mentality either by arguing that the perceived moderates on each side have been selling out 'their community' or by claiming that they can negotiate a 'fairer deal'.
>
> (Farry, 2004)

Whether or not the election result was due to 'institutionalised sectarianism within the Agreement' – and it is doubtful, as we now explore – the squeeze on the centre ground was clear. Alliance vote share fell from 6.5 per cent in 1998 to 3.6 per cent in 2001 (Westminster) and 3.7 per cent in 2003 (Assembly).

How credible were Alliance's arguments that the nature of the Agreement institutions was the cause of political polarisation and that the Agreement entrenched sectarianism? Would the party's alternatives have produced a different outcome? Alliance strongly asserted that the Agreement misunderstood ethnic identities as frozen and fixed – not chosen and changing – and that the Agreement's deference towards unionism and nationalism only served to refreeze them. However, McGarry and O'Leary (2009: 74–5) argue, first, that recognising that unionism and nationalism are the two, long-expressed preferences of most people in Northern Ireland, as does the Agreement, does not amount to an assumption that these preferences or identities are immutable and, second, that the liberal, non-communal dimensions of the Agreement are underappreciated. For example, there is the proportional representation–single transferable vote voting system that allows cross-community transfers; d'Hondt, which allows any party of sufficient strength to take a place in the Executive; duties of impartiality placed on ministers; and powerful human rights protections (see also Ruane and Todd, 1999b; Dixon, 2005; Higson, 2008). Indeed, McGarry and O'Leary (2009: 83) argue, just as Alliance do, that 'if the current institutions endure, a common Northern Irish identity may come to be shared by most unionists and nationalists; but that will be the work of at least two decades'. In a similar vein, Higson (2008) emphasises that rather than enshrining certain notions of identity, the overwhelming emphasis in the Agreement is on taking measures to *decrease* the salience of ethnicity, i.e. addressing the realities that caused groups to seek security in opposing identity blocs. These include police reform, demilitarisation, recognising victims and ensuring the protection of rights, measures that will encourage trust and undermine the ethnic binary.

Schwartz (2010) investigates Alliance's claim that the voting system which requires communal designations is not only distasteful, but unfair – it penalises parties designated 'other' due to the requirement of a quota only of MLAs designated 'unionist' and 'nationalist'. Based on voting simulations, Schwartz argues that there is some merit in this argument but that, assuming parties vote en bloc, the voting rules are unfair to *all* smaller parties, not simply 'other' parties, since any smaller party's votes may not be required to meet the unionist and nationalist thresholds. He also argues that this unfairness is offset to some degree by the 'super-legitimacy' provided by parallel consent rules, an important mechanism given the backdrop of constitutional conflict. In a submission to the Assembly and Executive Review Committee investigation into reforming voting/designation procedures, McGarry and O'Leary, along with Schwartz and McCrudden, caution against weighted majority voting due to the impossibility of determining the right threshold. A low threshold risks unduly endangering a minority, while a high threshold risks unduly empowering a single party with veto powers. Moreover, they argue that the d'Hondt method of appointing an all-inclusive coalition has been effective in bringing stability after a history of political exclusion and violence and should be retained pending cross-community consensus; parties are free to not sit in the Executive if they so wish (McCrudden *et al.*, 2013).

In sum, Alliance's criticisms regarding the illiberal and polarising nature of the Agreement, though understandable in the context of the party's philosophy and need to distinguish itself, were overstated. While there is an obvious crudity to sifting people into 'unionist', 'nationalist' and 'other' categories, it is unlikely that these designations and associated voting rules have influenced the choices of the electorate. It is unclear how much voters are even aware of designations; it is the divided party system and ethnic political appeals that are most visible. And, as Tonge (2005: 218) points out, voting that reflects the ethnic divide has persisted for generations in Northern Ireland regardless of prevailing political arrangements. In any case, communal designations, parallel consent and mandatory coalition may well be reformed in time, albeit more slowly than Alliance would prefer. The Assembly and Executive Review Committee concluded in 2013 that no consensus existed for changing d'Hondt and community designations or making more formal provisions for an opposition. The SDLP and Sinn Féin were the main opponents for obvious historical and political reasons, though even these parties accepted that such reforms may be a desirable evolution in the future (Assembly and Executive Review Committee, 2013).

Nevertheless, while Alliance's criticisms of aspects of the Agreement were problematic, unionist–nationalist wrangles at Stormont, and tensions and divisions at street level, lent weight to the overall Alliance critique that the new politics fell far short of what was needed if the social divisions at the heart of the conflict were to be overcome. This allowed the party to craft a distinctive and powerful discourse calling for a more integrated and shared society. Eradicating sectarianism and segregation had been one of the party's founding principles. The Agreement had been accepted by Alliance as a stepping stone that *might* lead to a less group-divided society. Accordingly, the contention that the implementation of the Agreement – as it was being conducted by the unionist and nationalist parties – was failing to advance the accord's transcender, reconciliatory potential was present throughout the party's post-Agreement policy and rhetoric. The goal was a 'shared future'. This phrase entered wide usage after the publication by the Office of the First Minister and Deputy First Minister (OFMDFM) in 2005 (during the suspension of devolution) of *A Shared Future: Policy and Strategic Framework for Good Relations in Northern Ireland* (OFMDFM, 2005). The document, based on extensive public consultation, sought to advance the vision set out in the 1998 Agreement that 'an essential aspect of the reconciliation process is the promotion of a culture of tolerance at every level of society, including initiatives to facilitate and encourage integrated education and mixed housing' (Agreement, 1998: 18). Thus, very much in line with Alliance's outlook, *A Shared Future* made clear that 'separate but equal is not an option. Parallel living and provision of parallel services are unsustainable both morally and economically' (OFMDFM, 2005: 15).

With the restoration of devolution in 2007, the Executive initiated the process of formulating its own community relations strategy, yet the DUP and Sinn Féin were unable to agree a document. Alliance made progress on the shared future agenda a condition of taking the Justice Minister post in April 2010 (Bell, 2012). (Alliance had voted against three Programmes for Government, in 2000, 2001 and 2008, claiming that the documents did not contain adequate provisions for tackling sectarianism.) This pressure led to the publication in July 2010 of an agreed Executive document, *Programme for Cohesion, Sharing and Integration* (OFMDFM, 2010), which went out for consultation. The document was widely criticised; the independent analysts of the consultation responses reported that many submissions highlighted, inter alia, the document's poverty of vision, apparent contentment with managing division between supposedly immovable unionist and nationalist identities, and failure to address the past (Wallace Consulting, 2011). Following the consultation, the parties met in private for eight months to seek consensus on a replacement community relations strategy but Alliance representatives actually walked out of these talks in May 2012. Ford explained that his party 'did not believe that the process was either effective or inclusive. It was not reflecting the many worthy contributions that were made to the CSI consultation. Moreover, the process was heading towards a lowest common denominator, with many critical issues either being ignored or downplayed' (Ford, 2013). The other parties, he said, were not prepared to commit to targets on integrated education, segregated housing or the removal of illegal flags and emblems. Peter Robinson responded to Alliance's withdrawal by saying that the party was 'unable to work with anybody but themselves' (BBC, 2012a).

In January 2013, Alliance published its own shared future proposals, *For Everyone* (Alliance, 2013a), which it described as a 'blueprint' for a future Executive strategy. At seventy-four pages, *For Everyone* was Alliance's most comprehensive document on community relations yet, incorporating and expanding various lines of argument the party had been making since the Agreement. With its overall emphasis on reconciliation, interdependence and the evolving, un-fixed nature of identity, the document echoed the thrust of *A Shared Future*. The strategy led with a pragmatic argument for a more shared society: the 'inextricable relationship between the creation of a shared future and the economic transformation of Northern Ireland' (p. 5). To address this, Alliance proposed 'Shared Future Policy Proofing' for all new major policies and a commitment that all new public facilities should be built to ensure optimal public use. In keeping with a long history of support for integrated education, Alliance proposed a target of 20 per cent of children to be educated in integrated schools by 2020 (Alliance had previously given a target of 10 per cent by 2010; the actual figure in 2013 was 6 per cent). Alliance accepted that separate school sectors would exist for the foreseeable future but encouraged as much collaboration and mixing between sectors as possible. A wide range of measures and targets were proposed to address segregated housing, 'peace' walls, problems at interface areas, territorial marking and hate crime. Alliance reiterated its policy of flying the Union flag on designated days from public buildings, and called for a consultation on developing shared symbols for Northern Ireland. *For Everyone* also called for talks encompassing all parties and civic society to agree mechanisms to regulate parading and address the legacy of conflict, a call met by the ill-fated Haass/O'Sullivan talks in autumn of 2013.

As Ford admitted in the Foreword to the document, Alliance had no power to implement any of this. The purpose was to show what was possible, spark debate and pressurise the DUP and Sinn Féin to come up with a plan of their own. And the document did meet with criticism. The DUP claimed that *For Everyone*'s target of reducing the number of 'peace' walls by 20 per cent by 2023 was actually 'unambitious'; Ford called it 'realistic' (Devenport, 2013). Others claimed that

Alliance's proposal that all new-build schools should be integrated amounted to eliminating parental choice; the *Irish News*'s interpretation of Alliance's plan was, according to its headline, 'End Catholic Education' (*Irish News*, 2013). Indeed, Alliance's calls for deliberate and targeted measures to overcome segregation have often been dismissed as social engineering, though the party's contention is that prevailing conditions are far from 'natural': 'people need to realise that there's been some serious social engineering to drive people apart in the first place' (interview with Chris Lyttle MLA, 4 April 2014). The DUP and Sinn Féin eventually published their own shared future document, *Together: Building a United Community* (OFMDFM, 2013) in May 2013. Unlike *For Everyone*, it pledged to remove all interface barriers by 2023 but was less radical in other areas, notably education. Alliance acknowledged this strategy as progress but accused OFMDFM of stealing its ideas. The subtitle, 'Building a United Community', was actually the name of Alliance's previous major community relations document of 2003, while *Together*, like *For Everyone*, proposed all-party talks under an independent chair to resolve flags, parades and past (Alliance, 2013b).

An Alliance renaissance?

While Alliance reached an electoral nadir in 2003 (3.7 per cent), subsequent Assembly elections saw an upturn in performance. In 2007 Alliance candidates won 5.2 per cent of the vote, giving the party seven seats, and in 2011 the vote share rose to 7.7 per cent, yielding eight seats. In the 2011 local government election, forty-four Alliance candidates were elected, an increase of fourteen from 2005. In the 2010 Westminster election, Naomi Long dramatically decapitated the DUP by defeating Peter Robinson in East Belfast, a seat he had held since 1979. Meanwhile, other developments further boosted the party's profile. In April 2010, Alliance joined the Executive when David Ford became Justice Minister, and in May 2011, the party's eight seats entitled it, under d'Hondt, to another Executive place; Stephen Farry became Minister for Employment and Learning. Thus, with just eight Assembly seats, Alliance held two Executive positions after May 2011, while the UUP and SDLP, despite having thirteen and fourteen seats respectively, held only one Executive place each. In the 2011 local election, Alliance overtook the UUP in Belfast, the former jumping from four to six councillors, and the latter dropping from seven to three councillors.

These successes were described by some observers as amounting to a 'renaissance' of the party (Bell, 2012: 2; Nolan, 2012: 125). Yet while a resurgence of sorts was evident, there were obvious special circumstances to certain of these developments. The Ministry of Justice post fell to Alliance due to the political sensitivity of the post and the protracted controversy surrounding the devolution of policing and justice powers to the Assembly. The Agreement made a brief reference to the willingness of the British Government to devolve responsibility for policing and justice in the future, but in light of the distinct history of lawbreaking and law-enforcing in Northern Ireland, cross-community support for a unionist or nationalist Minister for Justice was impossible. The St Andrews Agreement of 2006 contained a date of May 2008 for devolution of policing and justice, but the DUP claimed that this was a target rather than a deadline, and maintained that there was not sufficient public confidence for devolution to happen. When the date came and went, Sinn Féin boycotted Executive meetings from June until November 2008 – that party also had grievances relating to Irish language issues and the proposed national sports stadium. To resolve the impasse, the DUP and Sinn Féin agreed a road map to devolution. This allowed the resumption of Executive meetings but lack of progress on agreeing an actual date for devolution eventually led to the British Government convening crisis talks at Hillsborough Castle in early 2010, amid fears that Martin McGuiness was close to resigning as Deputy First Minister.

Part of that 2008 understanding between the DUP and Sinn Féin was that they would not nominate individuals from their own parties for the Justice Minister post, and that any such minister should have cross-community confidence (Bell, 2012: 12). This suggested that the biggest parties would not use d'Hondt to select the person for the role (this would have given it to the SDLP) and led to speculation that Alliance may take the job – an idea that dated at least to the St Andrews talks two years previously (McAdam, 2008). Alliance did not rule this out, but pointed to the dysfunctional Executive and the lack of clarity on the powers, conditions and budget of the Minister of Justice post as ruling out an Alliance minister in the near future (Ford, 2008). Bell's (2012) research on Alliance's eventual decision to join the Executive after the Hillsborough Agreement in February 2010 outlines three reasons for the move. First, the party was cognisant that, by early 2010, the institutions were on the verge of collapse and that Alliance was in a position to prevent this happening. Dissident republican violence in 2009 intensified the party's resolve that the Assembly should see out a full term. Second, Alliance wanted to use its Executive place to improve government, both in terms of enhancing co-operation within the Executive and delivering effective leadership in policing and justice. On the latter point, Alliance ensured that it had agreement from the DUP and Sinn Féin on a policy programme for the new department before taking on the role. Third, Alliance wished to use its leverage to force progress on an Executive shared future strategy.

The SDLP, the party that, had d'Hondt been used to allocate the job, would have been entitled to the Justice Ministry, was particularly incensed when David

Ford confirmed in February 2010 that he would put himself forward for the role. Alex Atwood claimed that a 'unionist shall be the Justice Minister come the middle of April' and that this was 'an offence to nationalism'. Furthermore, he condemned Alliance for pushing for shared future proposals and then taking the Ministry without these being made public (McAdam, 2010). Incidentally, certain voices in Alliance also believed the party should have used its leverage to make more and better progress on a shared future when it had the opportunity (Bell, 2012: 31). As noted above, the party did succeed in getting such a strategy, published by OFMDFM in July 2010, but was unhappy with its contents. However, the decision to take the Justice Ministry was not, on the whole, a controversial one within Alliance. Although the party saw itself as an unofficial opposition and supported voluntary coalition, abstaining from government was not actually a party principle. For this reason, joining the Executive did not stimulate the kind of internal opposition that had emerged in response to the decision to re-designate in 2001 (Bell, 2012: 50).

After Alliance took on the Justice portfolio, policing and justice, devolved, became a relatively uncontroversial aspect of administration in Northern Ireland, a considerable achievement after the prolonged stand-off that preceded the Hillsborough Agreement. Alliance party figures believed that joining the Executive enhanced the party's standing and credibility – it had certainly not damaged it – and may have contributed to Naomi Long's Westminster victory in May 2010 and the party's strong performance in the 2011 Assembly poll (Bell, 2012). In this, Long fulfilled a long-standing party ambition, and one that could reasonably have been regarded as beyond reach given the high bar of the first-past-the-post electoral system for Westminster constituencies. Nevertheless, there were a number of unique circumstances to Long's victory: East Belfast was strong Alliance territory; Long had built a reputation as a dedicated constituency worker and benefited from a successful year as Lord Mayor of Belfast in 2009–10; the UUP failed to inspire voters with their alliance with the Conservatives (the Ulster Conservatives and Unionists – New Force); and, most significantly, Peter Robinson had since the beginning of the year been mired in allegations surrounding property deals, expenses and his wife's personal and financial dealings with a young East Belfast entrepreneur. For these reasons, repeating the feat in other constituencies, or even in East Belfast, would be extremely difficult.

Alliance and the flag protests of 2012–13

One very unexpected consequence of Naomi Long's defeat of Peter Robinson in 2010 was contributing to what was described as 'the most serious challenge to the peace process in a decade' (Nolan, 2013: 160) and one of the most threatening periods for the Alliance Party itself: the flag protests of 2012–13. As we have seen in previous chapters, disagreement over whether, how and what flags and symbols should be displayed was a running theme in post-Agreement Northern Ireland, and was rooted in the unclear relationship in the Agreement between ongoing British sovereignty and the principle of parity of esteem for identities and cultures. Previous symbols controversies – the Police Service of Northern Ireland badge, the Assembly's emblem and the question of flag-flying on parliament buildings – had been resolved, and thus the vitriolic response to Belfast City Hall's decision on 3 December 2012 to bring the number of days the Union flag was flown on the building into line with practice at Stormont came somewhat out of the blue. However, as the protests continued, greater attention fell on the sequence of events that led up to the vote.

The issue had been placed on the agenda by Sinn Féin councillors who objected to the flying of the Union flag every day and the prevalence of British symbols in the City Hall. The Equality Commission carried out an Equality Impact Assessment and recommended a policy of flying the flag on designated days as the least divisive option; a public consultation in the summer of 2012 received polarised responses. Sinn Féin and the SDLP favoured removing the flag, the DUP, UUP and the Progressive Unionist Party (PUP) favoured no change and the Alliance Party policy was designated days. Critically, it was the six Alliance councillors that held the balance of power; the combined nationalist vote was twenty-four and the combined unionist vote was twenty-one. Tensions were raised in early November when DUP and UUP workers distributed 40,000 leaflets in East Belfast headlined, 'A shared future for who?' Printed in the black and yellow colours of Alliance, and not attributed to any organisation, the leaflet claimed that 'At the minute Alliance are backing the Sinn Féin/SDLP position that the flag should be ripped down on all but a few days. Contact the Alliance party and let them know we don't want our national flag torn down from City Hall. We can't let them make Belfast a cold house for unionists.' The leaflet contained the phone numbers of Alliance offices and specifically named Naomi Long, but – as unionists were forced to emphasise repeatedly in the media during the ensuing violence and threats – had a note at the bottom: 'please be respectful at all times.' In a foretaste of what was to come, Alliance personnel began to receive 'abusive and nasty' phone calls (BBC, 2012b).

On the night of the vote, one thousand protesters gathered outside the City Hall. As news of the unionist defeat reached the crowd, scuffles broke out, causing injury to a number of police officers; later, there were riots on the Lower Newtownards Road in East Belfast. Weeks of street protest, sporadic rioting and political recrimination followed; between the flag vote and the end of February

2013, 146 police officers were injured in rioting, 201 arrests were made and the cost of policing the riots and protests – many of which illegally blocked roads – was £20 million (Nolan, 2013: 163). It was estimated that the cost to businesses in Belfast over the Christmas period was around £15 million (BBC, 2013b). Unionist leaders condemned the violence but supported the protesters' view that a 'culture war' was being fought against the Protestant community, principally by Sinn Féin. Yet it was the Alliance Party that was the focus of the protesters' ire. In the days immediately following the vote, an Alliance councillor was intimidated from her home in East Belfast, the Alliance office in Carrickfergus was destroyed in an arson attack, the home of two Alliance councillors was attacked in Bangor, Naomi Long received a death threat and a petrol bomb was thrown at the car of a police officer who was guarding Naomi Long's office in East Belfast. Sporadic attacks and threats on Alliance offices and personnel continued throughout 2013 and 2014.

Unionists raged that Alliance had 'ripped down' their flag, a flag that in their view was causing offence to no one except republicans intent on erasing British culture from Northern Ireland. Alliance's argument that the motion that passed was a compromise to be celebrated was, said Peter Robinson, 'perverse': Alliance should have known where 'meddling with identity would lead' and instead of promoting a shared future, the vote had only set back community relations (Robinson, 2012c). In response to such accusations, Alliance argued that limiting the flying of the flag recognised the diversity of the city, and that there was no reason a policy of designated days should offend unionist sensibilities. The party asserted that by proposing the amendment (designated days) to the Sinn Féin motion to remove the flag, it had actually caused republicans and nationalists to do something that for them was unprecedented: vote *for* the Union flag to fly, albeit only at certain times. Moreover, designated days – rather than flying the flag every day – was, said Alliance, 'in line with British tradition as stated by the College of Arms' (Alliance, 2013c).

Alliance's arguments made little impact on the protesters. They were driven by a conviction that the removal of the British national symbol was itself symbolic of a general state of unionist besiegement. The flag protests may be understood as being stimulated by unionists' sense of loss at four inter-connected levels. First, unionists felt a sense of loss in relation to the city of Belfast. The flag had flown continuously over the City Hall for over one hundred years, throughout 'the Troubles' and the changes of the peace process, a steadfast reminder of unionist dominance/security in 'their' capital. Changing demographics and the failure of many Protestants to vote meant that unionists lost control of the council in 1997, and unionist defeat on the emotive issue of the flag came as a stinging indication of malaise. It is important to point out that the DUP, UUP and PUP had adopted different flag-flying policies in other times and places; notably, the UUP had supported designated days at Stormont, the DUP had supported designated days in Lisburn Council and the PUP had previously supported designated days at the City Hall. Thus, the tough policy pursued by these parties in late 2012 showed the special significance with which unionists accorded the British flag in Belfast.

Second, unionists felt that they were losing in a broader 'culture war'. The flag protesters, and the politicians who agreed with their analysis, believed that the City Hall vote was simply part of a wider attack on Protestant and British culture being fought principally by republicans, but also by public bodies such as the Parades Commission and Historical Enquiries Team, which were perceived to be biased against unionists. As we have seen in previous chapters, unionists' perception of a cultural war, and that they were losing, had been apparent almost before the ink had dried on the Agreement and stretched even further back into the Direct Rule period. The DUP/UUP leaflet had spoken of a potential for Belfast becoming a 'cold house for unionists'; notably, that emotive phrase had been used as long ago as 2001 by Secretary of State John Reid. A third sense of loss was felt by working-class Protestants in relation to the social vitality of their community – particularly, as they perceived it, relative to the Catholic/nationalist community. The flag protest drew attention to, and was partly caused by, a compound of social realities: educational underachievement, poor social cohesion, the demise of traditional sources of employment, general deprivation and a feeling of being inadequately represented politically.

Finally, to return to Alliance, unionists, in the form of the DUP, felt an acute sense of loss in relation to the East Belfast Westminster seat. Alliance was unequivocal about who was ultimately to blame and why: 'By directing the leaflet towards the Alliance Party, the DUP and UUP made Alliance the focus of those sinister elements who have since targeted the homes and offices of Alliance Party elected representatives.' The leaflets were put through people's letterboxes, said Alliance, for 'vindictive reasons of vengeance and self-interest against Naomi Long and the Alliance Party' and proof of this was the specific naming of Long – no longer a Belfast City councillor – on the leaflet (Alliance, 2013c). Moreover, as observers pointed out, the likelihood that unionists' true intention was to simply rouse unionist feeling against Alliance in East Belfast was indicated by the fact that it was very unlikely that a leaflet campaign could or would change the party's position in any case, since Alliance's stated and long-term policy was designated days (Fealty, 2012). Three days into the protests, Peter Robinson defended the leaflets, saying that they 'did not call on people to come on to the streets but asked people to engage in the democratic process. Their views were to be communicated by letter, email or telephone' (Robinson, 2012c).

While the personal unpleasantness suffered by the Alliance Party as a result of the flag protests was considerable, the political impact was less clear. The party would likely lose some Protestant votes, yet the period also witnessed a sharp increase in new members. Unionist targeting of Alliance ensured that the party received an unprecedented level of sustained media attention during the protests, attention that in normal circumstances gravitated towards the extremes. The party's decisive role and the repercussions it bore as a result arguably belied the notion that it was a bland or ineffectual option for voters, lending a degree of street credibility that had been lacking. As one 2014 Alliance Party candidate commented: 'I believe that if we survive electorally through the flags protest, Alliance is suddenly sharpened up ... I think Alliance is a better brand now than it has been for quite some time' (interview with Duncan Morrow, 20 May 2014). The first electoral tests since the flag protests did suggest that the party had emerged relatively unscathed electorally. In May 2014, the party actually increased its number of councillors on the new Belfast 'super council' from six to nine, while Anna Lo received 44,432 votes in the European poll, a significant increase on its previous result in 2009 of 26,699 votes. The party's approach on flags also gained support from the findings of the 2013 Northern Ireland Life and Times Survey, which found designated days to be by far the most popular policy among the public; 53 per cent chose this, compared with only 24 per cent who preferred the flag to be flown every day (ARK, 2014).

Conclusion

Although the Alliance Party has exhibited considerable internal diversity – liberal, conservative, Protestant, Catholic, pro-Union, pro-Irish unity – the core unifying idea has been reconciliation. In the current context of peace and constitutional stability but limited reconciliation, this is arguably an idea whose time has come, and the party has been successful at styling itself as the most credible and principal political exponent of the shared future agenda. The influx of immigrants into Northern Ireland since the expansion of the European Union in 2004 also boosts Alliance's argument that a politics dominated by just two identities is both insular and unreflective of reality. However, the contrast remains between the widespread currency of Alliance's ideas – more integration, less tribal politics – and Alliance's political weakness. Alliance has pursued the transcender logic, embodying within itself the partnership of Protestants and Catholics that was the goal of political talks throughout conflict and was the rationale of the Good Friday Agreement, with Protestants, Catholics and people of other ethnic and religious traditions and none, who may retain sympathy for different constitutional arrangements, working together to create a functioning, cohesive and prosperous society. However, while the Good Friday Agreement engendered considerable hope and optimism about the potential of a new form of politics, and attained widespread public support at the time, this was not translated into party political preferences; voters have remained, so far, with parties that speak to traditional group identities and anxieties. That is due to the enduring strength of unionism and nationalism, buoyed since 1998 by divisive issues emanating from the 'Troubles', but also to voters' wariness of Alliance's relative social liberalism.

Nevertheless, Alliance's vote share belies the significance of its ideas and role. The party has kept the reality of segregation before policy-makers and the electorate. Although other parties have had a vested interest in dismissing Alliance as 'really' unionist or nationalist, the party's credibility has been shown in significant appointments such as former party leader John Alderdice taking the role of first Presiding Office of the Assembly and sitting on the Independent Monitoring Commission. Most notably, Alliance became the very fulcrum of power-sharing through its occupation of the contentious Justice Minister post. Moreover, Alliance has held the balance of power in several councils, a role that of course proved all-important in the seminal Belfast flag decision. While it may appear that Alliance's forty-year struggle to surpass single-digit support represents failure, it can be argued that its very survival as a viable, cross-community political option, despite the centrifugal pull of the conflict, indicates success. Alliance has modelled cross-community harmony, though it has to a great extent been a harmony of the middle classes that have been relatively insulated from the fear and bloodshed of the 'Troubles'. Achieving greater socio-economic diversity remains a challenge for the party. That does not, however, make any less prescient the party's core critique that Northern Ireland remains handicapped by a sectarian politics of fear and exclusivity.

Conclusion

Fear, co-operation and trust after 1998

In Chapter 1, we described three 'logics of insecurity', or broad orientations to the insecurity problem faced by all, and we revisited them throughout the book. These were 'fatalist', 'mitigator' and 'transcender' – or, as Booth and Wheeler (2008) simplify them in the subtitle of their book, 'fear', 'co-operation' and 'trust'. Under the conditions of unresolvable uncertainty that characterise the human experience, this is the choice facing all political actors, and, indeed, everyone: to fear others and to attack and defend; to co-operate temporarily for mutual advantage; or to risk trust in recognition of human commonality and interdependence. Northern Ireland in 1998 was a creation of political actors' choices to fear, co-operate or trust in the past; Chapter 1 outlined how fatalist logic – fear, violence and nationalist exclusivity – drove the conflict, while others resisted the polarisation of the security dilemma in search of political common ground. A significant move towards mitigator logic on the part of unionists and republicans, encouraged by the Governments and other political parties, permitted the 1998 Agreement. Yet even among the parties who supported that accord, fatalist inclinations remained, meaning that critical issues were unresolved, and a new kind of battle for societal security began in the post-1998 years.

Fear and fatalism had always featured heavily in the unionist personality, part of the 'siege mentality' for which Ulster Protestants were famous; the siege was real, but so too was that of Northern Catholics who had to bear the consequences of unionist fears. But more open, less ethno-centric elements were always present in unionism too. Through the years of political impasse during the 'Troubles', the Ulster Unionist Party (UUP) remained reasonably united, but the IRA ceasefire, the talks process and the Agreement once again forced a choice: to fear and retreat and wish for a future of ethnic solidarity, without compromise, or to forge ahead in search of a new and uncharted shared security with nationalism. The UUP leadership held up the principle of consent as unionists' guarantee, the achievement that would allow them to endure the more difficult aspects of the deal. A more conservative faction, along with the Democratic Unionist Party (DUP), looked at the resilience of the IRA, and the uncertainty of the Agreement's constitutional and equality provisions, and decided that the Agreement was simply yet another plot hatched to weaken the Protestant position in Northern Ireland. The DUP's fatalist logic had a religious inflection. Its critique of the Agreement was reinforced by a theology that superimposed the eternal spiritual struggle onto the conflict in Ireland and that was incompatible with what the party saw as the ethical compromises required by the accord. The party expressed this worldview through a compelling moral critique of the political process, exploiting the not inconsiderable uncertainty that did surround the Agreement's implementation, with the aim of converting the fears of unionists into DUP votes.

In sum, the mitigator logic of the Agreement's unionist supporters led them to gamble in the hope of change in the nature of the conflict, while the opponents, in their fatalism, recognised only the continuity of threat. The overall ambivalence of unionism meant that the pro-Agreement UUP leadership, precarious from the outset, took an approach to implementation, particularly symbols and decommissioning, that sought to minimise the appearance of compromise. This had the effect of maintaining the nationalist image of unionism as imperious and ungenerous and nourished republican fatalism that unionists were congenitally incapable of treating Catholics with equality. Unfortunately for David Trimble, the approach did not satisfy the unionist electorate either, and the DUP profited.

Yet while the threat to the societal security of unionism from the Agreement was exaggerated by anti-Agreement unionist leaders, it was not a figment of their imagination either. Violent republicanism supplied unionists with ample fodder for their campaign of opposition to co-operation with Sinn Féin through the Agreement, a pact that allowed the IRA's Sinn Féin associates into government while the paramilitary group remained active and arming, and 'forgave' IRA prisoners without any sign of contrition; in fact, republicans celebrated their campaign of violence as getting them to where they were. Furthermore, Sinn Féin enthused that the Agreement could lead to the unification of Ireland. This was unlikely, but republican challenges to British culture and symbols encouraged unionist fears, and those fears encouraged republican hopes – the kind of hopes that had always been the essence of republican fatalism that imagined that the battle with British/unionist oppression would run by all means necessary until an Irish victory. To be sure, violent means had proved costly and ineffective for republicans, and a new approach combining electoral growth, co-operation with unionism and political persuasion was being attempted. But fatalism survived in republicanism's inability to be self-critical in relation to the past, frequent insensitivity towards unionists and its resilient and robust ethnic identity, all of which emboldened Protestant pessimism and weakened the mitigator impulses within unionism.

It was the destructive implications of ethnic nationalism that spurred John Hume and the Social Democratic and Labour Party (SDLP) to reframe Irish nationalism in less divisive form, a form that prioritised justice and good relations with unionists over immediate national sovereignty. The SDLP combined the articulation of Catholic grievances with the transcender strategies of trust-building and mediation. This approach emanated from an awareness of the self-fulfilling logic of fatalism that drove the cycle of violence, prevented trust and polarised identities, precluding security and political contentment all round. The party's desire for institutions that reflected the complexity of relationships and identities, and which could deepen cross-community co-operation over time, was partly inspired by the European example, and proved pivotal in the emergence of the 1998 Agreement. After the Agreement, however, the electorate did not thank the SDLP for its efforts, for Sinn Féin, its entanglement in violence loosening, persuaded voters that it was now the most effective and energetic champion of Catholic interests. Implementation of the SDLP's cherished Agreement depended on others – the axis of mistrust, unionists and republicans – but the SDLP exerted influence by protecting Sinn Féin's place in the Executive against calls for republicans' exclusion. It was a questionable stance but one that emanated from the party's desire to prevent the escalation of tension and potential unravelling of the process that may have resulted from exclusion. It was also a stance forced upon it by the IRA's behaviour.

A tacit cognisance of the security dilemma was also evident in the Alliance Party. Alliance contended that the Self/Other, 'us'/'them' split in Northern Irish society was at the heart of political instability, and, accordingly, both encouraged the co-operation of unionism and nationalism and modelled within itself the kind of ethnicity-blind politics that it hoped could eventually prosper more widely. Any Alliance hopes that peace and a political settlement would quickly stimulate its growth were disappointed, yet the party impacted the new politics in significant ways: for example, taking the Justice Minister post and providing a sustained critique of societal segregation.

The Agreement and its implementation, then, happened because sufficient elements of unionism and republicanism abandoned fatalist logic in favour of co-operation. Leaders on both sides judged that their community's societal insecurity would probably worsen if they continued to pursue the exclusive and undiluted vision of victory that they had long harboured. These judgements were part-forced by the determination of the British and Irish Governments to co-operate towards ameliorating the conflict. For unionists, continuing to hold out against compromise would likely weaken the unionist position, given Britain's desire to work with Dublin and assuage nationalist demands; this was recognised first by the UUP and then by the DUP several years later. For republicans, continuing to seek such a victory would cause further misery through violence, and preclude electoral growth and the creation of a pan-nationalist alliance that may prove more effective in meeting their goals than armed struggle. Thus, in the peace process, as framed by the British and Irish Governments, both sides could see and claim enough of a 'win' (unionists believing they were securing the Union and republicans believing they were weakening it) to make co-operation towards mutual security worth the risk involved in ceding ground in other areas.

Yet realpolitik was not the only factor in refashioning approaches. The context of closer British–Irish co-operation in which local actors made these strategic calculations was itself nurtured by European integration, a project that had at its heart the vision of transcending centuries of insecurity through interdependence and intermeshing identities. And the tight corners in which the Northern Ireland parties found themselves, plus the longevity of suffering through the 'Troubles', catalysed a degree of self-awareness regarding parties' role in causing the other side's fears – Booth and Wheeler's (2008: 7) 'security dilemma sensibility' – that encouraged fresh thinking about what kinds of shared solutions might be possible. Contact between political actors facilitated by track-two diplomacy, back-channel dialogue, the work of reconciliation groups and the forums of political talks and conferences helped foster mutual purpose and empathy, though perhaps not trust exactly. Nevertheless, there was a clear desire to create the conditions – the institutions and atmosphere – in which cross-party trust could be built. Successive, reciprocal and conciliatory moves, sometimes carefully choreographed to maintain an impression of balance, signalled each side to the other that they wished to revise the old conflict logic: for example, republicans accepting the ground rules of negotiations; unionists signing the Agreement; unionists 'jumping first' into devolution; republicans engaging with the Independent International Commission on Decommissioning; the DUP showing willingness to conditionally share power with Sinn Féin; republicans decommissioning and endorsing the police and courts. By making concessions, parties made it more difficult for opponents to regard them as aggressive or untrustworthy, repairing negative images, reversing the 'escalation' of identity that had resulted from the onset of physical insecurity, and allowing new conceptions of security to take root.

Applying 'lessons' from Northern Ireland to other arenas of conflict is beyond the scope of this book, but it must be said, at least, that the matrix of incentives and constraints that encouraged the parties' rethinks, produced by both the course of the conflict and the unique British–Irish and EU context, is clearly difficult to replicate elsewhere, a fact acknowledged by other discussants of possible 'lessons' from Northern Ireland (for example, Guelke, 2011; Mac Ginty 2011). Nevertheless, interest in the Irish experience around the world is due to the simple fact that people were being killed and now they are not, and people who were once enemies became, like Ian Paisley and Martin McGuinness, friends. The mere fact of change contradicts the fatalist logic that the future must follow the furrows of the past. And this may be the most powerful meaning of the Northern Ireland case – peace is possible – and it should incite hope in other regions of intractable conflict that they too may discover their own paths out of the consuming cycle of violence, enmity and insecurity.

Dealing with the future

'The parties made history yesterday', wrote Frank Millar (2007) in the *Irish Times* the day after devolution on 8 May 2007, 'but they didn't end it.' Indeed, as Chapter 1 explained and other parts of the book elaborated, identity insecurity has continued, notwithstanding the removal of physical threats and the relative robustness of the new institutions. Much of the debate about the unfinished work of the peace process has revolved around a single phrase: 'dealing with the past.' With political structures finally in place, there has emerged a widespread recognition of the need to confront the reality of the violent conflict just ended. Before moving on, society must first look back.

But look back how, and why? The physical and psychological needs of victims have been widely acknowledged, though of course who exactly is entitled to the 'innocence' that resides in the term 'victim' is far from agreed-upon. Then there are the legal and judicial questions. Should the past be dealt with through vigorous prosecution of 'Troubles'-related crimes, or should 'a line be drawn under the past' in order to avoid expensive, divisive and possibly futile investigations? Perhaps dealing with the past is ultimately a task for historians, requiring the knitting together of competing, colliding group memories into a narrative that both sides can own. As for why the past needs to be dealt with, some have argued that it is an unavoidable stage on the road to a united and peaceful future – finding consensus on the mistakes of the past would inoculate society from another outbreak of ethnic mayhem in the future. Others have more partisan motives.

Overall, then, 'dealing with the past' is shorthand for addressing the fact that the conflict ended without agreement on why it started. And understood this way, 'dealing with the past' is an apt description of the entire tumultuous process of implementing the Agreement examined in this book. Police reform, prisoner releases, demilitarisation, decommissioning, flags and emblems, 'on the runs', enquiries, including or excluding paramilitary-linked parties – all these issues were fraught and fought by the parties because the Agreement had drawn a moral equivalence between the two sides that was threatening to both. In contesting these issues, the residual fatalist tendencies of unionism and republicanism sought the victory that the Agreement had failed to indisputably award them. They wanted the problems of the past dealt with in such a way as to grant them historical vindication, their self-image of aggrieved innocent independently validated for all to see.

Moreover, given the future constitutional uncertainty, many in Northern Ireland have calculated that dealing with the past really means dealing with the future, and that any ground given on the past is a zero-sum loss that only assists the other side in pursuing its constitutional ideal. Exposure of the state's role in violently repressing the Catholic community supports republican arguments that the six-county entity has always been unjust and artificial. Exposure of the sectarianism of the IRA bolsters unionist arguments that Sinn Féin continues to work from a warped analysis that denies the strength and legitimacy of the unionist presence in Ireland. Victories on the past boost morale in the present and enhance the odds for the future. Or so it is thought.

This is not what was meant to happen. The Agreement did, unavoidably, fail to provide an explanation of the causes of the conflict and leave the constitutional future open, but the parties explicitly pledged not to let their divergent political projects prevent co-operation and the search for reconciliation. As the preamble states: 'We acknowledge the substantial difference between our continuing, and equally legitimate, political aspirations. However, we will endeavour to strive in every practical way towards reconciliation and rapprochement within the framework of democratic and agreed arrangements' (Agreement, 1998:1). The principle of majority consent, combined with the tenets of interdependency and non-violence, allowed both sides to retain their aspirations but did not allow both sides to realise those aspirations without taking account of the identity and fears of the other side. Unionists, in order to preserve the Union, would have to ensure that Northern Ireland was a place to which nationalists could feel belonging, while nationalists, to attain Irish unity, would have to convince unionists that they had something to gain, or at least nothing to fear, from a united Ireland. As Mark Durkan puts it: 'unionism and nationalism were going to have to compete for mutual assurance rather than compete in mutual attrition' (interview with Mark Durkan MP, 31 August 2012).

The problem was that for this to happen, parties would have to fully abandon fatalism in favour of the transcender tactics of trust-building, dialogue and empathy. It would require a unionism and a nationalism that were, first, confident enough be frank about past mistakes and sensitive towards the sensibilities of the other side, and, second, open to abandoning their exclusivist, tribal baggage. Perhaps, more than anything, it would require enlightened leadership all round. But instead of undertaking the self-examination and change that might win over those of a different political point of view, unionists and nationalists have, to a great extent, nursed their own wounded identities and defended their borders. This has not been the entire story; parties on both sides have made some efforts towards becoming more inclusive organisations. Yet the repeated detonation of disputes stemming from the 'Troubles' has worked against the unwinding of conflict identities, refuelled the mutual fatalisms of the past and stoked the suspicion that preferred constitutional futures are best guaranteed, not through generosity and rational arguments as the Agreement intended, but through communal solidarity and power. As a result, the growth of non-ethnic party politics has been stunted.

Indeed, in a land apparently obsessed with the question of what state it should belong to, reasoned arguments setting out why exactly the Union and Irish unity are good ideas are relatively rare. Instead, political leaders fixate on the political and cultural fortunes of their respective communities. Thus, while the idea that Northern Irish politics continues to be defined by a divergence of opinion on the national question is true, it is also misleading. It is, at bottom, defined by a rivalry of tribal identities. That rivalry has continued to be provoked by the political, legal and psychological legacy of inter-communal violence and clashing views of the origins of the 'Troubles', with a simple guiding principle: no advantage should be given to people who refuse to say sorry.

Hence the pall of negativity that has descended on the Northern Irish political scene, particularly since the flag protests began in late 2012. There has been failure to make progress on the three issues that are symptomatic of the underlying and ongoing identity conflict: flags, parades and the past. Logjam in Stormont is mirrored by logjam in a parading dispute in North Belfast. Question marks hang over Northern Ireland's acquired status as an international model for conflict resolution. The Executive has struggled with conflict legacy matters, but many of the famous 'bread-and-butter' issues have flummoxed it too; impasses have emerged in relation to a raft of policy areas, a state of affairs not eased by worsening financial austerity from 2014. Much of the media continues to work from an Orange–Green script, inflating minor political tensions. And the public has been paying attention. According to the 2013 Northern Ireland Life and Times Survey, the proportion of people who think relations between Protestants and Catholics are better now than five years ago has fallen from 65 per cent in 2007 to 45 per cent in 2013 (ARK, 2014).

Yet, at the same time, Northern Ireland is functioning and, in most respects, flourishing. If one were looking for a location that was symbolic of the new Northern Ireland, one might choose Ardoyne, centre of that bitter parading stand-off, to show that the new Northern Ireland is not really new at all but still known by the old impulses to monopolise and exclude, riven with political, economic and demographic insecurities. But an equally valid choice would be the Titanic Quarter. The rejuvenated site of the Belfast shipyards is now home to film studios, high-tech industries, a world-class visitor attraction in Titanic Belfast, international events such as the start of the Giro d'Italia cycle race, World Police and Fire Games, and MTV Awards, waterfront apartments, as well as acres of pregnant wasteland. To some degree, these two Northern Irelands represent class realities, with the working classes under pressure and held back by poverty, and the middle classes enjoying the consumerist fruits of peace. However, more broadly, these locations encapsulate the intermingling of continuity and change that defines post-Agreement Northern Ireland noted in the Introduction: the clash between anxiety and confidence, insularity and openness, and the sense of being beholden to the past and breaking with it.

Which of these places is the 'real' Northern Ireland? Both are and neither are, of course. But there is no doubt that 1998 was a decisive break with the past and the weight of evidence suggests that it is irreversible. The Agreement was the outworking of twin processes: strengthening ties between the evolving British and Irish states, and learning on the part of the parties in Northern Ireland that the long-imagined, exclusivist utopias were precisely that – utopian. The difficulties of implementing the Agreement were not inevitable, but neither were they surprising after decades of violence that left few families untouched. Now, it is reasonable to judge, based on the fact that previous 'insurmountable' issues have been surmounted, plus the prevailing favourable conditions, that the political challenges that remain will be overcome and, moreover, a common identification among the people of Northern Ireland can and will gather strength.

That may not manifest itself as a growing 'Northern Irish' identity. It may rather come as evolving formations of unionism and nationalism, Britishness and Irishness, that are more complex, overlapping and humble than in the past. It may also be very slow. While it is right and vital to point out the limited progress towards creating a less segregated society, it is also unwise to harbour excessive expectations of what should have been achieved in just a few years of power-sharing following immediately on the heels of thirty years of political bloodletting and several hundred years of social division and conflict before that. But if the societal security dilemma has indeed been decisively interrupted and the people of the North are finally 'sloughing off the dead weight of fatalism' (Arthur, 2000: ix), the prospects are good for a genuinely new Northern Ireland, one that understands its own diversity as a source of strength rather than insecurity, one that has found a measure of peace with its past, and one that, above all, faces the future without fear.

References

Unless otherwise stated, all electoral figures are taken from the ARK elections website (www.ark.ac.uk/elections). In the list below, where 'NIPC' appears after a reference, the material was sourced in the Northern Ireland Political Collection of the Linenhall Library, Belfast.

Adams, G. (1998a) *A Bridge to the Future* (Belfast: Sinn Féin). NIPC.
———(1998b) 'Leadership address by Gerry Adams MP and Martin McGuinness MP', Sinn Féin *Ard Fheis*, 18 April. Sinn Féin boxes, NIPC.
———(1999) 'A solid record of commitment to peace in Ireland', Sinn Féin press release, 26 March. Sinn Féin boxes, NIPC.
———(2000) 'Working for progress and stability', Sinn Féin press release, 27 January. Sinn Féin boxes, NIPC.
———(2001a) 'All citizens have right to equality of treatment', *Irish News*, 21 December.
———(2001b) Speech at Conway Mill, Belfast, 22 October. Sinn Féin boxes, NIPC.
———(2003) *A Farther Shore: Ireland's Long Road to Peace* (New York: Random House).
———(2007) Speech to commemorate Seán Sabhat and Feargal Ó hAnnluain, Co. Fermanagh, 1 January, CAIN Web Service, http://cain.ulst.ac.uk/issues/politics/docs/sf/ga010107.htm, accessed 14 January 2014.
Agreement Reached in the Multi-Party Talks (1998) Page numbers given in the text refer to the original printed copy distributed in 1998. Also available from the CAIN Web Service, http://cain.ulst.ac.uk/events/peace/docs/agreement.htm, accessed 2 June 2014.
Alliance (1970) *Declaration of Intent: A New Political Charter* (Belfast: Alliance Party). Alliance boxes, NIPC.
———(1988) *Governing with Consent* (Belfast: Alliance Party). NIPC.
———(1997) *Multi-Party Talks: Alliance Analysis of the Problem*, Alliance Party website, http://allianceparty.org/document/peace-process-papers/1997-multi-party-talks, accessed 23 February 2013.
———(1998a) *Assembly Election Manifesto* (Belfast: Alliance Party). NIPC.
———(1998b) *Election Communication from the Alliance Party*. Alliance boxes, NIPC.
———(2001) *Review of Assembly Designations and Voting System*, Alliance Party position paper, November. Alliance boxes, NIPC.

———(2004) *Agenda for Democracy: Alliance Party Proposals for the Review of the Agreement*, Alliance Party website, http://allianceparty.org/document/peace-process-papers/2004-good-friday-agreement-review/2004-01-07-agenda-for-democracy-alliance-proposals, accessed 4 January 2013.

———(2006) *Alliance Party of Northern Ireland Response to 'St. Andrews Agreement'*, 10 November, Alliance Party website, http://allianceparty.org/document/peace-process-papers, accessed 23 February 2013.

———(2013a) *For Everyone*, Alliance Party website, file:///C:/Users/Owner/Downloads/for-everyone%20(6).pdf, accessed 25 February 2013.

———(2013b) 'OFMDFM announcements are another missed opportunity', Alliance Party press release, 9 May, Alliance Party website, http://allianceparty.org/article/2013/007827/ofmdfm-announcements-are-another-missed-opportunity-alliance, accessed 23 June 2013.

———(2013c) 'Frequently asked questions about the recent vote on the Union flag at Belfast City Council', 11 January, Alliance Party website, http://allianceparty.org/article/2013/006960/frequently-asked-questions-about-the-recent-vote-on-the-union-flag-at-belfast-city-council, accessed 24 June 2013.

Alliance News (1998) 'Alliance wins six seats in new Northern Ireland Assembly', Alliance Party website, 1 June, http://allianceparty.org/article/1998/001390/alliance-wins-six-seats-in-new-northern-ireland-assembly, accessed 23 February 2013.

Alliance News (2001) 'Growing tribalism poses threat to future peace and stability', Alliance Party website, 9 June, http://allianceparty.org/article/2001/001200/growing-tribalism-poses-threat-to-future-peace-and-stability, accessed 23 February 2013.

An Phoblacht/Sinn Féin TV (2013) 'Gerry Kelly faces down PSNI aggression', YouTube, 22 June, www.youtube.com/watch?v=8K2juHYzDKs, accessed 30 June 2013.

ARK (2014) *Northern Ireland Life and Times Survey, 2013* [computer file]. ARK, www.ark.ac.uk/nilt [distributor], accessed 15 June 2014.

Arthur, P. (1999) 'Multiparty mediation in Northern Ireland', in C. Crocker, F. Hampson and P. Aall (eds), *Herding Cats: Multiparty Mediation in a Complex World* (Washington, DC: United States Institute of Peace Press), pp. 471–501.

———(2000) *Special Relationships: Britain, Ireland and the Northern Ireland Problem* (Belfast: Blackstaff).

———(2002) 'The transformation of republicanism', in J. Coakley (ed.), *Changing Shades of Orange and Green: Redefining the Union and the Nation in Contemporary Ireland* (Dublin: University College Dublin Press), pp. 84–94.

Assembly and Executive Review Committee (2013) *Review of D'Hondt, Community Designation and Provisions for Opposition*, Northern Ireland Assembly website, www.niassembly.gov.uk/Documents/Reports/Assem_Exec_Review/nia-123-11-15-Review-of-DHondt-Community-Designation-and-Provisions-for-Opposition.PDF, accessed 1 February 2014.

Aughey, A. (1989) *Under Siege: Ulster Unionism and the Anglo-Irish Agreement* (London: Hurst).

———(2005) *The Politics of Northern Ireland: Beyond the Belfast Agreement* (Abingdon: Routledge).

BBC (1998) 'IRA breaks silence on peace deal', BBC news website, 30 April, http://news.bbc.co.uk/1/hi/events/northern_ireland/latest_news/85905.stm, accessed 25 June 2007.

———(2005a) 'Trimble quits after poll defeat', BBC news website, 7 May, http://news.bbc.co.uk/1/hi/uk_politics/vote_2005/northern_ireland/4525407.stm, accessed 28 November 2013.

———(2005b) 'IRA statement in full', BBC news website, 28 July, http://news.bbc.co.uk/1/hi/northern_ireland/4724599.stm, accessed 25 June 2007.

———(2006a) 'SF, DUP will share power: Durkan', BBC news website, 15 July, http://news.bbc.co.uk/1/hi/northern_ireland/5182800.stm, accessed 6 December 2013.

———(2006b) 'Parties to respond within a month', BBC news website, 14 October, http://news.bbc.co.uk/1/hi/northern_ireland/6050454.stm, accessed 29 November 2013.

———(2006c) 'PUP-UUP link "against the rules"', BBC news website, 11 September, http://news.bbc.co.uk/1/hi/northern_ireland/5335004.stm, accessed 29 November 2013.

———(2009) 'Lady Hermon "under no pressure"', BBC news website, 27 February, http://news.bbc.co.uk/1/hi/northern_ireland/7913967.stm, accessed 13 May 2013.

———(2012a) 'Alliance pulls out of Stormont "shared future" group', BBC news website, 24 May, www.bbc.co.uk/news/uk-northern-ireland-18186505, accessed 23 June 2013.

———(2012b) 'Alliance Party "disgusted" at DUP/UUP flag policy leaflet', BBC news website, 13 November, www.bbc.co.uk/news/uk-northern-ireland-20317461, accessed 26 June 2013.

———(2013a) 'Conall McDevitt from SDLP quits politics over payment', BBC news website, 4 September, www.bbc.co.uk/news/uk-northern-ireland-23963979, accessed 4 September 2013.

———(2013b) 'Union flag protests cost Belfast businesses £15m', BBC news website, 10 January, www.bbc.co.uk/news/uk-northern-ireland-20972438, accessed 26 June 2013.

———(2014a) *Paisley: Genesis to Revelation*, first broadcast in two parts, 13 and 20 January 2014.

———(2014b) 'Anna Lo: "united Ireland" remarks "insulting" say unionists', BBC news website, 20 March, www.bbc.co.uk/news/uk-northern-ireland-26667174.

BBC Radio Ulster (2014) *Talkback* programme, 10 January.

Bean, K. (2002) 'Defining republicanism: shifting discourses of new nationalism and post-republicanism', in M. Elliot (ed.), *The Long Road to Peace in Northern Ireland* (Liverpool: Liverpool University Press), pp. 129–42.

———(2007) *The New Politics of Sinn Féin* (Liverpool: Liverpool University Press).

Belfast Telegraph (2005) 'Ford hits out at "rhetoric"', 14 February.

Belfast Telegraph (2013) 'Sinn Féin's Mairtin O Muilleoir on historic cenotaph gesture: the most difficult decision of my life, but the right one', *Belfast Telegraph* website, 12 November, www.belfasttelegraph.co.uk/news/local-national/northern-ireland/sinn-féins-mayor-mairtin-o-muilleoir-on-historic-cenotaph-gesture-the-most-difficult-decision-of-my-life-but-the-right-one-29745564.html, accessed 15 June 2014.

Bell, D. (2012) *Why Did the Alliance Party Decide to Join the Executive in 2010 and What Are the Possible Consequences for the Party?*, unpublished MA thesis, Queen's University Belfast.

Bew, J., M. Frampton and I. Gurruchaga (2009) *Talking to Terrorists: Making Peace in Northern Ireland and the Basque Country* (London: Hurst & Co.).

Bew, P. (2007) *Ireland: The Politics of Enmity, 1789–2006* (Oxford: Oxford University Press).

Bilgic, A. (2013) 'Towards a new societal security dilemma: comprehensive analysis of actor responsibility in intersocietal conflicts', *Review of International Studies*, 39:1, 185–208.

Blair, T. (1998) Speech to the Royal Ulster Agricultural Society, Belfast, 14 May, CAIN Web Service, http://cain.ulst.ac.uk/events/peace/docs/tb14598.htm, accessed 12 May 2013.

Booth, K. and N.J. Wheeler (2008) *The Security Dilemma: Fear, Co-operation and Trust in World Politics* (Basingstoke: Palgrave Macmillan).

Bourke, R. (2003) *Peace in Ireland: The War of Ideas* (London: Pimlico).

Bowcott, O. (2006) 'Dublin still split on Easter Rising', *The Guardian* website, 10 April, www.theguardian.com/world/2006/apr/10/ireland, accessed 20 January 2014.

———(2007) 'Historic vote ends Sinn Féin's long battle with the police service in Northern Ireland', *The Guardian* website, 29 January, www.theguardian.com/politics/2007/jan/29/uk.northernireland, accessed 14 January 2012.

Brewer, J., D. Mitchell and G. Leavey (2013) *Ex-combatants, Religion and Peace in Northern Ireland: The Role of Religion in Transitional Justice* (Basingstoke: Palgrave Macmillan).

Brock, L., J. Holm, G. Sorenson and M. Stohl (2012) *Fragile States: Violence and the Failure of Intervention* (Cambridge: Polity).

Brown, K. and R. Mac Ginty (2003) 'Public attitudes towards partisan and neutral symbols in post-Agreement Northern Ireland', *Identities: Global Studies in Culture and Power*, 10:1, 83–108.

Bruce, S. (1986) *God Save Ulster: The Religion and Politics of Paisleyism* (Oxford: Clarendon).

———(1994) *The Edge of the Union: The Ulster Loyalist Political Vision* (Oxford: Oxford University Press).

———(2001) 'Fundamentalism and political violence: the case of Paisley and Ulster evangelicals', *Religion*, 31, 387–405.

———(2007) *Paisley: Religion and Politics in Northern Ireland* (Oxford: Oxford University Press).

Bryan, D. and G. McIntosh (2007) 'Symbols and identity in the "new" Northern Ireland', in P. Carmichael, C. Knox and R. Osborne (eds), *Devolution and Constitutional Change in Northern Ireland* (Manchester: Manchester University Press), pp. 125–7.

Bryson, J. (2013) 'The way I see it…', Queen's University of Belfast Compromise After Conflict blog, 10 October, http://blogs.qub.ac.uk/compromiseafterconflict/2013/10/08/the-way-i-see-it, accessed 11 October 2013.

Bryson, L. and C. McCartney (1994) *Clashing Symbols?: A Report on the Use of Flags, Anthems and Other National Symbols in Northern Ireland* (Belfast: Institute of Irish Studies, Queen's University).

Butterfield, H. (1951) *History and Human Relations* (London: Collins).

Caldwell, J. (2007) 'No alternative to deal – Paisley', BBC news website, 4 April, http://news.bbc.co.uk/1/hi/northern_ireland/6527333.stm, accessed 23 November 2013.

Campbell, G. (2002) 'Peace and stability in Northern Ireland: a DUP perspective', Meath Peace Group Talks, 18 November. DUP boxes, NIPC.

Carmichael, P., C. Knox and R. Osborne (eds) (2007) *Devolution and Constitutional Change in Northern Ireland* (Manchester: Manchester University Press).

Carruthers, M. (2013) *Alternative Ulsters: Conversations on Identity* (Dublin: Liberties Press).

Clancy, M. (2010) *Peace Without Consensus: Power Sharing Politics in Northern Ireland* (Farnham: Ashgate).

Cochrane, F. (2000) 'Trimble's tough job', *Fortnight*, December, p. 13.

———(2013) *Northern Ireland: The Reluctant Peace* (New Haven, CT: Yale University Press).

Cooke, D. (1996) *Persecuting Zeal: A Portrait of Ian Paisley* (Dingle: Brandon).

Coulter, C. (1994) 'The character of unionism', *Irish Political Studies*, 9:1, 1–24.

Coulter, C. and M. Murray (eds) (2008) *Northern Ireland after the Troubles?: A Society in Transition* (Manchester: Manchester University Press).

Cox, M. (2006) 'Rethinking the international and Northern Ireland: a defence', in M. Cox, A. Guelke and F. Stephen (eds), *A Farewell to Arms? Beyond the Good Friday Agreement*, 2nd edn (Manchester: Manchester University Press), pp. 427–42.

Cox, M., A. Guelke and F. Stephen (eds) (2000) *A Farewell to Arms?: From 'Long War' to Long Peace in Northern Ireland* (Manchester: Manchester University Press).

———(eds) (2006) *A Farewell to Arms?: Beyond the Good Friday Agreement*, 2nd edn (Manchester: Manchester University Press).

Cunningham, M. (1997) 'The political language of John Hume', *Irish Political Studies*, 12:1, 13–22.

Cushnahan, J. (1979) 'The history and development of the Alliance Party: a centre party of Catholics and Protestants in Northern Ireland', lecture at the John F. Kennedy School of Government, Harvard University. Alliance boxes, NIPC.

Darby, J. and R. Mac Ginty (2002) *Guns and Government: The Management of the Northern Ireland Peace Process* (Basingstoke: Palgrave Macmillan).

Davidson, N. (2004) *Not by Might: A Journey in Faith and Politics – The Authorised Biography of Jeffrey Donaldson* (Belfast: Ambassador).

de Bréadún, D. (1999) 'Pitfalls and uncertainties should not be a surprise', *Irish Times*, 29 November.

Devenport, M. (2006) 'Poll indicates support for deal', BBC news website, 9 November, http://news.bbc.co.uk/1/hi/northern_ireland/6128536.stm, accessed 23 November 2013.

———(2013) 'Alliance shared future plans are ambitious', BBC news website, 29 January, www.bbc.co.uk/news/uk-northern-ireland-21247713, accessed 23 June 2013.

Dixon, P. (2004) '"Peace within the realms of the possible?" David Trimble, unionist ideology and theatrical politics', *Terrorism and Political Violence*, 16:3, 462–82.

———(2005) 'Why the Good Friday Agreement is not consociational', *Political Quarterly*, 76:3, 357–67.

———(2013) 'An honourable deception?: the Labour Government, the Good Friday Agreement and the Northern Ireland peace process', *British Politics*, 8:2, 108–37.

Donaldson, J. (2001) 'Unionism … a turning point in history?', *Belfast Telegraph*, 30 November.

Doran, N. (2013) Speech to the PUP party conference, 12 October, audio available on Audio Boo, https://audioboo.fm/boos/1656633-pupconf-irish_news-editor-noel-doran-telling-officialpup-how-to-be-more-credible-to-his-readers, accessed 10 March 2014.

DUP (1998) *Assembly Election Manifesto 1998* (Belfast: DUP). NIPC.

———(2001) *Westminster Election Manifesto 2001* (Belfast: DUP). NIPC.

———(2003a) *Assembly Election Manifesto 2003* (Belfast: DUP). NIPC.

———(2003b) *A Voice for Victims* (Belfast: DUP). NIPC.

———(2003c) *Towards a New Agreement* (Belfast: DUP). NIPC.

———(2005) *Westminster and Local Government Election Manifesto 2005* (Belfast: DUP). NIPC.

———(2006) *Your Verdict: What Is It to Be?*, CAIN Web Service, http://cain.ulst.ac.uk/issues/politics/docs/dup/dup231006consult.pdf, accessed 4 December 2013.

———(2007) *Assembly Election Manifesto 2007* (Belfast: DUP). NIPC.

Durkan, M. (2002) 'Address to the 32nd annual conference of the SDLP', 2 November. SDLP boxes, NIPC.

———(2003) Speech to the Ireland Institute, Pearse family home, Dublin, 27 February. SDLP boxes, NIPC.

———(2009) 'Irish unity', speech by Mark Durkan, Trinity College Dublin, 1 October. SDLP boxes, NIPC.

The Economist (2002) 'Keeping Sinn Féin out', 15 May, *The Economist* website, www.economist.com/node/1130124, accessed 20 January 2014.

Edwards, A. (2010) 'The Progressive Unionist Party of Northern Ireland: a left-wing voice in an ethnically divided society', *British Journal of Politics and International Relations*, 12:4, 590–614.

Edwards, A. and S. Bloomer (eds) (2008) *Transforming the Peace Process in Northern Ireland* (Dublin: Irish Academic Press).

Eggins, B. (2003) *The Contribution of the Alliance Party of Northern Ireland to Reconciliation*, unpublished MPhil thesis, Irish School of Ecumenics, Trinity College Dublin.

Elliott, M. (2009) *When God Took Sides: Religion and Identity in Ireland, Unfinished History* (Oxford: Oxford University Press).

Elliott, S. and W.D. Flackes (1999) *Northern Ireland: A Political Directory, 1968–1999* (Belfast: Blackstaff).

Empey, R. (2007a) Speech by Reg Empey at the Ulster Unionist Party annual conference, 27 October, CAIN Web Service, http://cain.ulst.ac.uk/issues/politics/docs/uup/re271007.htm, accessed 1 December 2013.

———(2007b) Speech by Reg Empey at an Extraordinary General Meeting of the UUP, 26 October, CAIN Web Service, http://cain.ulst.ac.uk/issues/politics/docs/uup/re261007.htm, accessed 1 December 2013.

English, R. (2006) *Irish Freedom: The History of Nationalism in Ireland* (London: Macmillan).

———(2011) 'Directions in historiography: history and Irish nationalism, *Irish Historical Studies*, 27:147, 447–60.

Evans, J. and J. Tonge (2001) 'Northern Ireland's third tradition(s): the Alliance Party surveyed', *British Elections and Parties Review*, 11:1, 104–18.

———(2003) 'The future of the "radical centre" in Northern Ireland after the Good Friday Agreement', *Political Studies*, 51:1, 26–50.

———(2013) 'From abstentionism to enthusiasm: Sinn Féin, nationalist electors and support for devolved power-sharing in Northern Ireland', *Irish Political Studies*, 28:1, 39–57.

Farren, S. (1999) 'Accord is not a one-way street', *Belfast Telegraph*, 18 August.
———(2000a) 'The SDLP and the roots of the Good Friday Agreement', in M. Cox, A. Guelke and F. Stephen (eds), *A Farewell to Arms?: From 'Long War' to 'Long Peace' in Northern Ireland* (Manchester: Manchester University Press), pp. 49–61.
———(2000b) 'Still the only show so the threats must go', *Belfast Telegraph*, 3 March.
———(2002a) 'Any United Ireland must be an agreed Ireland', *Irish News*, 8 January.
———(2002b) 'It's the Agreement and only the Agreement', *Belfast Telegraph*, 28 October.
———(2006) 'The SDLP: governing with uncertainty', in M. Cox, A. Guelke, and F. Stephen (eds), *A Farewell to Arms?: Beyond the Good Friday Agreement*, 2nd edn (Manchester: Manchester University Press), pp. 109–23.
———(2010) *The SDLP: The Struggle for Agreement in Northern Ireland, 1970–2000* (Dublin: Four Courts Press).
Farrington, C. (2006) *Ulster Unionism and the Peace Process in Northern Ireland* (Basingstoke: Palgrave Macmillan).
———(ed.) (2008) *Global Change, Civil Society and the Northern Ireland Peace Process: Implementing the Political Settlement* (Basingstoke: Palgrave Macmillan).
Farry, S. (1997) *Power-sharing: The Future for Northern Ireland?* Alliance Party discussion paper, August. Alliance boxes, NIPC.
———(2001) 'The right thing to do: comment on North Down decision', *Co. Down Spectator*, 24 May, reproduced on Alliance Party website, http://allianceparty.org/article/2001/003628/the-right-thing-to-do-comment-on-the-north-down-decision, accessed 23 February 2013.
———(2004) 'A return to the centre', *Alliance News*, 29 January, Alliance Party website, http://allianceparty.org/article/2004/000227/a-return-to-the-centre-by-stephen-farry, accessed 23 February 2013.
Farry, S. and S. Neeson (1999) 'Beyond the Band-Aid approach: an Alliance Party perspective upon the Belfast Agreement', *Fordham International Law Journal*, 22:4, 1221–49.
Fealty, M. (2012) 'This argument over the flags has been unnecessary and divisive from the outset', Slugger O'Toole website, 4 December, http://sluggerotoole.com/2012/12/04/city-hall-fleg-riots-this-argument-over-the-union-flag-has-been-divisive-and-unnecessary-from-its-outset, accessed 26 June 2013.
Feeney, B. (1998) 'Trimble can make yes sound like I don't know', *Irish News*, 13 May.
———(2005) 'Impossible dream of an SDLP merger', *Irish News*, 16 February.
Fitzgerald, G. (2003) 'Hope lies in inevitable evolution of DUP', *Irish Times*, 29 November.
Ford, D. (2001a) 'Truth is truth, crime is crime', *Belfast Telegraph*, 19 October.
———(2001b) 'Tough decision leaves Alliance with a role', *Irish Times*, 5 November.
———(2005) 'Coalition would break deadlock', *Irish News*, 20 January.
———(2008) Speech to the Alliance Party annual conference, 20 September, Alliance Party website, http://allianceparty.org/article/2008/003804/david-ford-s-party-leader-s-speech-at-conference, accessed 23 June 2013.
———(2013) 'Alliance unveils blueprint to deliver change for everyone', Alliance Party press release, 29 January, Alliance Party website, http://allianceparty.org/article/2013/006982/alliance-unveils-blueprint-to-deliver-change-for-everyone, accessed 23 June 2013.

Frampton, M. (2009) *The Long March: The Political Strategy of Sinn Féin, 1981–2007* (Basingstoke: Palgrave Macmillan).

Friel, L. and F. Lane (1998) 'Debating the future', *An Phoblacht/Republican News*, 23 April. Sinn Féin boxes, NIPC.

Ganiel, G. (2008) *Evangelicalism and Conflict in Northern Ireland* (Basingstoke: Palgrave Macmillan).

Galligan, Y. (2011) *Irish General Election 2011: Report and Analysis*, Electoral Reform Society website, file:///C:/Users/Owner/Downloads/irish-general-election-2011%20(1).pdf, accessed 20 January 2014.

Gibson, O. (1998) Speech at Omagh United Unionist meeting, 7 May. DUP boxes, NIPC.

Gillespie, P. (1998) 'European context helps underpin Northern accord', *Irish Times*, 11 April.

——— (2014) 'The complexity of British–Irish interdependence', *Irish Political Studies*, 29:1, 37–57.

Gilligan, C. (2003) 'Constant crisis/permanent process: diminished agency and weak structures in the Northern Ireland Peace Process', *Global Review of Ethnopolitics*, 3:1, 22–37.

Godson, D. (2004) *Himself Alone: David Trimble and the Ordeal of Unionism* (London: HarperCollins).

Gordon, D. (2010) *The Fall of the House of Paisley* (Dublin: Gill & Macmillan).

Gormley-Heenan, C. and R. Mac Ginty (2008) 'Ethnic outbidding and party modernization: understanding the Democratic Unionist Party's success in the post-Agreement environment', *Ethnopolitics*, 7:1, 43–61.

Graham, W. (2000) 'Angry McGuinness accuses Trimble of joining no camp', *Irish News*, 31 October.

——— (2001) 'SDLP "won't back SF eviction"', *Irish News*, 25 September.

——— (2004) 'SDLP "must remember its mandate and rebuild"', *Irish News*, 13 February.

Guelke, A. (2011) 'Lessons of Northern Ireland and the relevance of the regional context', in LSE IDEAS, *The Lessons of Northern Ireland*, LSE (London School of Economics) IDEAS website, www.lse.ac.uk/IDEAS/publications/reports/SR008.aspx, accessed 13 March 2013.

Harbinson, J.F. (1973) *The Ulster Unionist Party, 1882–1973: Its Development and Organisation* (Belfast: Blackstaff).

Hayes, B. and I. McAllister (1999) 'Ethnonationalism, public opinion and the Good Friday Agreement', in J. Ruane and J. Todd (eds), *After the Good Friday Agreement: Analysing Political Change in Northern Ireland* (Dublin: University College Dublin Press), pp. 30–48.

Hayes, M. (2010) 'UUP on life support as party goes down traditional route', *Irish Independent*, 27 September, www.independent.ie/opinion/analysis/maurice-hayes-uup-on-life-support-as-party-goes-down-traditional-route-26684268.html, accessed 12 May 2013.

Hayward, K. (2009) *Irish Nationalism and European Integration: The Official Redefinition of the Island of Ireland* (Manchester: Manchester University Press).

Hennessey, T. (1998) *Understanding the Agreement* (Belfast: UUP). NIPC.

——— (2005) *The Origins of the Troubles* (London: Gill and Macmillan).

Herz, J. (1951) *Political Realism and Political Idealism* (Chicago: Chicago University Press).

Higson, R. (2008) 'Anti-consociationalism and the Good Friday Agreement: a rejoinder', *Journal of Peace, Conflict and Development*, 12, www.brad.ac.uk/ssis/peace-conflict-and-development/issue-12/Anti-consociationalism-and-the-Good-Friday-Agreement,-A-Rejoinder.pdf, accessed 22 May 2010.

Horowitz, D. (2000) *Ethnic Groups in Conflict* (London: University of California Press).

Hume, J. (1996) *Personal Views: Politics, Peace and Reconciliation in Ireland* (Dublin: Town House).

———(2001) Speech to the annual conference of the SDLP, 10 November. SDLP boxes, NIPC.

IMC (2004) *First Report of the Independent Monitoring Commission* (London: The Stationery Office), available from CAIN Web Service, http://cain.ulst.ac.uk/issues/politics/docs/imc/imc200404.pdf, accessed 4 May 2014.

Independent Commission on Policing for Northern Ireland (1999) *A New Beginning: Policing in Northern Ireland – The Report of the Independent Commission on Policing for Northern Ireland* (London: The Stationery Office).

Intercomm and J. Byrne (2013) *Flags and Protests: Exploring the Views, Perceptions and Experiences of People Directly and Indirectly Affected by the Flag Protests*, www.thedetail.tv/system/uploads/files/353/original/Report.pdf?1386858265, accessed 23 January 2014.

Irish Independent (2008) 'Fianna Fáil and SDLP share breakfast in bed', 19 April.

Irish News (2013) 'End Catholic education', 29 January.

Irwin, C. (2002) *The People's Peace Process in Northern Ireland* (Basingstoke: Palgrave Macmillan).

Jervis, R. (1978) 'Co-operation under the security dilemma', *World Politics*, 30:2, 167–214.

Joint Declaration on Peace (1993) Available from CAIN Web Service, http://cain.ulst.ac.uk/events/peace/docs/dsd151293.htm, accessed 2 December 2012.

Kaufman, S. (1996) 'An international theory of inter-ethnic war', *Review of International Studies*, 22, 149–72.

———(2001) *Modern Hatreds: The Symbolic Politics of Ethnic War* (New York: Cornell University Press).

———(2006) 'Symbolic politics or rational choice?: testing theories of ethnic violence', *International Security*, 30:4, 45–86.

Kaufmann, C.D. (1996) 'Possible and impossible solutions to ethnic civil wars', *International Security*, 20:4, 139–75.

Kennedy, L. (2003) 'The SDLP must accept part of the blame', *Fortnight*, October, pp. 12–13.

Kerr, M. (2006) *Transforming Unionism: David Trimble and the 2005 General Election* (Dublin: Irish Academic Press).

Kinnvall, C. (2004) 'Globalization and religious nationalism: self, identity, and the search for ontological security', *Political Psychology*, 25:5, 741–67.

Kirby, S. (2013) 'Sinn Féin and the SDLP: resources, public relations and power in post-conflict Northern Ireland', paper presented at the European Communication Research and Education Association (ECREA) conference, Belfast, 14 June.

Kuran, T. (1999) 'Ethnic dissimilation and its international diffusion', in D. Lake and D. Rothchild (eds), *The International Spread of Ethnic Conflict: Fear, Diffusion and Escalation* (Princeton, NJ: Princeton University Press), pp. 35–60.

Lake, D. and D. Rothchild (1998) 'Spreading fear: the genesis of transnational ethnic conflict', in D. Lake and D. Rothchild (eds), *The International Spread of Ethnic Conflict: Fear, Diffusion and Escalation* (Princeton, NJ: Princeton University Press), pp. 3–32.

Leonard, A. (1999) *The Alliance Party of Northern Ireland and Power Sharing in a Divided Society*, unpublished MA thesis, University College Dublin.

LSE IDEAS (2011) *The Lessons of Northern Ireland*, LSE (London School of Economics) IDEAS website, www.lse.ac.uk/IDEAS/publications/reports/SR008.aspx, accessed 13 March 2013.

Mac Ginty, R. (1999) 'Biting the bullet: decommissioning in the transition from war to peace in Northern Ireland', *Irish Studies in International Affairs*, 10, 237–47.

———(2004) 'Unionist political attitudes after the Belfast Agreement', *Irish Political Studies*, 19:1, 87–99.

———(2006a) *No War, No Peace: The Rejuvenation of Stalled Peace Processes and Peace Accords* (Basingstoke: Palgrave Macmillan).

———(2006b) 'Irish republicanism and the peace process: from revolution to reform', in M. Cox, A. Guelke and F. Stephen (eds), *A Farewell to Arms?: Beyond the Good Friday Agreement*, 2nd edn (Manchester: Manchester University Press), pp. 124–38.

———(2011) 'Bad students learning the wrong lessons?', in LSE IDEAS, *The Lessons of Northern Ireland*, LSE (London School of Economics) IDEAS website, www.lse.ac.uk/IDEAS/publications/reports/SR008.aspx, accessed 13 March 2013.

Maginness, A. (2002) 'Redefining northern nationalism', in J. Coakley (ed.), *Changing Shades of Orange and Green: Redefining the Union and the Nation in Contemporary Ireland* (Dublin: University College Dublin Press), pp. 33–40.

Maillot, A. (2005) *New Sinn Féin: Irish Republicanism in the Twenty-First Century* (Abingdon: Routledge).

Mallie, E. (2012) Interview with Peter Robinson for HDnet Television, Eamonn Mallie website, 26 June, http://eamonnmallie.com/2012/06/peter-robinson-dealing-gerry-adams-killing-friend-ira, accessed 12 February 2013.

Mallon, S. (1998) Speech to the annual conference of the SDLP, 13 November. SDLP boxes, NIPC.

———(1999) 'Statement by Séamus Mallon on the announcement of his resignation', 15 July. SDLP boxes, NIPC.

———(2000) 'Mallon stands firm on Patten', transcript of interview on BBC Radio Ulster, 12 October. SDLP boxes, NIPC.

McAdam, N. (2000) 'Trimble set to say "back me or sack me"', *Belfast Telegraph*, 23 October.

———(2002) 'Trimble set for a test of his tactics', *Belfast Telegraph*, 20 September.

———(2008) 'Will Alliance break stalemate over the devolution of policing?', *Belfast Telegraph*, 29 July.

———(2010) 'Ford ready to take role as Justice Minister but SDLP cry foul over his accession', *Belfast Telegraph*, 26 February.

McAllister, I. (1977) *The Northern Ireland Social Democratic and Labour Party: Political Opposition in a Divided Society* (London: Macmillan).

———(2004) 'The armalite and the ballot box: Sinn Féin's electoral strategy in Northern Ireland', *Electoral Studies*, 23:1, 123–42.

McAllister, I. and B. Wilson (1978) 'Bi-confessionalism in a confessional party system: the Northern Ireland Alliance Party', *Economic and Social Review*, 9:3, 207–25.

McAuley, J., J. Tonge and A. Mycock (2011) *Loyal to the Core? Orangeism and Britishness in Northern Ireland* (Dublin: Irish Academic Press).

McCaffrey, B. (2003) *Alex Maskey: Man and Mayor* (Belfast: The Brehon Press).

McCall, C. (2006) 'From "long war" to "war of the lilies": "post-conflict" territorial compromise and the return of cultural politics', in M. Cox, A. Guelke and F. Stephen (eds) *A Farewell to Arms?: Beyond the Good Friday Agreement*, 2nd edn (Manchester: Manchester University Press), pp. 302–16.

McCallister, J. (2012) 'Speech by John McCallister MLA on the Covenant and civic unionism', 1 October, UUP website, http://uup.org/news/1167/Speech-made-by-John-McCallister-MLA-on-the-Covenant-and-civic-unionism#.Up22nNJdUdV, accessed 29 November 2013.

McCrea, B. and J. McCallister (2013) 'Politics and change in Northern Ireland', seminar presented in the Institute for Research in the Social Sciences, Ulster University, Jordanstown, 10 May.

McCrudden, C. (2001) 'Equality', in C. J. Harvey (ed.), *Human Rights, Equality and Democratic Renewal in Northern Ireland* (Oxford: Hart), pp. 170–86.

McCrudden, C., J. McGarry, B. O'Leary and A. Schwartz (2013) 'Memorandum for the Assembly and Executive Review Committee', in Assembly and Executive Review Committee, *Review of D'Hondt, Community Designation and Provisions for Opposition*, Northern Ireland Assembly website, www.niassembly.gov.uk/Documents/Reports/Assem_Exec_Review/nia-123-11-15-Review-of-DHondt-Community-Designation-and-Provisions-for-Opposition.PDF, pp. 230–8, accessed 1 February 2014.

McCusker, H., P. Robinson and F. Millar (1987) *An End to Drift: The Task Force Report* (Belfast: UUP). NIPC.

McDonald, H. (2000) *Trimble* (London: Bloomsbury).

———(2010) 'Unionists demand deal on 11-plus before backing power sharing', *The Guardian* website, 12 February, www.theguardian.com/politics/2010/feb/12/ulster-unionists-demand-11plus-powersharing, accessed 29 November 2013.

McGarry, J. (ed.) (2001) *Northern Ireland and the Divided World: The Northern Ireland Conflict and the Good Friday Agreement in Comparative Perspective* (Oxford: Oxford University Press).

McGarry, J. and B. O'Leary (1995) *Explaining Northern Ireland: Broken Images* (Oxford: Blackwell).

———(2004) *The Northern Ireland Conflict: Consociational Engagements* (Oxford: Oxford University Press).

———(2009) 'Power shared after the deaths of thousands', in R. Taylor (ed.), *Consociational Theory: McGarry and O'Leary and the Northern Ireland Conflict* (Abingdon: Routledge), pp. 15–84.

McGovern, M. (2004) '"The old days are over": Irish republicanism, the peace process and the discourse of equality', *Terrorism and Political Violence*, 16:3, 622–45.

McGrattan, C. and E. Meehan (eds) (2012) *Everyday Life after the Irish Conflict: The Impact of Devolution and Cross-Border Cooperation* (Manchester: Manchester University Press).

McGuinness, M. (1998) 'Leadership address by Gerry Adams MP and Martin McGuinness MP', Sinn Féin *Ard Fheis*, Dublin, 18 April. NIPC.

———(2007) 'Inaugural speech', reproduced in *Irish Times*, 9 May.

McIntyre, A. (1995) 'Modern Irish republicanism: the product of British state strategies', *Irish Political Studies*, 10:1, 97–121.

———(2001) 'Modern Irish republicanism and the Belfast Agreement: chickens coming home to roost, or turkeys celebrating Christmas?', in R. Wilford (ed.), *Aspects of the Belfast Agreement* (Oxford: Oxford University Press), pp. 202–22.

McKeown, L. (2001) *Out of Time: Irish Republican Prisoners, Long Kesh 1972–2000* (Belfast: Beyond the Pale Publications).

McKittrick, D., S. Kelters, B. Feeney and C. Thornton (1999) *Lost Lives: The Stories of the Men, Women and Children Who Died as a Result of the Northern Ireland Troubles* (Edinburgh: Mainstream).

McLaughlin, M. (1999) 'Speech delivered by Sinn Féin Chairperson Mitchel McLaughlin to Belfast rally', 28 February. Sinn Féin boxes, NIPC.

———(2000) 'Time to get off the roundabout', Sinn Féin press release, 29 March. Sinn Féin boxes, NIPC.

———(2002) 'Redefining republicanism', in J. Coakley (ed.), *Changing Shades of Orange and Green: Redefining the Union and the Nation in Contemporary Ireland* (Dublin: University College Dublin Press), pp. 41–7.

McLoughlin, P. (2010) *John Hume and the Revision of Irish Nationalism* (Manchester: Manchester University Press).

———(2014) 'A "mutually-hurting stalemate": using Zartman's "Ripeness Theory" to explain the Northern Ireland peace process', seminar presented in the Institute for Conflict Transformation and Social Justice, Queen's University Belfast, 7 February.

Meehan, E. (2006) 'Europe and the Europeanisation of the Irish question', in M. Cox, A. Guelke and F. Stephen (eds), *A Farewell to Arms?: Beyond the Good Friday Agreement*, 2nd edn (Manchester: Manchester University Press), pp. 338–56.

Melander, E. (1999) *Anarchy Within: The Security Dilemma Between Ethnic Groups in Emerging Anarchy* (Uppsala: Department of Peace and Conflict Research, Uppsala University).

Millar, F. (2007) 'Siege lifts but is power-sharing a final settlement?', *Irish Times*, 9 May.

———(2008) *David Trimble: The Price of Peace*, 2nd edn (Dublin: The Liffey Press).

Miller, D. (1978) *Queens Rebels: Ulster Loyalism in Historical Perspective* (Dublin: Gill and Macmillan).

Mitchel, P. (2003) *Evangelicalism and National Identity in Ulster, 1921–1998* (Oxford: Oxford University Press).

Mitchell, C. (2003) 'From victims to equals? Catholic responses to political change in Northern Ireland', *Irish Political Studies*, 18:1, 51–71.

———(2006) *Religion, Identity and Politics in Northern Ireland: Boundaries of Belonging and Belief* (Aldershot: Ashgate).

Mitchell, D. (2009) 'Cooking the fudge: constructive ambiguity and the implementation of the Northern Ireland Agreement, 1998–2007', *Irish Political Studies*, 24:3, 321–36.

———(2010) 'Conditions for peace in Northern Ireland and Israel-Palestine', *Peace Review*, 11, 280–7.

Mitchell, G. (1999) *Making Peace* (London: Heinemann).

Mitchell, P. (1995) 'Party competition in an ethnic dual party system', *Ethnic and Racial Studies*, 18:4, 773–96.

Mitchell, P., G. Evans and B. O'Leary (2002) 'The 2001 elections in Northern Ireland: moderating "extremists" and the squeezing of the moderates', *Representation*, 29:1, 23–36.

———(2009) 'Extremist outbidding in ethnic party systems is not inevitable: tribune parties in Northern Ireland', *Political Studies*, 57, 397–421.

Mitchell, T.C. (2002) *Indispensible Traitors: Liberal Parties in Settler Conflicts* (Westport, CT: Greenwood).

Mitzen, J. (2006) 'Ontological security in world politics: state identity and the security dilemma', *European Journal of International Relations*, 12:3, 341–70.

Moloney, E. (1984) 'Class, age and the SDLP: what the studies show', *Irish Times*, 31 January.

———(2007) *A Secret History of the IRA*, 2nd edn (London: Penguin).

———(2008) *Paisley: From Demagogue to Democrat?* (Dublin: Poolbeg).

Morgan, A. (2000) *The Belfast Agreement: A Practical Legal Analysis* (London: The Belfast Press).

Morris, A. (2014) 'Dissidents in disarray', *Irish News*, 3 February.

Morrison, D. (1999) 'Let the guns be beyond use', *Observer*, 28 November.

Morrow, D. (1997) 'Suffering for righteousness' sake?: fundamentalist Protestantism and Ulster politics', in P. Shirlow and M. McGovern (eds), *Who Are 'The People'?: Unionism, Protestantism and Loyalism in Northern Ireland* (London: Pluto Press).

———(2001) 'The elusiveness of trust', *Peace Review*, 13:1, 13–19.

Murray, G. (1998) *John Hume and the SDLP: Impact and Survival in Northern Ireland* (Dublin: Irish Academic Press).

Murray, G. and J. Tonge (2005) *Sinn Féin and the SDLP: From Alienation to Participation* (Dublin: The O'Brien Press).

Nesbitt, D. (2002) 'Redefining unionism', in J. Coakley (ed.), *Changing Shades of Orange and Green: Redefining the Union and the Nation in Contemporary Ireland* (Dublin: University College Dublin Press), pp. 48–56.

News Letter (2009) 'Alliance challenged over Union stance', 25 August.

Nolan, P. (2012) *Northern Ireland Peace Monitoring Report: Number One* (Belfast: Community Relations Council).

———(2013) *Northern Ireland Peace Monitoring Report: Number Two* (Belfast: Community Relations Council).

———(2014) *Northern Ireland Peace Monitoring Report: Number Three* (Belfast: Community Relations Council).

Norton, C. (2014) *The Politics of Constitutional Nationalism, 1932–1970: Between Grievance and Reconciliation* (Manchester: Manchester University Press).

O'Connor, F. (2002) *Breaking the Bonds: Making Peace in Northern Ireland* (London: Mainstream).

Ó Dochartaigh, N. (2011) 'Together in the middle: back-channel negotiation in the Irish peace process', *Journal of Peace Research*, 48:6, 767–80.

O'Doherty, M. (1998) *The Trouble with Guns: Republican Strategy and the Provisional IRA* (Belfast: Blackstaff).

———(2000) 'Glum faces in the SDLP', *Belfast Telegraph*, 4 May.

———(2014) 'New year ... but same sorry old story', *Belfast Telegraph*, 1 January.

O'Dowd, L. (1998) '"New Unionism", British nationalism and the prospects for a negotiated settlement in Northern Ireland', in D. Miller (ed.), *Rethinking Northern Ireland: Culture, Ideology and Colonialism* (Harlow: Longman), pp. 70–93.

OFMDFM (2005) *A Shared Future: Policy and Strategic Framework for Good Relations in Northern Ireland* (Belfast: OFMDFM), available on OFMDFM website, www.ofmdfmni.gov.uk/asharedfuturepolicy2005.pdf, accessed 24 June 2013.

———(2010) *Programme for Cohesion, Sharing and Integration Consultation Document* (Belfast: OFMDFM), available on OFMDFM website, www.ofmdfmni.gov.uk/reformatted_final_print_version_csi_-_26.07.10.pdf, accessed 24 June 2013.

———(2013) *Together: Building a United Community* (Belfast: OFMDFM), available on OFMDFM website, www.ofmdfmni.gov.uk/together-building-a-united-community-strategy.pdf, accessed 24 June 2013.

O'Kane, E. (2007) 'Decommissioning and the peace process: where did it come from and why did it stay so long?', *Irish Political Studies*, 22:1, 81–101.

Paisley, I. (1996) *An Exposition of the Epistle to the Romans* (Belfast: Ambassador Productions).

———(1998) 'Statement from DUP leader Dr. Ian Paisley', 15 April. DUP boxes, NIPC.

———(2001) Speech at the DUP annual conference, 24 November. NIPC.

———(2007a) 'Inaugural speech', reproduced in *Irish Times*, 9 May.

———(2007b) 'We can lay the foundation for a better future', *News Letter*, 31 March.

Paisley Junior, I. (1998) *Peace Deal?* (Belfast: DUP). NIPC.

———(2000) 'Appeasement has failed', DUP press release from Ian Paisley Junior, 16 February. DUP boxes, NIPC.

Paris, R. (2004) *At War's End: Building Peace After Civil Conflict* (Cambridge: Cambridge University Press).

Patterson, H. (1997) *The Politics of Illusion: A Political History of the IRA* (London: Serif).

———(1998) 'No vex please, we're British', *Parliamentary Brief*, 5:6, 10–11.

Patterson, H. and E. Kaufmann (2007) *Unionism and Orangeism in Northern Ireland since 1945: The Decline of the Loyal Family* (Manchester: Manchester University Press).

Peel, J. (2010) 'The shame of UCUNF', Jeffrey Peel website, http://jeffpeel.net/2010/05/05/the-shame-of-ucunf, accessed 29 November 2013.

Porter, N. (1998) *Rethinking Unionism: An Alternative Vision for Northern Ireland*, 2nd edn (Belfast: Blackstaff).

———(2003) *The Elusive Quest: Reconciliation in Northern Ireland* (Belfast: Blackstaff).
Posen, B. (1993) 'The security dilemma and ethnic conflict', *Survival*, 35:1, 37–47.
Powell, J. (2008) *Great Hatred, Little Room: Making Peace in Northern Ireland* (London: Vintage).
Purdy, M. (2002) 'Durkan was no fall guy', BBC news website, 1 November, http://news.bbc.co.uk/1/hi/northern_ireland/2388831.stm, accessed 5 November 2006.
———(2005) *Room 21: Stormont – Behind Closed Doors* (Belfast: The Brehon Press).
———(2008) 'Mallon toasts Good Friday Agreement', BBC news website, 20 March, http://news.bbc.co.uk/1/hi/northern_ireland/7305927.stm, accessed 6 December 2013.
———(2012) 'United unionism: are we about to see a DUP and UUP alliance?', BBC news website, 23 January, www.bbc.co.uk/news/uk-northern-ireland-16690694, accessed 3 December 2013.
Pyle, F. (1970) 'New party in North woos moderates', *Irish Times*, 22 April.
Rafter, K. (2005) *Sinn Féin 1905–2005: In the Shadow of Gunmen* (Dublin: Gill and Macmillan).
Ritchie, M. (2010a) Speech to annual conference of the SDLP, 6 November, CAIN Web Service, http://cain.ulst.ac.uk/issues/politics/docs/sdlp/mr061110.htm, accessed 6 December 2013.
———(2010b) Speech to Irish Labour Party conference, Galway, 17 April. SDLP boxes, NIPC.
Robinson, P. (1998) '"No" to Dublin rule – "no" to a united Ireland', DUP press release from Peter Robinson, 15 April. DUP boxes, NIPC.
———(1999a) 'Process corrupt and farcical', DUP press release from Peter Robinson, 4 August. DUP boxes, NIPC.
———(1999b) 'The ultimate betrayal', DUP press release from Peter Robinson, 9 September. DUP boxes, NIPC.
———(1999c) 'Trimble's trickery', DUP press release from Peter Robinson, 23 March. DUP boxes, NIPC.
———(2000) Speech to the DUP annual conference, 18 November. DUP boxes, NIPC.
———(2001a) 'There is no "safe harbour" – there are only "safe hands"', speech at the Young Democrats conference, Templepatrick, 17 January. DUP boxes, NIPC.
———(2001b) Speech to the DUP annual conference, 24 November. DUP boxes, NIPC.
———(2012a) 'Speech by First Minister Peter Robinson', OSCE Chairmanship Conference, Dublin, 27 April, OSCE website, www.osce.org/cio/90229, accessed 29 March 2014.
———(2012b) 'Reflections on Irish unionism', speech in Iveagh House, Dublin, 29 March, CAIN web Service, http://cain.ulst.ac.uk/issues/politics/docs/dup/pr290312.htm, accessed 23 January 2014.
———(2012c) 'Statement by Rt Hon Peter Robinson MLA', DUP website, 6 December, www.mydup.com/news/article/statement-by-rt-hon-peter-robinson-mla, accessed 26 June 2013.
Roe, P. (1999) 'The intrastate security dilemma: ethnic conflict as tragedy?', *Journal of Peace Research*, 36:2, 183–202.

———(2005) *Ethnic Violence and the Societal Security Dilemma* (New York: Routledge).

Rogers, B. (2000) 'Opinion', *Belfast Telegraph*, 23 February.

———(2001) 'Only IRA can save agreement', *Irish News*, 6 October.

Rose, W. (2000) 'The security dilemma and ethnic conflict: some new hypotheses', *Security Studies*, 9:4, 1–51.

Rowan, B. (2003) *The Armed Peace: Life and Death after the Ceasefires* (Edinburgh: Mainstream).

———(2005) *Paisley and the Provos: The Bugs, the Bank Job, the Broken Deal* (Belfast: The Brehon Press).

RTÉ (2002) 'Trimble brands Republic pathetic sectarian state', RTÉ News website, www.rte.ie/news/2002/0309/23893-north, accessed 5 March 2013.

Ruane, J. (2004) 'Contemporary republicanism and the strategy of armed struggle', in M. Bric and J. Coakley (eds), *From Political Violence to Negotiated Settlement: The Winding Path to Peace in Twentieth-Century Ireland* (Dublin: University College Dublin Press), pp. 115–32.

Ruane, J. and J. Todd (1996) *The Dynamics of Conflict in Northern Ireland: Power, Conflict, and Emancipation* (Cambridge: Cambridge University Press).

———(eds) (1999a) *After the Good Friday Agreement: Analysing Political Change in Northern Ireland* (Dublin: University College Dublin Press).

———(1999b) 'The Belfast Agreement: context, content, consequences', in J. Ruane and J. Todd (eds), *After the Good Friday Agreement: Analysing Political Change in Northern Ireland* (Dublin: University College Dublin Press), pp. 1–29.

———(2001) 'The politics of transition?: explaining political crises in the implementation of the Belfast Good Friday Agreement', *Political Studies*, 49:5, 923–40.

———(2007) 'Path dependence in settlement processes: explaining settlement in Northern Ireland', *Political Studies*, 55:2, 442–58.

Ruohomaki, J. (2001) *Two Elections, Two Contests: The June 2001 Elections in Northern Ireland* (Belfast: Democratic Dialogue), available on CAIN Web Service, http://cain.ulst.ac.uk/dd/papers/elect.htm, accessed 12 November 2007.

Ryder, C. (2006) *Fighting Fitt* (Belfast: The Brehon Press).

Scarcelli, M. (2014) 'Social cleavages and civil war onset', *Ethnopolitics*, 13:2, 181–202.

Schwartz, A. (2010) 'How unfair is cross-community consent? Voting power in the Northern Ireland Assembly', *Northern Ireland Legal Quarterly*, 61:4, 349–62.

SDLP (1971) 'SDLP draft proposals relating to negotiations on the present situation in Northern Ireland, September, 1971', Appendix 1 in G. Murray, *John Hume and the SDLP: Impact and Survival in Northern Ireland* (Dublin: Irish Academic Press), pp. 264–8.

———(1972) *Towards a New Ireland: Proposals by the Social Democratic and Labour Party* (Belfast: SDLP). NIPC.

———(1997) 'SDLP submission to Strands One and Two of the multi-party talks, constitutional issues', 20 October. SDLP boxes, NIPC.

———(1998a) *Assembly Election Manifesto 1998* (Belfast: SDLP). NIPC.

———(1998b) *SDLP: A Positive Approach* (Belfast: SDLP). NIPC.

———(1999a) 'Implementing the Good Friday Agreement: North-South economic and social development', SDLP discussion document. SDLP boxes, NIPC.

———(1999b) 'Policing: a new service for a new future – submission to the Independent Commission on Policing'. NIPC.
———(2000) 'Principles on the flying of flags: SDLP policy paper'. SDLP boxes, NIPC.
———(2002) 'New police legislation won by the SDLP', November. SDLP boxes, NIPC.
———(2003a) *Assembly Election Manifesto 2003* (Belfast: SDLP). NIPC.
———(2003b) 'A United Ireland and the Agreement: SDLP strategy document', November. NIPC.
———(2011) 'SDLP manifesto: Assembly and local government elections', CAIN Web Service, http://cain.ulst.ac.uk/issues/politics/docs/sdlp/sdlp_2011-05-05_man.pdf, accessed 12 June 2012.
Shanahan, T. (2009) *The Provisional Irish Republican Army and the Morality of Terrorism* (Edinburgh: Edinburgh University Press).
Shirlow, P., J. Tonge, J. McAuley and C. McGlynn (2010) *Abandoning Historical Conflict?: Former Political Prisoners and Reconciliation in Northern Ireland* (Manchester: Manchester University Press).
Sinnerton, H. (2002) *David Ervine: Uncharted Waters* (Dingle: Brandon).
Sinn Féin (1988) *Towards a Peace Strategy* (Belfast: Sinn Féin). NIPC.
———(1992) *Towards a Lasting Peace in Ireland* (Dublin: Sinn Féin). NIPC.
———(1996) Submission to the Review of Parades, Sinn Féin website, www.sinnfein.org/releases/reviewofparades.html, accessed 10 January 2014.
———(1998) *Assembly Election Manifesto 1998* (Belfast: Sinn Féin). NIPC.
———(1999) 'Interim response to the report of the Independent Commission on Policing', 30 November. Sinn Féin boxes, NIPC.
———(2001) *Westminster Election Manifesto 2001* (Belfast: Sinn Féin). NIPC.
———(2003) *Assembly Election Manifesto 2003* (Belfast: Sinn Féin). NIPC.
———(2007) *Sinn Féin Assembly Election Manifesto 2007*, Sinn Féin website, www.sinnféin.ie/files/2009/AssemblyManifesto2007small.pdf, accessed 14 January 2012.
———(2011) *Sinn Féin Assembly Election Manifesto 2011*, Sinn Féin website, www.sinnféin.ie/files/2011/AssemblyManifesto2011.pdf, accessed 6 January 2014.
Smith, J.G. (2006) 'Fighting fear: exploring the dynamic between security concerns and elite manipulation in internal conflict', *Peace Conflict and Development*, 8, www.brad.ac.uk/ssis/peace-conflict-and-development/issue-8/Fighting-fear.pdf, accessed 12 September 2012.
Smyth, C. (1986) 'The DUP as a politico-religious organisation', *Irish Political Studies*, 1:1, 33–43.
———(1987) *Ian Paisley: Voice of Protestant Ulster* (Edinburgh: Scottish Academic Press).
Smyth, M. (2000) 'Why Sinn Féin/IRA must be excluded', *Belfast Telegraph*, 24 October.
———(2001) 'Why the UUP must withdraw from the Executive', *Belfast Telegraph*, 2 February.
Snyder, J. and R. Jervis (1999) 'Civil war and the security dilemma', in B. Walter and J. Snyder (eds), *Civil Wars, Insecurity and Intervention* (New York: Columbia University Press), pp. 15–37.

Somerville, I. and A. Purcell (2011) 'A history of Republican public relations in Northern Ireland from "Bloody Sunday" to the Good Friday Agreement', *Journal of Communication Management*, 15:3, 192–209.

Southern, N. (2005) 'Ian Paisley and evangelical Democratic Unionists: an analysis of the role of evangelical Protestantism within the Democratic Unionist Party', *Irish Political Studies*, 20:2, 127–45.

St Andrews Agreement (2006) Available from CAIN web service, http://cain.ulst.ac.uk/issues/politics/docs/nio/bi131006.pdf, accessed 2 December 2012.

Sweeney, J. (2013) 'David Trimble: I should have quit in 2003… and why oh why did I rise to DUP baiting?', *Belfast Telegraph*, 3 August, www.belfasttelegraph.co.uk/news/politics/david-trimble-i-should-have-quit-in-2003-and-why-oh-why-did-i-rise-to-dup-baiting-29468865.html, accessed 3 August 2013.

Tang, S. (2009) 'The security dilemma: a conceptual analysis', *Security Studies*, 18:3, 587–623.

Taylor, R. (2009a) 'The injustice of a consociational solution to the Northern Ireland problem', in R. Taylor (ed.), *Consociational Theory: McGarry and O'Leary and the Northern Ireland Conflict* (Abingdon: Routledge), pp. 309–30.

———(ed.) (2009b) *Consociational Theory: McGarry and O'Leary and the Northern Ireland Conflict* (Abingdon: Routledge).

Thomson, A. (1998) *The Politics of Holiness* (Belfast: Evangelical Contribution on Northern Ireland).

———(2002) *Fields of Vision: Faith and Identity in Protestant Ireland* (Belfast: Centre for Contemporary Christianity in Ireland).

———(2004) 'It didn't have to be this way', *Fortnight*, January, p. 5.

Thornton, C. (2002a) 'Trimble: what now for Ulster Unionism?', *Belfast Telegraph*, 23 September.

———(2002b) 'SDLP pushes for new all-party talks', *Belfast Telegraph*, 2 November.

———(2004) 'Trio set to sing from the Big Man's hymn sheet', *Belfast Telegraph*, 6 January.

Todd, J. (1999) 'Nationalism, republicanism and the Good Friday Agreement', in J. Ruane and J. Todd (eds), *After the Good Friday Agreement: Analysing Political Change in Northern Ireland* (Dublin: University College Dublin Press), pp. 49–70.

———(2002) 'The reorientation of constitutional nationalism', in J. Coakley (ed.), *Changing Shades of Orange and Green: Redefining the Union and the Nation in Contemporary Ireland* (Dublin: University College Dublin Press), pp. 71–83.

Tonge, J. (2005) *The New Northern Irish Politics?* (Palgrave: Basingstoke).

———(2006) 'Polarisation or new moderation?: party politics since the GFA', in M. Cox, A. Guelke and F. Stephen (eds), *A Farewell to Arms?: Beyond the Good Friday Agreement*, 2nd edn, (Manchester: Manchester University Press), pp. 70–88.

Tonge, J., M. Braniff, T. Hennessey, J.W. McAuley and S. Whiting (2014) *The Democratic Unionist Party: From Protest to Power* (Oxford: Oxford University Press).

Tonge, J. and J. Evans (2001) 'Faultlines in unionism: division and dissent within the Ulster Unionist Council', *Irish Political Studies*, 16:1, 111–31.

———(2002) 'Party members and the Good Friday Agreement in Northern Ireland', *Irish Political Studies*, 17:2, 59–73.
Trimble, D. (1996) Speech at the UUC Annual General Meeting, 23 March. UUP boxes, NIPC.
———(1999a) 'Equality and Northern Ireland: speech delivered in New York City', 13 March, David Trimble website, www.davidtrimble.org/speeches_toraiseup10.htm, accessed 14 March 2014.
———(1999b) 'Progress can still be made', *Belfast Telegraph*, 8 October.
———(1999c) 'Eve of Unionist Council meeting message from Rt. Hon. David Trimble MP', 26 November. UUP boxes, NIPC.
———(2000a) 'My challenge to the DUP', *Belfast Telegraph*, 19 September.
———(2000b) Speech at the UUP annual conference, 7 October. UUP boxes, NIPC.
———(2001a) *To Raise up a New Northern Ireland: Articles and Speeches 1998–2000* (Belfast: The Belfast Press).
———(2001b) 'Unionism … a turning point in history?', *Belfast Telegraph*, 30 November.
———(2002) Letter to UUC delegates, 18 September. UUP boxes, NIPC.
———(2007) 'Reflections on the Belfast Agreement', Anthony Alcock Memorial Lecture, University of Ulster, Coleraine, 24 April, www.publicaffairs.ulster.ac.uk/podcasts/Trimble.doc, accessed 28 April 2007.
———(2008) 'Agreeing to differ', *The Guardian*, 5 April, www.theguardian.com/books/2008/apr/05/politics2, accessed 24 February 2013.
TUV (2014) *Manifesto 2014: Europe and Council Elections*, TUV website, http://tuv.org.uk/wp-content/uploads/2014/05/manifesto2014.pdf, accessed 4 June 2014.
TV3 (2013) *Sinn Féin: Who Are They?* First broadcast in two parts, 25 November and 2 December 2013.
UUP (1969) *Northern Ireland: Fact and Falsehood* (Belfast: UUP). NIPC.
———(1998a) 'Ulster Unionist voice', UUP referendum campaign advertisement. UUP boxes, NIPC.
———(1998b) 'Referendum communication from the Ulster Unionist Party'. UUP boxes, NIPC.
———(1998c) *Assembly Election Manifesto 1998* (Belfast: UUP). NIPC.
———(1999a) *Implementing the Agreement* (Belfast: UUP). UUP boxes, NIPC.
———(1999b) 'A response to "A new beginning: policing in Northern Ireland", the report of the Independent Commission on Policing for Northern Ireland', 9 September. UUP boxes, NIPC.
———(2001) *Westminster Election Manifesto 2001* (Belfast: UUP). NIPC.
———(2003) *Assembly Election Manifesto 2003* (Belfast: UUP). NIPC.
Waever, O. (1993) 'Societal security: the concept', in O. Waever, B. Buzan, M. Kelstrup and P. Lemaitre (eds), *Identity, Migration and the New Security Agenda in Europe* (London: Pinter), pp. 17–40.
Walker, B. (2012) *A Political History of the Two Irelands: From Partition to Peace* (Basingstoke: Palgrave Macmillan).

Walker, G. (1997) 'A most bitter pill for the doctor to swallow', *Belfast Telegraph*, 16 May.

——— (2004) *A History of the Ulster Unionist Party: Protest, Pragmatism and Pessimism* (Manchester: Manchester University Press).

Walker, S. (2009) 'Tories wanted to merge with the UUP', BBC news website, 30 March, http://news.bbc.co.uk/1/hi/northern_ireland/7971533.stm, accessed 13 May 2013.

——— (2013a) 'SDLP commissioned report says party "resting on its laurels"', BBC news website, 29 November, www.bbc.co.uk/news/uk-northern-ireland-politics-25147178, accessed 30 November 2013.

——— (2013b) 'SDLP should leave Executive says former minister Brid Rogers', BBC news website, 28 February, www.bbc.co.uk/news/uk-northern-ireland-foyle-west-21621582, accessed 6 December 2013.

Wallace Consulting (2011) *Programme for Cohesion, Sharing and Integration Consultation Analysis*, OFMDFM website, www.ofmdfmni.gov.uk/final_web_version_-_csi_analysis_report_-___pdf_1.12_mb_.pdf, accessed 24 June 2013.

Wallis, R., S. Bruce and D. Taylor (1986) *'No Surrender!': Paisleyism and the Politics of Ethnic Identity in Northern Ireland* (Belfast: Department of Social Studies, The Queen's University of Belfast).

Walter, B. (1999) 'Designing transitions from civil war', in B. Walter and J. Snyder (eds), *Civil Wars, Insecurity and Intervention* (New York: Columbia University Press), pp. 38–69.

Walter, B. and J. Snyder (eds) (1999) *Civil Wars, Insecurity and Intervention* (New York: Columbia University Press).

Weir, P. (1998) 'Statement by Peter Weir to the Northern Ireland Forum', 30 January. UUP boxes, NIPC.

Wendt, A. (1992) 'Anarchy is what states make of it: the social construction of power politics', *International Organisation*, 46:2, 391–425.

White, B. (1999) 'Nesbitt: why he's the exception to the rule', *Belfast Telegraph*, 11 September.

Whyte, J. (1991) *Interpreting Northern Ireland* (Oxford: Clarendon).

Wilford, R. (ed.) (2001a) *Aspects of the Belfast Agreement* (Oxford: Oxford University Press).

——— (2001b) 'The Assembly and the Executive', in R. Wilford (ed.), *Aspects of the Belfast Agreement* (Oxford: Oxford University Press), pp. 107–28.

——— (2010) 'Northern Ireland: the politics of constraint', *Parliamentary Affairs*, 63:1, 134–55.

Wilson, R. (2010) *The Northern Ireland Experience of Conflict and Agreement: A Model for Export?* (Manchester: Manchester University Press).

Woodward, B. (1999) 'Bosnia and Herzegovina: how not to end civil war', in B. Walter and J. Snyder (eds), *Civil Wars, Insecurity and Intervention* (New York: Columbia University Press), pp. 73–115.

Wright, F. (1973) 'Protestant ideology and politics in Ulster', *European Journal of Sociology*, 14:2, 212–80.

Zartman, I.W. (1985) *Ripe for Resolution: Conflict and Intervention in Africa* (Oxford: Oxford University Press).

Index

Adams, Gerry 65, 74, 87, 101, 105, 111, 119, 126, 137, 159, 169
   Agreement and 113–15
   arrest in 2014 46
   elections and 131–2
   IRA and 128–30
agreed Ireland 88–91, 107
Ahern, Bertie 133
Alderdice, John 192
Alliance Party
   Agreement and 175–6, 181–3
   electoral fortunes 169, 181, 185, 187
   flag protests and 187–91
   ideology 169–74, 191–2
   Justice Ministry and 185–7
   origins 168–9
   re-designation affair (2001) 151, 178–80
   shared future and 183–5
Allister, Jim 160, 162
Anglo-Irish Agreement 27, 30, 53, 54, 58, 70, 87, 90, 111, 138, 141–2, 173
Ardoyne 200
Assembly
   design 29–30
   suspensions 67–8, 94, 95, 180, 183
Assembly election
   (1973) 169
   (1998) 58–9, 69, 93, 101, 115, 131, 145, 154, 176–7
   (2003) 64, 70–1, 78, 138, 155, 179
   (2007) 161, 185
   (2011) 5, 108, 131, 170, 185
Attwood, Alex 187

Belfast City Hall 100, 120, 148, 167, 172, 188–91

Blair, Tony 57–8, 60–1, 68, 76, 83, 94, 97–8, 105, 145, 149, 180
   pre-referendum pledges 41, 62, 128
British Government
   Agreement and 30, 32, 34, 57, 61, 74, 114
   approach to republicans 60, 62, 67–8, 97–8, 125
   Direct Rule and 119
   management of the peace process 5, 26, 27, 28, 41, 94, 143, 155, 158, 186
British–Irish Council 30, 91, 147, 158
British–Irish Intergovernmental Conference 30, 142
Brooke/Mayhew talks 57, 90, 141

Campbell, Gregory 117, 146–8, 157
Carson, Edward 52
Catholic Church 139
ceasefires 31, 33, 39, 60, 90, 96, 112, 113, 125, 126, 129, 149, 174, 193
Chinese finger trap 19
Close, Séamus 178
Cold War 11, 14, 17, 28, 111
Collins, Michael 85, 109
Colombia 4, 67, 128, 130
colonialism 25
Conservative Party 78, 80
consociationalism 5, 46–7, 174
constructive ambiguity 33–4, 59, 61, 64–5, 151
Council of Ireland 107

decommissioning
   Agreement and 30, 32–3, 37, 38
   Alliance Party and 174–6
   completion of (2005) 43, 130
   DUP and 150, 151, 157

first act of (2001) 63, 128, 151, 178
  SDLP and 93–8
  Sinn Féin and 42, 123–30
  UUP and 57–70
Democratic Unionist Party
  Agreement and 141–5
  Comprehensive Agreement (2004) and 157
  ethnic outbidding and 40, 153
  flag protests and 163, 165
  FPCU links 138–40
  ideology 138–41
  modernisation 153–4
  power-sharing with Sinn Féin 43–4, 78–9, 162–3
  St Andrews Agreement and 157–61
  TUV and 162
  unionist unity and 81
Deputy First Minister 29, 43, 44, 94, 151, 155, 158, 178, 183, 186
Derry 43, 110
designations (in Assembly) 29, 82, 158, 175, 178–82
De Valera, Éamon 52, 109
d'Hondt 29, 79, 82, 146, 175, 181–2, 185–6
Direct Rule 7, 27, 51, 53, 56, 66, 75, 119, 146, 159, 161, 190
Dodds, Diane 162
Dodds, Nigel 151, 165
Donaldson, Jeffrey ix, 44, 57
  decommissioning and 63–7
  joining DUP 153
Doran, Noel 24
Downing Street Declaration 9, 27, 90, 112
DUP *see* Democratic Unionist Party
Durkan, Mark ix, 44, 89, 92, 106, 137, 151, 178–9
  Agreement interpretation 46, 198
  potential exclusion of Sinn Féin and 94, 96, 97–8
  Trimble assessment 64, 76
  united Ireland and 89, 102–3

ECHR *see* European Convention on Human Rights
elite manipulation 12, 19
Elliott, Tom 81
Empey, (Sir) Reg 79–81, 84

equality
  Agreement and 29, 30, 32
  Alliance Party and 174
  SDLP and 87, 91–3
  Sinn Féin and 111, 113, 114, 116, 118–24
  unionists and 57, 74–6
Equality Commission 30, 61, 91, 120, 147, 188
ethnic outbidding 40, 153
EU *see* European Union
European Convention on Human Rights 30, 87, 91
European election
  (2009) 162
  (2014) 82, 133, 167
  Paisley victories 138
European Union 14–15, 26, 147, 191
ex-combatants 49, 112

Farren, Séan 89–90, 92–3, 94–5
Farry, Stephen 176–8, 181, 185
fatalist logic
  DUP and 138, 148, 164
  meaning 13
  Northern Ireland parties and 24, 28, 34, 36, 41, 43, 47, 50, 170, 193, 195, 197
  security dilemma and 15–16, 18, 20, 23
  UUP and 55, 66, 76, 83
  Sinn Féin and 109, 111, 134–5
Fianna Fáil 106, 109, 132, 133
fifty-fifty recruitment (police) 73, 75, 148, 158, 176
First Minister 43, 44, 59, 63, 81, 151, 155, 158, 159, 165, 178
Fitt, Gerry 86
flag protests 199
  Alliance Party and 187–91
  DUP and 163, 165
Florida 67, 130
Ford, David 171, 179, 180, 184
  Justice Minister 185, 187
Foster, Arlene 153
FPCU *see* Free Presbyterian Church of Ulster
Framework Document 90, 142
Free Presbyterian Church of Ulster 138, 140

Gaelic Athletic Association 81, 165
Game of Thrones 164

Garland, Roy 77
Giro d'Italia 200
Green Party 5, 82

Haass, Richard 45, 47, 184
Hain, Peter 161
Hayes, Maurice 81
Hermon, (Lady) Sylvia 79, 80, 162, 178
Higgins, Michael D. 133, 134
Hillsborough Castle 186
Historical Enquiries Team 190
Hoey, Kate 58
Home Rule 21, 52
Human Rights Commission 30, 75, 91
Hume, John 7, 69, 85–90, 101, 105, 107, 132

IICD *see* Independent International Commission on Decommissioning
IMC *see* Independent Monitoring Commission
Independent International Commission on Decommissioning 30, 32, 62–4, 126–8, 130
Independent Monitoring Commission 41, 79, 129, 130
IRA *see* Irish Republican Army
Irish Government 30, 76, 100
   British–Irish Council and 20
   change of Irish constitution 27, 31, 55
   management of peace process 5, 25, 26, 123–4, 157, 195–6
   NSMC and 29
Irish language 32, 82, 91, 113, 120, 147, 158, 162, 186
Irish News 24, 167, 180, 185
Irish Republican Army
   history 22, 109, 110
   political purpose and impact after 1998 24, 124–30
   see also decommissioning, ceasefires
Irish Times 1, 160, 179, 197
Irish tricolour 72, 120

Joint Authority 5, 28
Justice Minister 183, 185–7, 192, 195

Kelly, Gerry 121
Kelly, Delores 106

Labour Party (Britain) 56, 58, 80, 125

Labour Party (Ireland) 24, 106
Leeds Castle 157
Lo, Anna 167, 172, 191
local government election
   (1981) 169
   (2011) 185
   (2014) 84, 101, 162
Long, Naomi 169, 185, 187–90
Loyalism 104, 139, 163
Loyalist paramilitaries 28, 65, 96, 110, 112, 122, 125, 141, 143
   see also UDA, UVF
Lyttle, Chris ix, 172, 185

McCallister, John 81–2
McCann, Eamonn 24
McCartney, Bob 141, 178
McCartney, Robert 130, 157
McCrea, Basil 81, 82
McDevitt, Conall 105
McDonnell, Alasdair 105
McDowell, Michael 133
McGuinness, Martin 123, 126, 128, 137
   Agreement and 114, 116
   handshakes with Queen Elizabeth II 108
   IRA and 130
   Irish Presidency bid 133–4
   relationship with Paisley 43, 162, 197
McLaughlin, Mitchel ix, 58, 69, 161
   decommissioning and 125, 127
   Irish unity and 117
   Trimble assessment 77
Maginness, Alban 121
Mallon, Séamus 79, 86, 92–3, 100, 105
   resignation as Deputy First Minister 94, 151
   St Andrews Agreement and 106
Mandelson, Peter 63, 68, 74, 98, 100, 120, 150
Maskey, Alex 120
Maze/Long Kesh 162
Mitchell, George 62
Mitchell Principles 112, 117
Mitchell Review (1999) 61–2, 93
mitigator logic
   Agreement and 29, 174, 193
   DUP and 164
   meaning 13–15
   Sinn Féin and 135

UUP and 60, 66, 78, 83, 194
Molyneaux, James 53, 55
Morrow, Duncan ix, 171–2, 191
MTV Awards 200

Napier, Oliver 168, 169
nationalism (Irish) 9, 22–4
   intra-nationalist party competition 41, 85, 93, 97, 100–6, 130–2
   SDLP expression of 86, 89, 91, 102–3, 107, 195
   Sinn Féin expression of 119
   unionist fear of threat from 52, 56, 70, 76, 142
Nationalist Party 22, 86
Nesbitt, Dermot ix, 64, 69, 77, 84, 126, 153
Nesbitt, Mike 82
new unionists 54, 73, 89
News Letter 160
NI Conservatives 5
NI21 5, 82
Nobel prize
   Hume and Trimble awarded 85
   Trimble's lecture 22, 59
North–South Ministerial Council 29, 30, 31, 58, 63, 91, 114, 122, 146, 147, 158
Northern Bank robbery 130, 157
Northern Ireland Act (2000) 158
Northern Ireland Labour Party 169
Northern Ireland Life and Times Survey 116, 156, 170, 191, 199
NSMC *see* North–South Ministerial Council

Ó'Muilleoir, Mairtín 121
O'Neill, Terence 53, 138, 150
Orange Order 78, 144
   see also parades
Orange Standard 144
O'Sullivan, Megan 45

Paisley, Ian
   assessments of 24, 141
   condemnation of Agreement 142–5, 150–2
   founding of DUP 138
   opposition to civil rights 24, 53, 164
   power-sharing and 3, 43, 137, 145, 160–2, 164
   relationship with Martin McGuinness 43, 197
   religious beliefs 138–40
   resignation as party leader 165
Paisley, Ian Junior 142, 165
Palestine 111
parades 45, 102, 158, 185, 199
   Drumcree 55
   republican opposition to Orange parades 102, 121
   republican parade in Castlederg (2013) 135
   unionist defence of Orange parades 147, 148
Parades Commission 190
parallel consent 29, 143, 175, 178, 179, 182
parity of esteem
   Agreement and 32, 173
   SDLP and 87, 89, 91, 93, 95, 98, 99, 100
   Sinn Féin and 119, 120, 124
   unionists, flags and symbols and 71–5
partition 21, 24, 52, 56, 58, 86, 109, 111–13, 118–19, 167
Patten (policing commission and report)
   see policing
Peace Monitoring Reports 3
Pearse, Patrick 1, 109
Pledge of Office 29, 37, 61, 158
Police Service of Northern Ireland 64, 74, 122, 128
   see also policing
policing
   Agreement and 30, 32–4, 37, 45
   DUP and 145, 148, 150, 159, 162
   SDLP and 98, 100
   Sinn Féin and 98, 118, 121–2, 126
   UUP and 57, 61, 69, 72, 74, 79, 80
Powell, Jonathan 68, 94, 128, 154
principle of consent 32, 37
   Alliance Party and 167, 171–4
   DUP and 143
   SDLP and 89, 91, 99
   Sinn Féin and 37, 42, 112, 114, 117
   UUP and 52, 59, 70, 72, 83–4
prisoners 29, 34, 49, 61, 198
   linkage of releases with decommissioning 41, 61–2, 69, 176
   releases in Agreement 30, 194
   republican support for releases 37, 113
   unionists and releases 35, 37, 57, 75, 145, 150, 156

Programme for Cohesion, Sharing and
    Integration 183
Progressive Unionist Party 79, 188, 189, 190
Proportional Representation 29, 181
PSNI *see* Police Service of Northern Ireland
PUP *see* Progressive Unionist Party

Queen Elizabeth II 108
Quinn, Ruairí 24

re-designation *see* designations
referenda (1998) 2, 31, 39, 61, 88, 91, 93–4,
    131, 145
Reid, John 147, 150, 155, 179, 190
Reiss, Mitchell 159
Republican Sinn Féin 131
Ringland, Trevor ix, 80–1
Ritchie, Margaret 103, 104, 106
Robinson, Iris 165
Robinson, Peter 43, 142, 146, 150–1, 153–4,
    157, 160–1, 164–5
  flag protests and 187, 189, 190
  inclusive unionism and 165–6
  Westminster defeat 185, 187
Rogers, Bríd 94–6, 106
Royal Ulster Constabulary *see* RUC
Royal Ulster Constabulary 35, 98, 143

St Andrews Agreement 8, 9, 44, 79, 106–7, 128,
    138, 158–61, 179, 186
Scotland 56, 171
SDLP *see* Social Democratic and Labour Party
security dilemma 6
  Alliance Party and 168, 170, 174
  DUP and 138
  historic conflict in Ireland and 20–2
  meaning 10–13
  new definition 16
  peace process and 25–8
  post-Agreement politics and 34–42
  post-settlement security dilemma 47–50
  resolution of in Northern Ireland? 6, 26–8,
    46–7, 195–7, 200
  SDLP and 93
  Sinn Féin and 118
  'Troubles' and 22–5
  UUP and 64, 83

security dilemma sensibility 43, 83, 196
Shared Future, A (2005 document) 183–4
Sinn Féin
  Agreement and 113–18
  electoral progress 42, 93, 100–5, 111, 130–4
  equality and 118–24
  IRA and 124–30
  Orange parades and 120
  origins and development 109–13
  policing and *see* policing
  principle of consent and 37, 42, 112,
    114, 117
  St Andrews Agreement and 138, 157–9
Smyth, Martin 64, 66–9
Social Democratic and Labour Party
  Agreement and 90–3
  decommissioning and *see* decommissioning
  electoral contest with Sinn Féin 100–6
  flags and symbols and 98–100
  ideology 87–90
  mooted mergers 106
  origins 86–7
  policing and *see* policing
societal security 17
societal security dilemma 17–20
  see also security dilemma
South Africa 111
Stormont *see* Assembly
Sunningdale 53, 79, 86, 107, 141–2,
    164, 169

Titanic Quarter 200
track-two diplomacy 28, 196
Traditional Unionist Voice 162
transcender logic 6, 13, 17, 50, 198
  Alliance Party and 191
  May 2007 and 43
  meaning 14–15
  SDLP and 95, 107
  Sinn Féin and 135, 195
Trimble, David 22, 36, 37, 42, 51
  Agreement and 55–60
  approach to decommissioning 57–70
  assessment of 77–8
  election as leader 55
  policing and symbols and 70–6
  resignation as leader 76

trust 11, 14–15, 29, 43, 47, 196
TUV *see* Traditional Unionist Voice

UCUNF *see* Ulster Conservatives and Unionists – New Force
UDA *see* Ulster Defence Association
Ulster Conservatives and Unionists – New Force 80–1
Ulster Defence Association 39
Ulster Scots 32, 147, 158
Ulster Unionist Council 63, 64, 66, 67
Ulster Unionist Party
   Agreement and 55–60
   decommissioning and *see* decommissioning
   leadership 53–5, 76–82
   Orange Order and 78
   origins and development 52–5
   policing and *see* policing
   safeguarding Britishness of Northern Ireland 70–6
   UCUNF and *see* UCUNF
Ulster Volunteer Force 39, 79
unionism
   intra-unionist party competition 40–1, 58–60, 69–70, 81–2, 138, 153, 156–7, 162
   nature of identity 24, 35, 52–5, 73, 81–2, 138–41
   origins 20–1, 52

see also Democratic Unionist Party, Ulster Unionist Party
United Kingdom Unionist Party 5, 59, 141, 178
United States 27, 104, 111, 113, 140
UUC *see* Ulster Unionist Council
UUP *see* Ulster Unionist Party
UVF *see* Ulster Volunteer Force

Vanguard Unionist Party 53, 55, 138
victims 30, 58, 75, 133, 148, 176, 182, 197

Wales 56
Washington 63
weak state 18, 39
Weir, Peter 75, 178
Westminster election xi
   (1918) 109
   (1997) 101
   (2001) 41, 63, 70, 101, 154, 178, 181
   (2005) 70, 76
   (2010) 80, 169, 185
   Mid-Ulster by-election (2013) 80, 82
Weston Park 98, 122
Women's Coalition 5, 151, 178
World Police and Fire Games 200

YouTube 121
Yugoslavia 11, 16, 19